HOLD YOUR TEEN CLOSE

How to Understand and Connect with your Teenage Son: The Cognitive-Friendly Parenting Method.

Penny Goodwin

Alex Pezaro Press

First published in 2025 by Alex Pezaro Press.

On Children excerpt from *The Prophet* by Khalil Gibran, used with permission. *The Prophet* (1923 version) is in the public domain. Special thanks to the Gibran National Committee and Penguin Books for confirming the public domain status of this work.

Some names and identifying details in this book have been changed to protect the privacy of the individuals involved. The experiences shared are based on real events and relationships, but the names and certain details have been altered for confidentiality.

Disclaimer: The information in this book is for general informational purposes only and is not intended as medical or psychological advice. The author is not a healthcare professional, and the content should not be used as a substitute for professional medical, psychological, or therapeutic advice. Always consult with a qualified healthcare provider for any medical or mental health concerns.

A CIP record for this title is available from the British Library.
ISBN 978-1-0369-3157-5
Cover design by Tom Shelley and Lilly Flanagan
Diagrams by Tom Shelley and Lilly Flanagan
Cartoons and Cover image by Tom Shelley
Printed in the United Kingdom
Website: www.alexpezaro.com Email: connect@alexpezaro.com
LinkedIn https://www.linkedin.com/in/penny-goodwin-7b79a331

"This is a very important book.** It is well written, clear, lucid, and concise. The challenges facing our children and in turn their parents are immense. The post COVID era has thrown up a range of challenges combined with pressures that previous generations have not had to face. The impact of social media can be devastating for some children and parents struggle to help their children navigate their way through these difficulties. However, there are solutions, and* ***this book offers both parents and their adolescent children some helpful insights on how to meet these and other challenges."

Dr Peter Carter, OBE PhD MBA FRCN MCIPD RCGP (Hon) Ad Eundem RCSI RMN RGN
Independent Healthcare Consultant

"As a Cognitive Behavioural Psychotherapist specialising in anxiety, I often see first-hand how both anxiety and the challenges of parenting an anxious teenager can affect families. The section on anxiety in this book serves as ***an invaluable resource, offering practical strategies*** *and a* ***clear roadmap*** *that helps parents* ***build a healthier relationship with their anxious teen****, while also empowering them to develop effective* ***coping skills****. In CBT, we emphasise the critical role of the relationship between therapist and client. This book mirrors that concept by focusing on the parent-teen relationship, stressing the importance of creating an open space. When teens feel comfortable expressing their anxieties, it opens the door to real, lasting change,* ***making this approach a crucial tool for fostering sustained progress****."*

Dawn Kett, BSC (Hons) MSc PGCert PGDip MBABCP
Cognitive Behavioural Psychotherapist

ACKNOWLEDGMENT AND THANKS TO OUR ENDORSERS

Dr Peter Carter

Dr Carter OBE PhD MBA FRCN MCIPD RCGP (Hon) Ad Eundem RCSI RMN RGN is a key Independent Healthcare Consultant. In 2020, Dr Carter received the Chief Nursing Officers' Award for Lifetime Achievement, recognising his major contributions to nursing and healthcare leadership.

Dr Carter was Chief Executive and General Secretary of the Royal College of Nursing from 2007 to 2015. Prior to that, for 12 years, Dr Carter was Chief Executive of the Central and North West London NHS Foundation Trust.

A fellow of the Royal College of Nursing, an honorary fellow of the Royal College of General Practitioners, and an Ad Eundem of the Royal College of Surgeons of Ireland, Dr Carter was regularly cited in the Health Service Journal as one of the NHS's most influential leaders during his tenure as Chief Executive of the Royal College of Nursing.

In 2011, Dr Carter was awarded the inaugural President's Medal of the Royal College of Psychiatrists. In 2006 he was awarded the OBE.

Dr Carter has held visiting professorships at several universities: King's College, Canterbury Christ Church, Chester and Anglia Ruskin. Featured twice on BBC's Hardtalk, he has written articles for journals, newspapers, and book chapters, appeared in TV documentaries, and been interviewed numerous times on TV and radio.

In 2024, Dr Carter had his first sole-author book published, *My Asylum Days* (available on Amazon Books).

Keith Lowe

Keith Lowe is the author of several major history works, best known for *Savage Continent*, an international bestseller that won the Hessell-Tiltman Prize and Italy's Cherasco History Prize. The book is a standard account of post-World War II violence in Europe.

His 2017 book, *The Fear and the Freedom*, exploring the global aftermath of the war, was praised by the Wall Street Journal as one of the best WWII books of the decade. It was shortlisted for the Historical Writers' Association Non-fiction Crown and was adapted into a 12-part Czech radio series.

Keith Lowe has written widely acclaimed historical books on WWII monuments and the 1943 Hamburg bombing. His latest, *Naples* 1944, covers Italy's liberation and ensuing turmoil.

He regularly appears on TV and radio, lectures worldwide, and contributes to major international newspapers including The Times, Daily Telegraph, and Wall Street Journal. Keith Lowe is a Fellow of the Royal Historical Society and serves on the advisory board for Liberation Route Europe.

Dawn Kett

Dawn Kett BSc (Hons) MSc PGCert PGDip MBABCP is an accredited Cognitive Behavioural Psychotherapist and member of the British Association for Behavioural and Cognitive Psychotherapies (BABCP). Dawn Kett holds a BSc (Hons) in Psychology, an MSc in Developmental Psychology, and also postgraduate qualifications in Cognitive Behaviour Therapy. She specializes in treating anxiety disorders, including social anxiety, health anxiety, panic, OCD, phobias, and generalised anxiety.

AUTHOR BIO

With two decades of hands-on experience as a mother and many years as a youth mentor, Penny Goodwin has gained deep insight into the needs, desires, and challenges of today's teenagers.

In her role as a youth mentor, she has had the privilege of working closely with young people, guiding them through personal challenges and supporting their growth in key areas such as emotional intelligence, self-esteem, confidence, education, decision-making, and relationships. This support has empowered them to navigate life's complexities with resilience and confidence. She sees the power of accepting young people for who they truly are, rather than who we expect or want them to be. This acceptance has led many of those she has supported to express that, for the first time, they felt truly heard and understood.

In a previous role as Community Ambassador for The Children's Society, Penny wrote and delivered speeches on youth-related subjects such as mental health, young carers, and county lines, deepening her insight into the complex issues today's youth face. Her earlier experience as a child portrait photographer, one of the several businesses she has built, allowed her to apply her understanding of young people in a very practical way.

Penny is a self-professed foodie with a lifelong interest in food and nutrition. Early in her career, she worked as a chef, even cooking for His Royal Highness Prince Michael of Kent, a skill that she has passed onto her son, in preparation for adulthood.

Based just outside London, Penny enjoys spending time with her family and friends, cooking, gardening, or rambling through the countryside whenever she gets time away from work.

TABLE OF CONTENTS

"When we embark on our parenting journey into early adolescence, we know it won't always be easy. But the more prepared we are, the better our children's chances, and the brighter their future. This book is the first step."

CHAPTERS:

DEDICATION

I dedicate this book to my son, whom I'm in awe of every single day. You are truly amazing and an inspiration to me. Thank you for coming into my life. I love you more than words can describe.

I also dedicate this book to all parents and carers, whether you have helped as a stopgap in supporting a young person or have spent years raising several children.

NOTE TO READER

This book is based on my experiences of raising a son. While many of the tools and ideas here are equally relevant to girls and young people in general, the focus throughout this book is on understanding and raising boys.

That said, many of the ideas and strategies in this book are also helpful for all teenagers, including those who are transgender, non-binary, genderfluid, or intersex teenagers. Parents, carers, and professionals working with teenagers of any gender may find useful insights within these pages.

The word 'parent' means both parent and carer. The word 'school' is interchangeable with the word 'college' or 'university'. So please use whichever suits your situation.

The use of the word 'ego' in this book refers to the general term, relating to your own sense of self, your abilities, your intelligence, and how important you feel, as opposed to Freud's definition.

Quotes used at the beginning and throughout the chapters are original reflections and are written by the author. These are not attributed to any other sources.

The Cognitive-Friendly Method definition:

Drawing on my research from psychology and brain science, I developed the Cognitive-Friendly Method to effectively equip parents, carers, and professionals with a practical approach for understanding and connecting with teenagers. This framework highlights teenagers' cognitive limitations and guides adults to act with compassion and empathy, fostering more positive and harmonious relationships during adolescence.

PREFACE

The idea for this book was born a few years ago, when I combined my desire to support my son through adolescence with a deep commitment to becoming the best parent I could be. Each night, I lay in bed analysing the conversations I'd had with my teenage son, dissecting every word and asking myself what I could do differently next time. I realised some scenarios needed slightly tweaking and others drastically re-thinking. At every step, I made a conscious effort to remove my ego from the equation and replace it with pure love. A few weeks into this journey, it became clear that if I could find ways to strengthen our relationship, I had a responsibility to share what I had learned so others could benefit. I believe, that by learning from one another, we can improve our world. So I grabbed pen and paper and quickly outlined the structure of this book within just a few minutes. I didn't have to stop and think, the words just flowed. Somehow, I instinctively knew how this book should be written. The more I wrote, the more I saw the need for a new approach. One that was not only rooted in an understanding of teenage brain development, but one that emphasised the need for compassion and empathy. This became the basis for the Cognitive-Friendly Method. A framework that helps parents understand their sons' cognitive limitations and emotional needs, fostering deeper connections, mutual respect, and more harmonious relationships during the often-turbulent teen years. The Cognitive-Friendly Method was originally developed to help parents, but it has since proven valuable for professionals working with teenagers as well. This book wasn't written on a whim; it was written from my heart to yours. My goal was to create lasting, positive changes for both parents and teens, whether subtle or profound.

I have relished every minute of writing this book. Loved getting lost in thought as I read many fascinating medical research papers. Enjoyed talking to teens and asking their opinions on life, and interviewing experts like Ashley Leenders and Helen Trenoweth on their insightful experiences. Editing this book was full of serendipitous moments. Time and again, I found myself working on sections that mirrored situations unfolding in my life. Each one gently guiding me towards the best course of action.

My hope is that this book becomes a trusted companion, something you can return to whenever you feel the need. While much of the contents may offer new insights, some parts may simply serve as gentle reminders of things once known but perhaps forgotten. Unless stated otherwise, the theories and principles within these pages have evolved from my reflections, experiences, interactions and observations as a hands-on mother. I have also applied these same principles in my role as a dedicated youth mentor and have witnessed the positive impact they can have on young lives.

Although this book is written from the perspective of raising a son, much of the advice, insights, and tools included are equally relevant to girls and to young people of all genders, making it a helpful resource for any parent or caregiver.

Thank you for investing your precious time in buying and reading this book.

INTRODUCTION

"The teenage years aren't something to 'get through', they are something to enjoy and cherish."

According to UNICEF, there are around 1.3 billion adolescents in the world today, equating to approximately 16 percent of the world's population and the largest ratio ever recorded. Yet, these young people are still often seen but not heard. Too old to be the number one-star attraction, akin to when they were tiny, and too young to be taken seriously, as not yet an adult. So, there they sit, caught in the void between childhood and adulthood, struggling to adjust to their rapidly evolving life (UNICEF, n.d.).

From the moment they were born, we pampered and adhered to our child's every whim. As babies, when they cried, we would spend ages working out what was wrong. Were they hungry, did their nappy need changing, were they scared, cold or sick? As they grew into toddlers we asked similar questions. Sometimes, they would help with our investigations, and at other times, they would throw us a red herring. Every time we thought something was amiss, we would wrack our brains to investigate why they were behaving so.

Yet now, as teenagers, this attention appears to have faded. We expect them to perpetually behave flawlessly, and when they don't, we find their behaviour unacceptable and place blame upon them. We say that they are 'acting up', 'not being reasonable' or are 'pushing the boundaries'.

The fact that they may be hurting, scared, or confused doesn't often come into the equation. In truth, they may not even know why they are feeling the way they do, as they can't always formulate their feelings. We wouldn't scold a baby for crying, so why do we do expect our teens to stay composed when they are overwhelmed? Instead, we should investigate why they are acting so and support them.

These once precious babies that we cradled in our arms are still the same people standing in front of us today. Our beloved child who posed for more photos than the Queen, who brought us such joy, even when they were simply sleeping. No embarrassment here, who hasn't tiptoed into their young child's room just to see their beautiful little bodies cocooned in slumber, and to listen to their soft, relaxing breath as though it was a mantra?

There are plenty of books available on the topic of 'Dealing with a Teenager'. However, most seem to treat teens as though they are dealing with a terrible disease. In fact, one book on my shelf describes having a teenager as one of the most stressful things you can have. Not sure where having a terminal disease or going through a bereavement fits into the author's mindset. The fact that we need to 'deal with them' in itself is such a negative starting point. If we take this stance, then surely we are only looking at the symptoms of parenting teenagers and ignoring the sensible, *holistic* approach of starting with the cause? Which brings me onto my next point, the crux of the book. You may not want to hear this, but trust me, it's good news. In the majority of cases, the 'problem' with teenagers is ... *how they are parented.* I understand that this is rather an unusual statement, and I don't mean to offend, but without realising, this could be the best news you've heard for a while because if you are willing to be open to change, your relationship with your teenager can vastly improve. But, for this to come into fruition, you have to be prepared to work on yourself. Be willing to be open and honest, eat humble pie, admit you are wrong and go within and meet some of your own demons. Let's rise to the occasion, for it's our responsibility as parents and keyholders for future generations.

It's easy to forget that our teenage sons are the next generation, that their significance is vital to the human race, and that our impact will affect not only our children, but our grandchildren, and great grandchildren too. Which is why if we asked ourselves what we want for our sons, most of us would answer that we want them to be happy and healthy. But, being complex human beings, the process isn't always straightforward. Hence, the need to put our parenting style under the microscope.

In scenarios where teens have fallen in with the wrong crowd or ended up on the wrong side of the law, parents can still be proactive, as it's never too late for them to have a significant influence on their son. We are all critical to the development and moulding of our young people, but it's the parents' contribution that is vital to the relationship between parent and child.

As you delve into the book, you will examine mindsets and discover catalysts for positive changes, enabling you to challenge the age-old 'teen blame' culture, where teens are 'obviously' the cause of their own angst. Along the way, you will find a plethora of unparalleled information, from the workings of the teenage brain to the obstacles they encounter, including mental health conditions. There are insightful interviews from experts on the subject, valuable citations from peer-reviewed medical papers and umpteen vital tools and techniques to improve communication. Additionally, there are helpful tips on parental needs, to assist you on your parenting journey.

By implementing the concepts in this book, you will experience a happier and more fulfilling relationship with your son, whilst creating a more harmonious family environment. At times, you may feel like throwing in the towel, for it's much easier to lay down the law and take total control or ignore your teen and always put yourself first. Change takes time and patience, and in today's busy world this isn't easy. But the good news is that by taking one step at a time even the smallest efforts can eventually lead to significant change. And, if you truly respect and deeply love your child then this is the only path. So, when your patience runs out, take a deep breath, praise yourself for choosing this path, put on a brave face and take up the challenge, and you will reap the rewards. And never, *ever*, give up on your teen.

Note: *Throughout the book, I use the word 'teen' or' teenager' for flow, but I'm always referring to teenage boys. The focus is on parenting sons.*

CHAPTER 1: UNDERSTAND AND CHALLENGE

"When we see teenagers, we are guilty of merely observing their behaviours, rarely do we look behind their masks to discover the reasons behind our perceptions."

SEEING THROUGH THEIR EYES

We are accustomed to being at the centre of our son's universe, offering strength and security through our strong bond. For years, they've looked up to us for advice on many levels: how they should act, feel, and even think. But during the tough pre-teens stage, reality kicked in and our sons were forced to see life and the world for what they truly are, rather than what they believed them to be. It was at this mind-blowing point that they started to work things out for themselves. For the majority, it was around 11 years old, but for those who had faced significant challenges, it was several years earlier. Comparing their interpretation of life with reality, led many to believe their parents were hypocrites, as this 'false' interpretation had initially been instilled by parents. That's why some began to challenge and cross-examine parents, questioning all aspects of our parenting and who we are as individuals.

It was at this point, during the pre-teens, that they would have had to face the stark reality that their parents weren't perfect, don't know everything, don't think the same and have a different personality to them, which isn't pretty, as up till now we had been put on a pedestal. Our teens believed that we always told them the gospel truth, or at least their interpretation of it, and could do no wrong. Their thought process would have taken a pounding when they found out that their parents were only human, and not superhuman. They would have experienced feelings of sadness, disappointment, isolation, and betrayal, as if the roof of their entire existence had just caved in, leaving them wondering if they could carry on relying on us. The pedestal our children had placed us upon had now been whisked away, leaving a smaller, less significant parent in its place on the floor, in a heap of normality. Albeit painful, this is an important stage that our pre-teens needed to go through in order to become independent adults.

UNDERSTANDING OUR TEENS

"How we perceive our sons is our choice. But we need to make sure our perception is true."

In the Introduction to this book, we learnt that it's time to challenge people's thoughts and attitudes and that the ethos of 'blame the terrible teens' needs to be put to bed. We need to stop listening to these untruths as they can be damaging to both us and our teens. As parents, if we fail to do so, our job will become much harder than it needs to be, and for our sons, their journey will be a far less enjoyable one.

For most of us, it has been a long time since we were teenagers, so understandably we may have forgotten what it feels like. Forgotten the challenges that we faced, the way we were treated and how we felt about life and ourselves. Which is why it's vital to question whether we are treating our teens the way they deserve to be treated.

Today, we *have* to parent differently than in the past as we are living in unusual times. We can't just carry on as we did before the days of Covid-19. Our teens have suffered greatly, physically and mentally, and still are today, thanks to the pandemic and its aftermath, cost-of-living crisis, and the war between Russia and the Ukraine. And when it comes to the cost-of-living crisis, data in *The Children's Society's Annual Household Survey* 2023, revealed that 82% of children aged 10-17 years indicated that they were either 'very' or 'quite' concerned. This makes me wonder about the conversations being held in households around the country and the impact of these conversations on our young peoples' lifestyles and mental health. These frightening issues leave most teens feeling powerless, making their lives seem far more challenging compared to the relatively care-free days of our own childhood. This means they need our love and support now more than ever. They can't even escape these terrifying events as they are rammed down their throats when they turn on a screen, are in the playground or are attending lessons in school. With this in mind, we *must* make their mental health our top priority. Just as we would support a friend through a tough time such as bereavement or divorce, we need to support our children through one of the toughest stages of their lives: the teenage years.

Loving our sons isn't enough. To truly understand them we need to listen and connect with them on a daily basis. And instead of making assumptions about their behaviour, we must first figure out why they are acting so. The roller-coaster ride they are on means that their emotions will at times run wild. We will witness confusion and frustration during ups and downs, and even periods of silence as they struggle to make sense of their thoughts. Their challenging journey into adulthood is further compounded by their innate drive for independence, often leading to rifts with their parents. Yet, these rifts can be greatly reduced, and often prevented, if we truly understand them. Therefore, being patient as they navigate their way through life is crucial.

To support our teens, we need to be curious about them so we can see the real person inside. They need to know that we value them and that we are invested in who they are as individuals. That we understand how they think, feel and connect to both their world and ours. When we fulfil their fundamental desire to be accepted for who they are and address their innate need for us to be proud of them, we instil positive attributes such as confidence, self-esteem, courage, kindness, persistence, hope, and a sense of worth, enabling them to open up to both us and the world around them.

The more we get to know our teens, the more we can see how our actions affect them. Sometimes, we will need to tweak our own actions depending on theirs. And, if we really listen, we will find that they can ground us and bring us back from our busy states of mind to a calmer place, allowing us to focus on what's really important.

It's no secret that by the time our children become teenagers they no longer want to hang out with us. This is often due to embarrassment on their part, their natural inclination to pull away from us, or our own behaviour. Teens can be very sensitive to some situations, such as witnessing a parent belittling or arguing with another, or a parent being treated disrespectfully in front of others. These situations can cause them stress and play on their minds for quite a while. But their reluctance to hang out with us on a regular basis should not be interpreted as a complete aversion to spending time with us.

Teen boys' abstract thinking skills are still developing, so there will be times when they ponder and feel anxious about the ramifications of various issues, such as political, scientific, financial or social, and may form opinions that differ greatly from ours. This period is further complicated by their tendency to yo-yo between adult-like thought patterns and child-like ones, often reverting to childish behaviours when feeling stressed, anxious, or vulnerable.

Although we need to respect our teens' desire for independence, we shouldn't let them push us away, as this can create a void which, without intervention, is likely to grow. Nor should we use their separateness as an excuse to ignore them as this can lead to family disconnection, which, fuelled by the overuse of technology, can cause total isolation. Instead, we need to seek opportunities to spend time with them, one-on-one or as a family. Which is why being patient and flexible with our own plans will go a long way in improving relationships.

Children are unique individuals, and their needs will vary depending on their circumstances. The same child brought up in two different households will be shaped into two different individuals. Just as two different children growing up in the same household will shape into two different adults.

At times, it seems like our teens are on another planet, zoned out and unreachable. When we are running around like crazy, juggling millions of tasks, they seldom notice or offer a helping hand. Being in their own world, they often don't realise what we are up to. But let's not forget that adults can be just as guilty of this as teens. For example, recently, I went for a walk. I'd been walking for about 20 minutes when it dawned on me that everyone had their rubbish bins out for collection, which was rather unusual as it wasn't the normal collection day. Due to a recent public holiday, I knew the collection day had changed, but it had taken me 20 minutes of walking past numerous bins to realise this. It hadn't dawned on me that they were all in the street for a reason! So, it's not just our teens that don't see the obvious in front of them due to their mind buzzing with thoughts.

It's good practice to regularly take time out to think about all the conversations and arguments you are having with your teen. Fathom out what he's thinking and what he's trying to convey, amidst the entanglement of his fragile emotions. Look for patterns and think about how you can best support him.

COMPASSION

"Once we step into the shoes of compassion, we no longer see the other person as a problem, nor a threat."

To get on in life, we often need to bite our tongue. Never is this truer than when we are conversing with our teens. Before we respond to what may seem like irrational outbursts, we may have to eat humble pie, count to ten, or even twenty. But it's worth noting that these so-called outbursts are, in fact, uncontrollable feelings, and by applying both compassion and empathy, life becomes easier for all involved.

Compassion, along with empathy, are our secret weapons, enabling us to understand others on a deeper level, breaking down invisible barriers. Although the practice of compassion is easier for some, it's something we all need to strive for as it deepens our relationships, making our parenting journey a lot smoother.

The teenage years are just as important as the first few months of life, yet, finding the time and energy for our teens is often seen as an inconvenience. When they were babies, we didn't mutter "I really couldn't be bothered to get up in the night and give my son a feed as it's very inconvenient". Nor did we suggest our baby would have to miss their naps as we had more important things to do, such as shopping or meeting friends. So why do we act this way now? We know that our teens are not yet adults and not fully independent, therefore, we need to find both the time and energy to devote to them.

Aiding them on their journey, being by their side, guiding them and lending a hand when things get tough is all part and parcel of our role as parents. And although they may look mature on the outside, and are nearing physical maturity, inside they aren't as strong as we think as they often even struggle to comprehend what they are thinking, let alone feeling.

Protecting our teens from harm and providing them with the tools needed for adulthood is part of our job description. Our role does not include:

- Berating them.
- Disrespecting them.
- Exploiting them.
- Hassling them.
- Ignoring them.
- Nagging them.
- Neglecting them.
- Putting them down.

- Regularly punishing them – unless they've committed an illegal/immoral act or put themselves or others in danger.
- Shouting at them.
- Verbally or physically abusing them.

Problems

"Empathy is a window to another's soul."

Struggling with serious issues is all part of life. Upon doing so, we need to remember that our teens may also be struggling with their own issues too. And although compared to ours, we may think that theirs are minimal, in their eyes they are colossal and extremely serious. Masking their feelings and keeping problems to themselves as they go around smiling or laughing doesn't mean that they are okay as they may, unbeknown to us, be handling tough circumstances. As they age, they will want to solve problems privately and we may not even be aware of the conversations they are having, nor aware of the situations they've fallen into. If we are privy to their problems, we need to be careful not to belittle them or compare theirs to ours, making them feel insignificant. Furthermore, if we don't take their worries seriously, they won't rush to us for advice or use us as a listening ear or sounding board in the future.

RESPECT

We should be respectful when talking to, or about, our teens. Whether they are in earshot or not. Just because we are upset or annoyed at them doesn't mean that the whole world needs to know.

The Anna Freud Centre, a UK based world-leading mental health charity for children and families, was started by Anna Freud, a pioneering child psychoanalyst and daughter of the famous Sigmund Freud. Anna firmly believed that every child should be recognised as a person in their own right, that they deserve to be heard no matter their age, and that having a voice is not only their human right but also their innate desire. She observed their need to interact, something that most of us noticed when our children were young. For example, when our sons' joyous words erupted after something exciting happened. Just because children grow up, doesn't mean this innate need for connection disappears.

Anna's belief brings us onto the subject of respect. We want our teens to respect us, but to gain respect, we first must give it. Parents need to earn respect from their teens as they would from their friends. If we treat our friends badly, they will realise and vote with their feet. So why should we expect our teens to act differently? Only perhaps out of fear.

In the case of a malicious or abusive parent, surely a badly treated teen should not automatically be expected to respect them? Compared to previous generations, who taught their children to respect elders no matter how they behaved, I would like to think that our generation has made significant progress in challenging this behaviour.

For our teens to follow suit and respect us, we first need to respect ourselves. Otherwise, it becomes easy for them to shrug off any respect that they think should come our way.

We can send our sons to the best school, provide them with a private tutor for every subject, offer endless after school activities or lavish them with expensive gifts, but if we don't respect and listen to them it's all in vain. The teen that is treated as a second-class citizen, intimidated, ignored or bullied at home will not lead a successful life, especially where his mental health is concerned.

At times, you may need to use a filter when conversing with your teen, as this helps eliminate any non-essential waffle, including moans and groans, which are more appropriate for a partner or friend.

Alongside our teens' innate yearning for independence and their need to take control and make decisions, there is also their desire for privacy, a desire that should be respected.

WHAT YOUR TEEN REALLY NEEDS

"Teenagers may have what they want, but do they have what they need?"

"The biggest gift a child can have is not the best trainers. The biggest gift is a secure home with a family that loves them and allows them to be themselves. Children thrive when they are surrounded by people that love them unconditionally." Mark Russell, CEO The Children's Society.

Teenagers' bedrooms around the world may be equipped with all the latest gadgets, but is this what they really need, or indeed really crave? In the western world, on the surface, most teenagers seem to have everything. Sadly, in reality, this is often not the case. It's pointless buying your teen a top-of-the-line flat screen TV if you're just going to ignore him.

Aside from unconditional love, more than anything else, teenagers need us to *listen* and *connect* with them. They need families that support them, *understand* who they are, and acknowledge that they are constantly changing. In addition, they need the following (in no particular order):

Physiological Needs:

- Food, warmth, and shelter.
- A safe environment to live in, away from any harm.
- Regular exercise to keep healthy and feel good.
- The chance to have a healthy diet.

Emotional Needs:

- A firm but caring hand.
- A safe environment to air their feelings.
- Compassion.
- Emotional support.
- Empathy.
- Honest parents.
- Kind and gentle parents.
- Positive parents.
- Non-judgmental parents.
- Parents that have total faith in them.
- Respect.
- Space to learn and grow.
- Time to relax and wind down when needed.
- To have their feelings accepted without question.
- To be allowed to keep making mistakes and not be reprimanded unless the mistakes are illegal, immoral, or dangerous.
- Parents with no preconceived ideas about what they may want or feel.

Social Needs:

- A support network.
- Boundaries, rules, and consequences.
- Good role models.
- Someone to talk to, even if outside the family unit.
- The opportunity to be a teenager and not a child nor adult.
- The opportunity for education.
- The opportunity to make friends.

TEEN NEEDS MODEL

The model below depicts teenagers' basic needs.

A Teen has an unmet need.

This need could be Physiological, Emotional, or Social.

Physiological needs include food, water, air, good health, warmth, sleep, and shelter.

Emotional needs include love, respect, attention, a sense of self, achievement, a safe space, protection, acceptance, validation, independence, and privacy.

Social needs are the sense of belonging and the need to fit in and be accepted by peers, family, friends, community, and country.

↓

This need triggers a behavioural response, which the teen expresses outwardly.

↓

Parents decipher the need in order to support and guide.

Help includes setting boundaries, teaching that actions have consequences, being a good role model, offering a listening ear, communicating effectively, and boosting confidence and self-esteem. It also involves providing love, respect, compassion, and a safe environment – nourishing their mind, body, and soul.

"Positive family relationships are key to children's subjective well-being. A greater focus is needed on family well-being as a whole." The Children's Society, Good Childhood Report Summary 2022.

CHAPTER 2: NEUROLOGICAL, BIOLOGICAL, AND PSYCHOLOGICAL CHALLENGES

"The teen years are a time when the brain fine-tunes itself."

While much of the brain science in this chapter applies to all teenagers, the focus here is on how these changes affect boys, and how parents can better understand and support their sons as a result.

The essence of the Cognitive-Friendly Method lies in understanding the teenage brain. This understanding is arguably the most vital piece of the parenting puzzle. When paired with patience, empathy, and compassion, these strengths equip us with the tools needed to build a harmonious relationship with our sons. Armed with this knowledge, we can gain valuable insight into the reasons behind our teens' often puzzling and unpredictable behaviour, enabling us to better navigate overwhelming moments such as mood swings, impulsive decisions, and emotional outbursts.

After infancy, adolescence is the most crucial time of development in a human being's life. During adolescence, there are a whole host of challenges that present themselves including:

NEUROLOGICAL, BIOLOGICAL, AND PSYCHOLOGICAL CHALLENGES

- Additional pressure at school e.g. important exams.
- Change in body shape as it grows and develops.
- Change in priorities including the importance of peers.
- Detachment from parents – the need for independence.
- Development of values, beliefs, ethics and morals.
- External influences – fewer parental influences and more from individuals outside the family unit.
- Heightened emotional activity.
- Heightened sense of self-consciousness.
- Life events such as moving onto secondary school.
- Neurological development.
- Additional responsibility.
- Puberty – increase in hormonal production, development of sexual organs, muscle development, physical growth: height and weight, facial and body hair, body odour.
- Search for identity.
- Increased demand for complex decision-making skills.
- Changes in the deepening of the voice.

NEUROLOGICAL, BIOLOGICAL, AND PSYCHOLOGICAL CHALLENGES

For adults, changes to the body are slight and gradual, often occurring over several years, but for our sons, they happen rapidly, which can be unsettling, especially as they frequently notice changes in their appearance. Being image conscious, these changes can be a big deal for them. According to research, and contrary to belief, boys worry about their body image as much as girls. Moreover, to make the situation more challenging, teens are often reluctant to discuss their bodies with either parents or friends, leaving them feeling alienated, especially if their friends are at different stages of development.

EMOTIONS

Emotions are brief, complex psychological states that arise from changes in thoughts, feelings, and behaviours, in response to both external stimuli and internal processes. As homo sapiens, we experience a whole range of emotions, both positive and negative. Which is why it's acceptable for our sons to express emotions such as frustration, sadness, doubt, annoyance, or anger. And any anxieties. During puberty, due to heightened emotions, our teens will traverse through every emotion possible, often peaking and troughing in a very short space of time.

As babies, it was acceptable to cry or scream as a way of expressing our emotions, but as soon as we became children, we were told to keep our emotions in check. Some were taught that it was not acceptable to have feelings, let alone express them. Yet, suppressing emotions is unhealthy as it can lead to violent outbursts or low self-esteem. It can also stop us from really knowing ourselves and really knowing what we are feeling at any given moment.

Akin to living in a fog, the teenage years are confusing times. Experiencing frightening and bewildering issues simultaneously can lead to the odd wobbly moment, as the transition from childhood to adulthood raises countless unanswered questions. With emotions like confusion, self-doubt, fear, guilt, anger, sadness, embarrassment, disgust, excitement and joy being juggled daily, if not hourly, it's no surprise that we might receive a thumbs-up from them one day, only to find they've completely changed their mind the next. Everyday worries including school, family and crime weigh heavy on their young minds. And due to their natural detachment from parents, thoughts about losing their childhood can trigger separation anxiety.

It's hard to imagine that many teens enjoy the daily struggles that are part and parcel of being a teenager. The confusion and frustration of trying to control their emotions, feeling elated one minute and sad the next, isn't only exhausting but can't be much fun either.

When it comes to feeling positive about their life, naturally, teens tend to err on the side of caution, preferring to think in a negative manner and recalling negative thoughts or emotions, rather than positive ones. This is known as 'negative bias' and is present in both teens and adults alike. For this reason, it's important to install hope and optimism into their mindsets whenever we can.

Researchers have discovered that adolescents experience a wide range of emotions simultaneously, but they struggle with emotional differentiation. In effect, an adolescent may consistently feel angry and sad at the same time, indicating that they struggle to discriminate between the two.

"Our results suggest that adolescence is a period in which emotions co-occur with greater frequency, but these emotions are poorly differentiated. This finding contributes to basic understanding of the social and emotional changes that arise during adolescence. The novel experience of simultaneous emotions could produce meta-emotions such as confusion or potentially interfere with effective emotion regulation as adolescents struggle to select optimal strategies for regulating simultaneously experienced emotions" (Nook et al., 2018).

"Although speculative, our results suggest that low emotion differentiation, which has previously been associated with psychopathology, may be one factor that contributes to the increased onset of mental illness in adolescence" (Nook et al., 2018).

There will be times when our teens' emotions will be out of sync with their actions, and times when their feelings are intense, such as when they are attracted to others romantically, including having their first crush. However painful it is to witness, it's necessary for testing the waters for adult relationships.

Being adults, we have the benefit of years of experience in managing our emotions, although there will be times when we all struggle. Our teens haven't had this luxury, so we need to teach them how to exercise self-control to reduce anger and avoid angry or violent outbursts. Like us, they can use strategies such as exercise, breathing techniques, alone time, a listening ear, grounding techniques, or distract themselves in activities such as music, sport or T.V.

Due to our teens black and white thinking patterns, things are either right or wrong, good or bad, with not much grey in between. And as they are not yet mature enough to think in an adult-like manner all the time, we shouldn't take everything they say literally.

Teenage boys don't always understand their own feelings, so they hide them. When the world tells them that they need to be tough and strong, how do they accept the feelings of vulnerability, anxiety, fear, feebleness, weakness, tenderness and uncertainty? Everywhere they look, men are depicted as macho and unemotional human beings and often the rock that women hold on to. As women are still often seen as the gentler and less aggressive sex, it implies that men are perceived as the tougher one. Perhaps this is one of the reasons why boys aren't as open with their feelings as girls as their need to be tough suggests that they need to 'hold it all in' and refrain from displaying emotions as this would reveal their weaknesses and vulnerabilities. All of which leads us to question whether society is responsible for how we shape our sons.

When conversing with our sons, it's useful to keep in mind the saying, 'They can dish it out, but they can't take it', as often they can verbalise exactly how they feel, but can't deal with our responses, especially when treated as adults. In short, we need to respect them, understand them, be aware of our words, and not overreact to their responses. Remember, the words that we use will have a lifelong impact on our teens, so we need to choose kind ones. Fans of the late, great Louise Hay will know that she believed that there is power in our words, and we need to pay close attention to them.

PUBERTY

The primary objective of puberty is to produce sexually active adults, capable of reproducing. In males, it begins when the pituitary gland, the gland responsible for testosterone production, signals the testes to produce testosterone, triggering sperm production.

Typically, the onset of puberty for males is between the ages of 9 and 14 years, with an average of 11.5 years. Some will experience early onset and some a late one. Usually, boys go through puberty a couple of years later than girls.

NEUROLOGICAL, BIOLOGICAL, AND PSYCHOLOGICAL CHALLENGES

During puberty, the entire body undergoes change and growth. Bones, organs, muscles, and limbs strengthen, genitals increase in size, and body hair becomes more visible in the armpit and groin areas, with the growth of moustaches and sideburns. Lung capacity and height increases, the male voice 'breaks' before it permanently deepens and the larynx grows in size. Due to hormonal changes, acne and spots are common, so too is body odour due to increased activity of the sweat glands.

THE BRAIN

"An understanding of the teenage brain could help everyone cope better with adolescence, from teenagers themselves to parents, carers, and teachers" (BBC, n.d.).

Years ago, while reading a book on psychology, I came across a chapter on the brain. It felt so complex that I decided to skip it, just for the time being. Embarrassingly, I never returned to it. Over time, I've had to teach myself how the brain works because it's far more relevant to parenting, especially during adolescence, than I ever imagined. It can make a huge difference to how we communicate, connect, and guide our teens on their journey into adulthood. Comprehending their thought processes, capabilities, and limitations, helps us realise that behaviours we might consider 'unacceptable' are in fact 'reasonable' and expected during this stage of development.

NEUROLOGICAL, BIOLOGICAL, AND PSYCHOLOGICAL CHALLENGES

BRAIN TASKS

Below is a list of brain functions. Note that some aren't yet possible due to teens' underdeveloped brains.

Sensory Functions

- Balance.
- Danger recognition.
- Hearing.
- Sensory skills such as touch, taste, and smell.
- Smell recognition.
- Sound recognition.
- Spatial awareness.
- Temperature regulation.
- Vision.

Cognitive and Physical Functions

- Ability to learn and understand.
- Actions such as coughing, sneezing, vomiting, and swallowing.
- Controlling breathing, heart rate, blood pressure, circulation, and digestion.

NEUROLOGICAL, BIOLOGICAL, AND PSYCHOLOGICAL CHALLENGES

- Decision making.
- Facial recognition.
- Hormone regulation.
- Hunger and thirst.
- Language and formulation of words.
- Logic and reasoning.
- Memories – short- and long-term.
- Motor skills tasks such as writing, walking, jumping, and running.
- Movement.
- Numerical skills.
- Oxygen and carbon dioxide levels.
- Planning.
- Risk assessment.
- Sleep/Wake cycles.

Behavioural and Emotional Functions

- Attention span.
- Neurodevelopmental Disorders.

- Emotional regulation.
- Facial expressions.
- Impulse control.
- Personality development.
- Reward system.
- Social behaviour.
- Stress levels.

So, you can see why the brain is often referred to as the most complex item in the universe!

The brain, part of the central nervous system, is often referred to as our 'command centre' because it plays a crucial role in controlling and coordinating all of the body's functions. Consisting of three main components, namely the cerebrum, the brainstem, and the cerebellum, the brain is malleable, adapting and responding to stimuli from both the internal and external environment, which are influenced by life experiences, hormones and sex.

The most crucial part of our body, our brain only weighs about 2% of our total body weight. Being a very sensitive organ, it floats in a protective liquid called cerebrospinal fluid (CSF), which acts as a shock absorber. Not symmetrical, the brain consists of two hemispheres, one on the right and one on the left, not mirroring each other, but with similarities. The right hemisphere develops significantly during the first 18 months of life and controls the movement for the left side of the body, while the left hemisphere controls the movement for the right side of the body. Visual information processing involves a crossover at the optic chiasm, where the right visual field is processed by the left hemisphere and the left visual field by the right hemisphere.

Generally, the left hemisphere is believed to be associated with written language, critical thinking and analysis, number skills, spoken language, logic and reasoning. And the right hemisphere with our imagination, tone of voice, creativity, insight and spatial awareness.

Located in the cerebrum, the corpus callosum is the brain's largest white matter structure, consisting of approximately 250 million axons. It connects the two hemispheres, efficiently transferring cognitive, motor and sensory information between them via the neural highway.

Despite MRI and fMRI advancements in recent decades, brain research is still in its infancy, leaving many questions unanswered, particularly when it comes to the limbic system and its structures. Previously, we were under the impression that each region of the brain worked independently. However, modern day research has now taught us that some regions work together to perform certain tasks.

The brain undergoes rapid development during the first 6 years of life, and by our 7th birthday it's approximately 90% of its adult size. Throughout adolescence, the brain continues to grow and change significantly, where, aside from the ages of 1-3 years, there are more changes during this time than at any other time. As thought patterns change, so too do emotional behaviour and dexterity. Despite acting mature and wise at times, a teen's brain isn't fully developed until he's nearing adulthood, at approximately 25 years of age. During adolescence, teens acquire new intellectual, emotional and social skills. However, to make matters even more challenging for them, different regions of their brain *develop at different rates, requiring time* for these regions to *synchronise effectively.*

BRAIN PLASTICITY

Brain plasticity, otherwise referred to as 'neuroplasticity' or 'the moulding of the brain', is the brain's ability to reorganise its functions and structures. The teenage brain can physically, chemically, and biologically change and adapt in response to environmental factors, experiences, skill development, and memory formation. Cognitive development can be impaired by environmental influences like trauma, chronic stress, substance abuse, or emotional abuse, all negatively altering the brain. For this reason, if a teen is struggling due to an unhealthy home environment, major issues at school or elsewhere, his brain can be adversely affected.

Although heightened during childhood, brain plasticity extends into adulthood, where its astonishing capabilities have been linked to chronic pain relief and recovery from various brain injuries and disorders.

In an interesting medical research paper titled *Maturation of the adolescent brain*, the authors state that "Plasticity permits adolescents to learn and adapt in order to acquire independence, however, plasticity also increases an individual's vulnerability toward making improper decisions because the brain's region-specific neurocircuitry remains under construction, thus making it difficult to think critically and rationally before making complex decisions" (Arain et al., 2013).

NEURONS

The human brain contains approximately 86 billion neurons, also known as nerve cells. Neurons form networks that transmit information through electrical or chemical signals, both within brain regions and throughout the body. Different signals are used for different brain processes, such as hunger or sadness. Not all neurons make it to their final destination, approximately a third die en-route during development, and some survive the journey but end up in places they should not be. Neurons never touch each other as there is a gap between them called a synapse which allows messages to be passed from one neuron to another.

In our spinal cord, three types of neurons exist: sensory, motor and interneurons. Sensory neurons, which detect and respond to external sensory information gathered from our environment, e.g. smell, taste, touch, etc., transmit signals to the brain. Motor neurons, which transmit signals to muscle cells or glands for movement. And interneurons, which serve as links between the sensory and motor neurons.

Neurons have two main types of extensions: axons and dendrites. Axons form long projections that transmit electrical impulses away from the neuron's cell body to other neurons, muscles or glands. Some axons are extremely long and can stretch from the spinal cord down to the toes. These nerve fibres are extremely thin, several times thinner than a human hair strand. Dendrites, on the other hand, are branched extensions that receive electrical or chemical signals from other neurons. They are crucial for receiving and integrating information, allowing effective communication within the nervous system. This process supports everything from basic reflexes to complex cognitive functions.

SYNAPTIC PRUNING

Synaptic pruning, essential for brain maturation, eliminates weaker connections, strengthens important ones, increases grey matter density, and results in a faster, more efficient, and more effective brain. Starting at the prenatal stage and tailing off in our mid-20s, pruning also occurs in adulthood, albeit at a slower, less active, pace. Helping to 'rewire' the brain's connections in readiness for adulthood, synaptic pruning eliminates excess by decluttering and reorganising the brain, pruning away any unnecessary synapses. Though new neurons continue to develop and form new synaptic connections, pruning eliminates unnecessary or unused synapses, optimising the connections that are actively involved in neural networks.

We can apply the classic phrase 'if you don't use it, you lose it' during adolescence as actively engaged neural circuits are strengthened, while inactive ones are eliminated through synaptic pruning. Learning a new skill, such as a language or an instrument, strengthens your teen's synapses and improves the efficiency of his neural connections. To support the development of faster and more confident decision-making, encourage him to make his own choices, helping engage and reinforce his brain pathways.

External influences play a significant role in neuron development during adolescence. According to Dr Jay Giedd, Neuroscientist and Professor at John Hopkins Bloomberg School of Public Health, USA, most of the learning that allows adolescents' brains to form and adapt takes place through everyday actions, such as travelling by bus, going shopping or even just queuing up at the post office.

If you're struggling to deal with your teen's words or behaviour, use a non-judgemental voice to explain 'cause and effect' to help him understand his actions and encourage his synaptic pruning. For example, the next time he appears selfish, remind him that there are other people to consider. Or if he's hurt your feelings, explain kindly, but firmly, that you too have feelings and that his words have hurt you.

Myelination occurs when remaining neurons develop a myelin sheath, enabling them to transmit electrical signals more quickly, using less energy. This process takes place after axons have finished growing, forming new offshoots, and trimming away any excess. Starting at the back of our brain and progressing forward, the prefrontal cortex is the last area to become myelinated. This process is impacted by life experiences such as diet, exercise, sleep, and stress. Overlapping with synaptic pruning, myelination is believed to begin just before birth but is not fully laid until a person is 25-30 years old, with myelin plasticity occurring throughout adulthood.

THE BRAINSTEM

The brainstem, located at the base of the brain, connects the cerebrum and cerebellum to the spinal cord. Composed of the midbrain, pons, and medulla, it plays a crucial role in relaying information between the brain and the body. It controls vital functions such as breathing, blood pressure, heart rate, and sleep, as well as coordination, balance, and reflexes like coughing and swallowing.

THE CEREBRUM

The cerebrum, the largest part of our brain, forms part of the forebrain and accounts for two-thirds of our brain's mass. Consisting of white and grey matter, it's responsible for our conscious thoughts and actions, including elements that demand thinking such as learning, memory, logic, reasoning, language, planning, and our five senses. Comprising two cerebral hemispheres: the right and the left, it contains our limbic system and works together with other parts of our brain to carry out essential daily functions.

Just because your teen knows something intellectually, doesn't mean he can apply it consistently. Since his cerebrum, particularly his prefrontal cortex, is still maturing, his decision-making may be hit-and-miss at times. To support the areas of the brain that are still developing, offer structure, gently repeat instructions, and help him talk through his thoughts.

THE CEREBELLUM

The cerebellum, also known as 'Little Brain' in Latin, sits behind the brainstem and consists of two hemispheres: the right and the left, connected by a central structure called the vermis. Despite containing only approximately 10% of our brain mass, it houses over half of the brain's neurons. It's the second largest part of our brain and forms part of the hindbrain. It contains three lobes: the anterior lobe, posterior lobe and flocculonodular lobe, along with two fissures: the primary and posterolateral fissures.

Primarily responsible for motor coordination and motor learning, the cerebellum governs processes such as voluntary movements, balance, posture, muscular activity, reflex memory, and learning movement sequences. It also fine-tunes motor actions to improve accuracy and timing.

Ongoing research at Johns Hopkins Medicine, USA, is exploring the cerebellum's role in other areas such as emotions, social behaviours and cognition, as they believe that the cerebellum may contribute to a broader range of brain functions than previously thought (Hopkins Medicine, n.d.).

Even though your teen might look grown up, his cerebellum is still developing. Since this part of his brain helps with physical coordination as well as emotional and social timing, you may witness him blurting something out in public or forgetting to follow through on a task. This isn't necessarily rudeness, it's just that his brain is still learning how to time and sequence things. Repeating steps calmly and helping him slow down will support his development.

THE CEREBRAL CORTEX

With our brain containing around 86 billion neurons, approximately 16 billion are found within the cerebral cortex, (CC), the outermost surface of our brain. Primarily composed of grey matter, the CC is divided into two hemispheres, the right and the left. Each hemisphere is further divided into four lobes: the frontal, parietal, occipital, and temporal lobes. Each lobe is responsible for processing different types of sensory information. These lobes develop back to front, literally! With the prefrontal cortex, (PFC), situated within the frontal lobe, being the last part of the brain to develop.

Responsible for numerous processes such as memory, reasoning, learning, decision-making, language, emotion, intelligence, and personality, our CC constitutes more than half the volume of the human brain, despite its thinness of approximately 3 millimetres. Ingeniously designed, its wrinkly convoluted appearance contains numerous folds and grooves, cleverly adding to its total surface area, allowing more information to be processed compared to a flat surface.

As the CC continues developing during the teen years, this can contribute to impulsive decisions, heightened emotional responses, inconsistent decision-making, and difficulties with sensory processing and long-term planning. To support our teens, we can offer structure, encourage critical thinking, and create opportunities for emotional regulation. By creating a calm environment, encouraging the reduction of overstimulation, and by maintaining open communication, we can help foster our teen's emotional and cognitive growth.

THE LIMBIC SYSTEM

Developing relatively early in life, the limbic system, (LS), is a collection of interconnected core structures located within the cerebrum, buried under the cerebral cortex. Playing a vital role in emotion, memory, learning, and motivation, including behaviour and emotional responses, gratification, aversion, hunger (food) satisfaction, sexual arousal, and reproduction, these structures chiefly communicate messages via neural highways. The LS composes many components, such as the septum, mammillary bodies, cingulate gyrus, septal nuclei, fornix, thalamus, hippocampus, hypothalamus, amygdala, and prefrontal cortex although many experts are still deciding which structures make up this system.

THE HIPPOCAMPUS

Due to its shape, the hippocampus was named after the Greek word meaning 'seahorse'. Located within our medial temporal lobe, it's part of our limbic system. Involved in memory formation, learning, emotions, and our survival behaviour, it plays a crucial role in formulating spatial memory, which is associated with our navigation skills. We have two hippocampi, one in each hemisphere. The hippocampus plays a vital role in converting short-term memories into long-term ones. It consolidates new information, then helps transfer it to the cerebral cortex for long-term storage. The hippocampus also aids in retrieving memories, and quality sleep plays a crucial role in this entire process.

Although it's thought unlikely that we can exhaust the vast capacity of long-term memory, our short-term memory's capacity is limited, and information that isn't processed or understood is typically lost. Stress has a profound and multifaceted impact on memory, including the potential to shrink the hippocampus and disrupt both short- and long-term memory systems.

The hippocampus continues to develop during the teenage years, affecting memory, learning, emotional control, and spatial navigation. Stress, a lack of sleep, and emotional turmoil can all impede its growth. To support your teen's hippocampal development, encourage good sleep hygiene, as quality sleep strengthens memory. Promote structure and routines, as repeated learning aids memory consolidation. Reducing stress by taking time to connect with your teen, helping manage any anxiety, and repeating information while using visuals will help your teen remember it more effectively, supporting both memory formation and emotional regulation.

NEUROLOGICAL, BIOLOGICAL, AND PSYCHOLOGICAL CHALLENGES

MEMORY

Memory is a complex subject. Our minds are selective in what they choose to remember. To protect ourselves, our brain sometimes uses the process of disassociation, which is where our minds choose to block out unwanted memories.

Memories are stored in various parts of our brain, incorporating inputs from visual, tactile and auditory areas. Bizarrely, under a microscope, the associated interconnections resemble a network or spider's web since they are encoded from all different brain regions.

Experiments with mice and other animals are currently being conducted to see whether we can externally manipulate the brain's memories by overwriting, erasing or adding to them, in the hope of treating illnesses such as depression, PTSD, Alzheimer's, or schizophrenia. However, scientists are considering the ethical standpoint. In the case of treating diseases, they think it may be acceptable, but in the case of deleting painful memories, some are unsure since the implications could be dire, especially when it comes to evidence and the law.

Memory plays a vital role in how we learn, store, and recall information. During the teenage years, memory systems are still developing, meaning our teens may face challenges when retaining and recalling details, especially when under pressure. Memory struggles can manifest in different ways, such as forgetting tasks, misplacing important items, or difficulty with retaining information over the long term. To support your teen, try providing consistent routines and give them plenty of chances to practice and repeat things. Encourage active recall, like quizzing them or breaking tasks down into smaller, more manageable steps over time. Creating a calm, low-stress environment will also help with memory retention, as stress can really affect the brain's ability to process and store information.

THE AMYGDALA

Due to its shape, the amygdala was named after the Greek word for 'almond'. Located within our temporal lobe, it's part of our limbic system. Even though a paired structure, it's considered as one brain area, enabling us to have separate memory systems for each hemisphere. Working in conjunction with other regions like the hippocampus, the amygdala is responsible for attaching emotional content to memories, forming new memories, and processing emotional responses. The amygdala is adept at evaluating incoming information and generating appropriate responses, such as a defensive reaction to a perceived threat.

Our amygdala plays a vital role in our emotional learning and behaviour, including instinctive behaviour. A major player in detecting and responding to fear or threats in the environment, it's constantly on the lookout for these signals. If danger is sensed, the amygdala will initiate the 'fight-flight-freeze' response, and we may even find ourselves reacting to a fearful situation before we are even consciously aware that we are being threatened.

Historically, the amygdala is thought to be primarily responsible for responses linked to intense negative emotions. However, more recently, research suggests that this structure is also involved in the processing of strong, positive emotions. The right amygdala is believed to be primarily associated with negative responses, while the left, to both negative and positive ones. Research informs us that our amygdala is thought to be involved in systems responsible for reward-based learning, food intake, sex, addictive drugs and decision making.

In some instances, overreaction from our amygdala leads to 'amygdala hijacking', during which time sudden, intense, emotional reactions are displayed that are out of proportion for the situation. When this happens, we often regret our actions. For example, we might suddenly lose our temper and verbally lash out a someone. During such moments, our amygdala is attempting to protect us from perceived danger.

Research led by Joseph LeDoux, a Neuroscientist at New York University and a leading specialist in this field, indicates that our amygdala isn't directly responsible when we experience feelings of fear, but instead contributes to these feelings by detecting and responding (Le Doux, 2015).

Experts suggest that while individuals with amygdala removal may experience increased violence and a 180-

degree turn in their personality, others, particularly those with epilepsy, have shown to benefit from this procedure, experiencing reduced seizure activity and improved quality of life in some cases. However, such outcomes can vary significantly depending on the individual and the underlying condition.

Until the prefrontal cortex is fully developed, teens tend to rely more heavily on their amygdala for emotional responses. This explains why teens tend to act on their emotions, displaying strong emotional outbursts. Since their amygdala isn't yet connected efficiently to the logical part of their brain (the prefrontal cortex), they are more likely to engage in negative thought patterns, often assuming the worst-case scenario.

It's worth noting that our teens can struggle to correctly decipher social cues and emotions, which can lead to misinterpretations. Perhaps this is why they are more prone to amygdala hijacking.

If your teen frequently experiences negative emotions, you can help him transform these feelings into neutral or positive ones by teaching him how to pause, reflect, and weigh up his thoughts, while keeping the bigger picture in mind. To support his developing brain, encourage him to build emotional awareness by naming and talking about his feelings. Teach him deep breathing or grounding techniques to help settle his brain's alarm system and encourage plenty of downtime to reduce emotional overwhelm. You can also model emotional control by staying calm throughout any outbursts.

THE PREFRONTAL CORTEX

"Right now, we have a unique opportunity to nurture our teens by fostering a positive impact on their mindset, one they will carry into adulthood."

The prefrontal cortex (PFC), located just behind the forehead, forms the front part of the frontal lobe and accounts for about 30% of the frontal lobe of the cerebral cortex. Broadly divided into functional regions, including the ventromedial (such as the orbitofrontal) and lateral PFC, each region is responsible for different cognitive processes. Although neurons in the PFC begin developing before birth, the most significant growth and refinement take place during childhood and adolescence, especially around puberty.

The PFC is our brain's key decision-making hub and moderator for complex goal-oriented functions, including emotional control, self-regulation, self-awareness, social behaviour, planning, organisation, time management, and executive skills like maintaining focus and anticipating outcomes. Our teen's sense of the passage of time is still developing, partly because the prefrontal cortex and its connections to other brain regions like the cerebellum and parietal lobes are still maturing. This can make it harder for teens to estimate how long tasks will take or to manage time effectively.

Our PFC plays a crucial role in rational thinking, receiving input from various cortical regions to process information in real-time. It supports our ability to exercise judgment, logic, and reasoning, as well as to multi-task and anticipate consequences. In collaboration with other brain regions, it helps organise and retrieve memories.

According to the University of Queensland's Brain Institute, there are functional differences between our PFC's left and right hemispheres. The right being more active in spatial working memory, and the left in verbal working memory.

The PFC is one of the most talked about regions of the teenage brain. As it's still developing, structurally and functionally, teens' capabilities, in the areas of decision making and behavioural regulation, including emotional control, are limited. Until their PFCs are fully developed, our teens must rely heavily on their amygdala as the neural connections between the emotional and decision-making areas are still being established. Unfortunately, their neural connections don't always develop at the same pace as their PFC. This is important to understand as it explains why our teens' immediate reaction to most situations is to exhibit an *emotion* as opposed to a *thought*. Elucidating why they can't later explain what they were thinking as, in actual fact, they were *feeling* more than they were *thinking*. **Therefore, often teens don't think, they feel.**

Adults, on the other hand, have the advantage of possessing a fully developed PFC, enabling them to respond to situations in a rational way, using planning and reasoning. As our teens are yet to experience this luxury, they *respond emotionally* and often on their *gut reactions*, before they've even thought about the subject at hand. Akin to riding a bike before the brakes have been fitted. Until their PFC has developed, controlling their impulses becomes near impossible for them, which justifies why they tend to act on their *impulses* rather than using rational thinking. Once their PFC has developed, they will be able to make rational judgements.

To plan out what we are going to say before we speak, adults collect real-time information, which avoids inappropriate behaviour, such as saying or doing something foolish. Yet, for our teens, this would be very challenging. Perhaps this is why they are often accused of speaking without thinking.

"The prefrontal cortex is one of the last regions of the Brain to reach maturation, which explains why some adolescents exhibit behavioural immaturity."

"Behavioral control requires a great involvement of cognitive and executive functions. These functions are localised in the prefrontal cortex, which matures independent of puberty and continues to evolve up until

24 years of age. It has been suggested that, during this period, adolescents should not be overprotected, but be allowed to make mistakes, learn from their own experiences, and practice self-regulation. Parents and teachers can help adolescents through this period by listening and offering support and guidance" (Arain et al., 2013).

To support our sons' PFC's development and to help their brains build the necessary neural connections, encourage them to make decisions at their own pace. The more they practise executive functions, the more efficient these connections become. As they refine these skills, they will be better prepared for adult-related tasks like securing a job or managing finances. When your teen makes a mistake, you can, in a supportive non-blaming way, gently point it out if he hasn't already identified it himself. If he's struggling with tasks such as his to-do list, assist by walking him through it, suggesting that he breaks it down into smaller, more manageable steps, and, if needed, enlists the help of a friend.

The following illustrates the judgemental capacity of our PFC. Not long ago, I was driving down a main road with the intention of turning into a side street. I slowed down and waited for the oncoming traffic to clear. While watching the approaching car, I was debating whether or not there was enough time to turn safely, feeling impatient as I was running late. My initial thought was that I could make the turn, but just a couple of seconds later, I felt my PFC step in. It told me to wait and act sensibly, as there might not be enough time to turn safely.

GREY MATTER AND WHITE MATTER

GREY MATTER

The Central Nervous System is composed of grey and white matter. While some areas of grey matter are found deep within the brain, grey matter (GM) predominantly makes up the outermost layer of the brain, the cerebral cortex. Grey matter is primarily made up of neuronal cell bodies, glial cells, dendrites, and synapses, and contains relatively few myelinated axons compared to white matter.

GM's main function is to process and interpret information in the brain. It plays a critical role in daily activities such as emotional regulation, memory retention, muscle control, decision-making, speech, self-control, and processing sensory inputs like sight and sound. GM's volume peaks in late childhood and gradually declines through adolescence, partly due to synaptic pruning. While GM tends to develop earlier than white matter in some regions, myelination continues into adulthood. GM contains mostly unmyelinated or lightly myelinated axons, which can lead to slower signal transmission compared to the heavily myelinated axons in white matter.

In the past, scientists believed that teens lose GM during adolescence. However, recent research carried out at Penn State University, USA, has shown that although the overall volume of grey matter decreases, its density actually increases, reflecting a more refined and efficient brain structure. Until this developmental stage is complete, particularly in areas such as the prefrontal cortex, our teens may find it harder to regulate emotions, make decisions, or control their impulses. Since much of this brain development occurs during sleep, it's essential that our teens get enough high-quality sleep to support healthy brain maturation.

"If we are puzzled by the behavior of adolescents, it may help to know that they need to adjust to a brain that is changing in its size and composition at the same time that demands on performance and acceptable behavior keep scaling up" (University of Pennsylvania School of Medicine, 2017).

WHITE MATTER

White matter (WM), found mainly in the deeper regions of the brain, is primarily composed of myelinated axons and glial cells, although some unmyelinated axons are also present. Glial cells play a key role in supporting and maintaining neural function. Derived from the Greek word for 'glue', glial cells are found in both the central and peripheral nervous systems and are integral to their proper functioning. Glial cells play crucial roles in supporting neurons, aiding in recovery from nerve injury, and producing myelin. They provide structural support, protection, and nutrients to neurons, helping to maintain and regulate neural networks.

WM derives its name from myelin, the white, fatty substance that coats and insulates the nerve fibres. Unlike GM, WM contains relatively few synapses and neuronal cell bodies. WM plays a crucial role in functions such as learning, memory, reading, motor coordination, visuospatial processing, and the acquisition of new skills. During childhood and adolescence, WM density increases, particularly in the prefrontal cortex and corpus callosum, contributing to enhanced brain connectivity and cognitive development.

Excessive screen time, especially when it leads to reduced sleep and limits activities like exercise or social interactions, can negatively affect WM development in teens. Research has shown that too much screen use can weaken the quality of WM, slowing the formation of important brain connections. This can impact attention, decision-making, and memory. Furthermore, pre-bed screen time can disrupt sleep, which is crucial for healthy brain development. Finding a healthy balance of screen use, quality sleep, and real-world engagement is key to supporting WM growth.

NEUROLOGICAL, BIOLOGICAL, AND PSYCHOLOGICAL CHALLENGES

RISK-TAKING

We all want to protect our children and shield them from pain when we see them struggling, but this ultimately does them a disservice as it doesn't prepare them for adulthood. Instead, we need to loosen the reins so they can explore and experience new opportunities, as decision-making is important for cognitive growth. Unquestionably, freedom may come at a price, bringing potential risks, but this is a natural part of life, and with proper guidance, these risks can be managed.

There are numerous activities that tempt our teens. From the thrill of trying new experiences to the participation in age-old activities, such as initiation ceremonies held by students at universities, which can unfortunately have disastrous consequences. However, not all result in negative outcomes. Provided that we've taught them right from wrong, by discussing scenarios such as speeding, unprotected sex, consuming alcohol before driving or carrying out illegal or immoral acts, our teens should know what is and isn't acceptable in our eyes.

The words 'risky behaviour' and 'teenagers' seem to go hand in hand, especially male teens. Although some engage in it wittingly and are more influenced by outside factors such as their peers, many do not. Not that I'm condoning it, but engaging in risk-taking activities helps teens understand how the world operates, highlights their strengths and weaknesses, provides insight into their self-perception and gives them an opportunity to learn new skills, thus preparing them for future challenges. Some believe that it's beneficial if teens make mistakes whilst still in the nest, when parents are around to help and advise, rather than waiting until they've left home. But we must remember that it's not just teens that take risks, adults do too. Whether it's speeding, having unprotected sex or just failing to turn off the lawnmower whilst emptying the grass box.

Teen's risk-taking actions are often due to enticing rewards, which, in their minds, outweigh any potential losses. Ergo, the emphasis is on the rewards. Even though risks may be high, a teen's focus will be on the positive outcome he *hopes* to achieve. Among professionals in the field, there are various schools of thought regarding the reasoning behind teenage involvement in risky behaviour. The majority attribute it to their developing PFC, which is logical as they are yet to fully grasp the implications of actions and consequences. If this holds true, it's important to understand it's not necessarily our teens' fault. At the same time, some professionals believe that teenagers are capable of making decisions but are more motivated by the rewards than the losses, e.g. being seen as 'cool' by their friends when smoking, versus getting lung cancer.

Teens will take greater risks if they have an audience. Being watched by their peers, especially by people they admire or aspire to, magnifies their reward. As humans, our motivation for approval is innate and linked to our need to belong. Akin to adults, teens don't want to be socially excluded, which is why they go along with the crowd to avoid being the odd one out. But we must remember, adults often act this way too. Recently, while completing my laps in the pool, a man started swimming in the lane next to me. I then noticed my innate desire to swim faster, not just to keep up with him but to outdo him.

Then there are professionals who believe that, even if teens understand the risks, their decisions are complex, as they face confusing thoughts and feelings. These include weighing their need and desire to look cool in front of their friends, a significant pull for them, against the desire to stay safe. With thoughts like, 'Should I face my fears and go with the crowd, or risk being rejected by my peers and branded a coward, but stay safe?' crossing their minds, it's no wonder that common sense often doesn't prevail. This helps explain the disparity between the desire to take on risky activities and the ability to make sensible decisions, or possibly, their inability to avoid inappropriate behaviour.

"The observation that adolescents know that they are engaging in risky behavior is not supported by the sole explanation of a less developed prefrontal cortex. In this context, our model suggests that the adolescent is capable of making rational decisions, but in emotionally charged situations the more mature limbic system will win over the prefrontal control system" (Casey et al., 2008).

"It's not a question of intellectual maturity. Most studies show that abstract reasoning, memory, and the formal capacity for planning are fully developed by age 15 or 16. If teenagers are asked hypothetical questions about risk and reward, they usually give the same answers as adults. But the emotional state in which they answer questionnaires is not necessarily the one in which they make important choices. In real life, adolescents, compared to adults, find it more difficult to interrupt an action under way (e.g. stop speeding), to think before acting (learn how deep the water is before you dive), and even to choose between safer and riskier alternatives. It's easy for them to say that they would not get into a car with a drunk driver, but more difficult to turn down the invitation in practice. Adolescents' judgment can be overwhelmed by the urge for new experiences, thrill-seeking, and sexual and aggressive impulses. They sometimes seem driven to seek experiences that produce strong feelings and sensations" (Harvard Health Publishing, 2011).

An alternative professional standpoint is that risky behaviour is due to a lack of experience of being an adult, and not related to an underdeveloped PFC. You can make up your own mind on which theories sit more comfortably with you. In the meantime, I believe that we shouldn't overlook the idea that a lack of sleep may be a large contender for risky behaviour due to the inability to think clearly, along with the idea that FOMO may play a part in all of this. Nor can we ignore the influences of social media and the internet.

Although teenage risk-taking is often viewed negatively by the public, many young people are making great strides.

Examples include Swedish activist Greta Thunberg and American artist and activist Nadia Nazar.

BRAIN FUEL

As with our body, our brain needs good-quality food to fuel it so that it can function optimally. Using up approximately 20% of our calorie intake, the brain needs a combination of high-quality carbohydrates, healthy fats, vitamins, minerals and proteins. If it doesn't get enough, we suffer. Hunger can lead to adverse effects such as nausea, bad breath, lack of focus, lack of concentration, irritability, drop in blood pressure and fainting can take over. Long-term damage may occur if food intake or fluids are insufficient, leading to mild dehydration, which can affect attention, memory, and executive functions.

SEX DIFFERENCES IN BRAIN DEVELOPMENT

In the paper titled *Sex differences in the developing brain: insights from multimodal neuroimaging*, researchers confirmed that males' brains are generally about 9–12% larger than females, including greater overall volumes of both grey and white matter. However, when it comes to specific brain regions such as the hippocampus, the evidence is mixed. Before puberty, males and females have similar hippocampal volumes, and although some studies suggest that after puberty females may have larger hippocampi, when overall brain size is considered, these differences diminish. Additionally, the amygdala appears to develop differently between sexes. In females, its volume increases rapidly before peaking and then decreases, whereas in males, it continues to increase during puberty (Kaczkurkin et al., 2018).

An earlier paper, *Sex differences in the structural connectome of the human brain*, indicates that females show greater interhemispheric connectivity, and males more localised intrahemispheric connections (Ingalhalikar et al., 2014).

As with both papers, these results vary between studies and depend on analysis methods and whether brain size is adjusted for, highlighting that while some sex differences in brain development are well-established, many details remain uncertain, and further research is needed to clarify them. So, what does this mean for parents? Research discussed in Scientific American (2016) highlights that while boys and girls show some differences, most psychological sex differences are relatively small.

The Scientific American article explores how early life experiences and parenting styles shape brain development and behaviour. Early life experiences can alter gene functions, leading to significant behavioural outcomes. The quality of maternal care has been linked to neural and psychological consequences. Likewise, the way we parent boys versus girls may shape children's developing brains. For example, mothers tend to discourage physical risk-taking more in daughters than in sons. (Fathers encourage more risk taking in children than mothers do, but no one has tested the likely hypothesis that dads pressure sons more than daughters in this respect.)

Boys are more physically active than girls from infancy through childhood. Research shows that the average boy is more active than about 69 per cent of girls.

Peers also shape behaviour: in all-boy groups, lively boys tend to energise each other, while energetic girls usually gather in smaller groups of calmer friends. In organised sports, girls start playing later, quit earlier, and join fewer teams overall than boys, reflecting cultural factors that amplify differences in physical skills.

Many studies show that boys tend to be more physically aggressive than girls. This difference is associated with prenatal testosterone levels but, interestingly, is not related to the rise in testosterone during adolescence.

One challenge boys face is that, as they mature, they are often encouraged to suppress expressions of fear, sadness, and tenderness. This 'toughening up' process is less common for girls, resulting in boys being less emotionally expressive and often also less sensitive to others' feelings. Such social conditioning likely affects the amygdala, a highly adaptable part of the brain. Encouraging greater resilience in girls and greater emotional sensitivity in boys is both achievable and beneficial for everyone.

Language differences appear early. Girls start talking about a month earlier than boys and are around 12 per cent ahead in reading by kindergarten. Their advantage in reading and writing grows through school, so by 12th grade, 47 per cent more girls than boys graduate as proficient readers, with an even bigger gap in writing, based on decades of U.S. Department of Education data.

There is little evidence that girls are neurologically more advanced in reading; it's more likely due to the fact that girls read more than boys, which boosts their long-term academic performance.

From birth, a child's language exposure is the key factor shaping their verbal skills. Studies show gender explains only about 3 per cent of the differences in toddlers' language ability, while environment and exposure account for over 50 per cent. So, the more parents engage boys with talking, reading, songs, and stories, the better their language and literacy development.

While girls tend to excel in verbal skills, boys often have an advantage in spatial abilities. Spatial skill differences are among the largest cognitive gaps, with the average man outperforming up to 80 per cent of women in mental rotation tasks.

Most sex differences aren't as fixed as people often think. While genes and hormones start some differences, culture and upbringing play a bigger role in shaping both sexes. Understanding this can help reduce stereotypes and encourage parents and teachers to support children in developing a wider range of skills (Scientific American, 2016).

The above article from 2016 provides valuable insights into early brain differences and their interaction with environment and culture. Building on this, more recent research analysing newborn brains confirms that some structural differences are present prenatally. For example, females show more grey matter in regions linked to memory and emotion, while males have more white matter in sensory and motor areas. These findings further support the idea that biology lays the groundwork, but environmental and cultural influences continue to shape development (Neuroscience News, 2025).

BRAIN FACTS

The following is a list of interesting facts about the brain:

- As your brain is constantly changing, reading this book may help consolidate memories and leave a lasting memory trace.
- At least 50% of our brain is made up of fat.

NEUROLOGICAL, BIOLOGICAL, AND PSYCHOLOGICAL CHALLENGES

- Experts say that the more familiar you are with a subject, the easier it is to remember related information.
- It has been said that if we laid out just one person's myelinated fibres, they would stretch around the world three times.
- Our 5 senses can unconsciously take in approximately 11 million pieces of information at any given moment, but we can only process around 40 of them (Wilson 2022).
- Our 5 senses can process approximately 40 pieces of information per second consciously (Wilson 2022).
- Our brain develops from the back to the front.
- Our brain never really rests; even during deep sleep the brain remains active.
- Research suggests that substance abuse, cigarette use, and alcohol can significantly affect brain development.
- Signals travel up to 100 times faster through myelinated axons compared to unmyelinated ones.
- Some nerve impulses can travel up to 100 metres per second, approximately 200 miles an hour.
- Teen brains develop at breakneck speed, highlighting the teenage years as a critical stage of life.
- The brain is composed of approximately 75% water.

NEUROLOGICAL, BIOLOGICAL, AND PSYCHOLOGICAL CHALLENGES

- The teenage brain is strongly influenced by its environment, which, in turn, is influenced by the teenager.
- The average brain contains around 86 billion brain cells. Each cell connects to roughly 1,000 other cells, forming a network of about 86 trillion connections.
- The brain uses about 20% of the body's total blood supply.
- The brain of the average adolescent is only about 80% developed.
- The plasticity of the teenage brain allows for adaption to its environment, which can lead to both positive and negative outcomes.
- Myelinated axons transmit signals far more efficiently than unmyelinated ones.
- Since the brain runs on electrical signals, stimulating it electrically can actually change the way it functions.
- We use our brain to work out how our brain works!

MENTAL HEALTH

'Covid was difficult. Not talking to my friends.' Young person.

The teenage brain is malleable, adapting and evolving in response to its environment. Trauma can cause the brain to become hypervigilant and alter information processing, leading to increased risk of anxiety and behaviour problems later in life. According to MQ Mental Health Research, 75% of mental illnesses start before a child reaches their 18th birthday, while 50% of mental health problems in adult life (excluding dementia) take root before the age of 15 (MQ Mental Health, 2021). Unfortunately, most cases go undetected and untreated, including early signs of psychotic disorders, which can be missed as they resemble normal adolescent development and hormonal changes.

High levels of long-term stress can impact the teenage brain, causing impairment of developing neurons, leading to behaviour problems and learning difficulties, affecting mental and physical well-being. Due to either impaired neurons or an immature prefrontal cortex, some teens are unable to control emotions, or understand or express their feelings, leaving them susceptible to depression and self-harm.

During adolescence, neurons are maturing in the stress-sensitive region of the corticolimbic system. This system comprises the prefrontal cortex, amygdala and hippocampus. Although there is no conclusive evidence, most probably due to the infancy of brain research, experts believe that long-term exposure to stress can lead to dysfunctions such as depression, anxiety, sleep problems, digestive problems, PTSD, weight gain, heart problems and high blood pressure. It's also thought that stress can alter the physical shape and size of the structures within this system. With the knock-on effect that stress can play havoc with our bodies.

NUTRITION

Regular exercise, coupled with good nutrition, contributes to a healthy body. During the teenage years, whilst the body and brain are developing rapidly, the importance of a healthy diet goes without saying. A well-balanced diet supplies essential nutrients crucial for immune function, cognitive abilities, muscular and skeletal development, sexual health, organ function, energy levels, focus, mood regulation, and heart health. Iron, an essential mineral at this stage of growth and the most frequently occurring micronutrient deficiency, promotes healthy myelination, maintains brain functions, transports oxygen and aids neurotransmitter production. Due to the heightened levels of physical growth and muscular development, teens need an increased amount of iron. Research suggests a possible link between low iron levels and psychological disorders, including mental health conditions. Calcium is another vital nutrient needed at this stage of life, approximately 50% of adult bone mass accrues during adolescence. And vitamin D is essential for the proper functioning of the immune system, as well as skeletal and muscle development. All three key nutrients are commonly known to be insufficiently consumed by UK adolescents. Other nutrients that require monitoring include B vitamins, zinc, vitamin A, folic acid, fibre, and magnesium.

One of the greatest actions we can undertake for our teens is to foster a healthy attitude to eating. A diet that includes protein, dairy, healthy fats, high-fibre foods including wholegrains, plenty of fresh fruit and vegetables, and limited amounts of sugar and refined carbohydrates will set them up for life. Teaching them how to cook is one of the best ways to accomplish this, throwing in some basic nutritional facts along the way. To make the process even more enjoyable, try introducing new foods and experimenting with different cuisines.

Happiness – Be Realistic

It's natural to experience fleeting moments of happiness or joy in our day, but when we reflect on this we realise that we only spend a small percentage feeling really happy. Therefore, it would be unrealistic to expect anything different from our teens, who are going through such turbulent times and constantly treading water.

Whilst it's important to keep happiness as our goal, we should not be defeated by our teens' low moods and use it as an excuse to beat ourselves up and worry excessively. Some days, like us, they just aren't feeling positive. That said, it's important to distinguish the difference between short-lived low moods and common mental health conditions such as anxiety and depression. It's prudent to seek help if your teen's low mood persists for a couple of months without any signs of improvement, or if he falls into depression, shows signs of anxiety, or acts in a way that you feel is a cry for help, such as self-harming.

MENTAL HEALTH CONDITIONS

"The 'state of youth' has become an increasingly popular subject of debate in academic, policy and media circles. Commentators fear that British youth are on the verge of mental breakdown, at risk from antisocial behaviour, self-harm, drug and alcohol abuse" (Dixon et al., 2006).

"Children and young people who are currently growing up in the UK are doing so in challenging times, from schools being a recurrent area of concern for their well-being, to long NHS waits when they need support. In addition, the recent Covid-19 pandemic was followed by large increases to the cost of living that have pushed many families into financial hardship, with a record number of UK children now living in poverty" (The Children's Society, 2024).

"UK Teenagers Are Facing a Happiness Recession", and "UK Teenagers Rank Last for Life Satisfaction in Europe." Sky News, August 2024, quoted Mark Russell from The Children's Society.

For several years, the UK has ranked as having the unhappiest children in Europe. Fear of failure is one of the main reasons, which isn't surprising as we've shifted away from focusing on our children and families to focusing on our careers. Although we cannot necessarily be blamed, as we need to provide for our families, we must admit that our need not only to keep up with the Joneses, but outdo them, is far too common. Yet, in our mad rush for consumerism, we've failed to notice the trail of disruption we've left behind.

The World Health Organisation states:

- "Globally, one in seven 10-19-year-olds experiences a mental disorder, accounting for 15% of the global burden of disease in this age group.
- Depression, anxiety and behavioural disorders are among the leading causes of illness and disability among adolescents.
- Suicide is the third leading cause of death among those aged 15–29 years old.
- The consequences of failing to address adolescent mental health conditions extend to adulthood, impairing both physical and mental health and limiting opportunities to lead fulfilling lives as adults" (World Health Organisation, 2024).

One in seven children experiencing a mental disorder equates to approximately 4.5 children in each classroom. Admittedly, we are more aware than previous generations, but we still need to ask ourselves if we've addressed this issue in a manner that has made enough impact yet. The frightening thought is that if these conditions aren't treated at this crucial stage of life, they will continue into adulthood, affecting our teens' lives for many years to come, and possibly their children's as well. Mental health conditions such as major depression disorder (MDD), are growing at an alarming rate and are now prevalent amongst teenagers, which, if not treated during the teenage years, are likely to become precursors for more serious conditions later in life.

Considering its prevalence among teenagers, it's a welcome relief that mental health conditions are no longer a taboo subject, allowing teens to openly discuss their struggles without being seen as 'odd,' unlike in previous generations. Yet, despite this progress, many still find it difficult to broach the subject.

Often, mental health issues affect our young people more than we realise. When teens reach out to express feelings of depression or anxiety, or verbalise that things are just not right, we need to make sure that we take them seriously. It's far too easy for cries of help to fall on deaf ears when parents either don't listen properly or find the conversation too difficult to handle, often causing them to shut the discussion down. However, it's essential that they are taken seriously and that we don't dismiss their feelings or put it down to 'having a bad day' or label their behaviour as 'normal teenage behaviour'. It's also easy to fall into the trap of assuming that if they seem OK then they must be OK, as this is not always the case, especially with boys, as they can be more fearful than girls when it comes to telling parents that something is wrong.

It can be difficult for adults, let alone teenagers, to motivate themselves to take action to get the support they need, which is why our teens need our full support. Seeking medical help, either on their own or with a parent, often, is not an option, as often they feel embarrassed or worry that they've done something wrong. Some find the whole experience far too traumatic, especially ones that are fearful of the possible medical outcome. Teens worry that conversations will not be kept confidential, and that the information will be fed back to their parents. Talking about their problems, especially to strangers, including their own GP, is really difficult for this age group. Which is why so many cases go untreated and undiagnosed professionally. Sadly, receiving help for a mental health condition, even when a diagnosis has been made, be it by the teen themselves or a family member, isn't usually straightforward as often there are further stumbling blocks along the way.

To make matters worse, apart from visiting their GP, many teens don't know where else to turn. According to the *Young People's Health and Wellbeing Survey* (2023), conducted by Hertfordshire County Council, 37.1% of all respondents answered 'Not sure' or 'No' when asked if they knew how to access support and services for mental health.

Researching mental health conditions online can easily lead to misinformation and can frighten teens. Even from a GP's perspective, it can be difficult to assess the situation when the teen sitting in front of them is unsure or not forthcoming with some of the pieces of the jigsaw puzzle. A more complete understanding of a teenager's mental health often requires input from multiple sources, including parents, teachers, caregivers, and the young person themselves.

In 2019, the charity YoungMinds commissioned a survey of 1,008 GPs regarding their experiences in treating young people who were struggling with their mental health. Below is Emma Thomas, Chief Executive of YoungMinds, reply:

"As these worrying results show, GPs are on the front line when it comes to mental health, but too often they don't believe that there is good enough early support in their community. That leaves them grappling with the difficult choice of trying to help young people themselves, or referring them to mental health services, even when those services are overstretched. This means many young people either receive support from GPs who have the best of intentions but may not feel equipped to provide the right help, or can face long waiting times for specialist services, which may then turn them away because of high thresholds for treatment" (YoungMinds, 2019).

We only have to glance at The Children's Society website to see that 1 in 8 children have low well-being, equivalent to 3-4 children in each class at school (The Children's Society, 2022).

The list of common mental health conditions that our teens face is troublingly long and includes:

- ADHD – Attention Deficit Hyperactivity Disorder.
- Anxiety Disorder.
- Borderline Personality Disorder.
- DID – Dissociative Identity Disorder.
- Depression.
- Eating Disorders.
- Gaming Disorder.
- HPD – Histrionic Personality Disorder.
- Insomnia.
- ODD – Oppositional Defiant Disorder.
- OCD – Obsessive Compulsive Disorder.
- Panic Disorder.
- PTSD – Post Traumatic Stress Disorder.
- Schizophrenia.
- Suicidal thoughts/attempts.
- SUD – Substance Use Disorder.

NEUROLOGICAL, BIOLOGICAL, AND PSYCHOLOGICAL CHALLENGES

Please note that it's important not to jump too quickly to conclusions or apply labels as sometimes what looks like a condition can be a normal part of development.

When it comes to the increasing number of mental health conditions that our teens face today, we must consider that there may be other challenges that put a strain on their mental health too, such as:

- Family health issues.
- Divorce or separation.
- Bereavement.
- Issues at school.
- Moving house.
- Moving school.
- Own underlying health issues.
- Issues with neighbours.
- Poor or unresolved relationships within the family or with friends.
- Upcoming exams.

With timetables often crammed full of school, chores, homework, extracurricular activities, and tutoring, it's hard for our teens to achieve a good work/life balance. While it's important to instil a good work ethic, it's equally important to teach our teens that life isn't just about work.

They need to understand balance in all areas of their lives: work, rest *and* play. If their work/life balance is out of sync it can lead to frustration, stress and mental health conditions, with a knock-on effect on other family members too. As the pressures on our young people have increased, they need to know that highly paid jobs don't automatically equate to happiness. Fun, time with friends and time to nurture and look after themselves is essential. Undoubtedly, when they become adults, there will be certain times when 'all work and no play' will be necessary, but this should only be a temporary measure and not how they spend the majority of their time.

Thanks to the pandemic, the recent impact on teenagers' mental health has been devastating. It was widely reported in the news that during the first year of Covid-19 self-harm rates soared.

Alongside the elderly, I believe teenagers suffered the most during Covid-19, especially since many had virtually no contact with their peers or friends.

"Record numbers of children and young people are being referred to mental health services for crisis and non-crisis care, as the toll of the pandemic on the country's mental health is revealed in a new analysis by the Royal College of Psychiatrists. Eighteen months after the first lockdown and after warnings from the mental health sector about the long-lasting mental health impact of the pandemic, the Royal College of Psychiatrists' analysis of NHS Digital data found that:

- 190,271 0–18-year-olds were referred to children and young people's mental health services between April and June this year, up 134% on the same period last year (81,170) and 96% on 2019 (97,342).

- 8,552 children and young people were referred for urgent or emergency crisis care between April and June this year, up 80% on the same period last year (4,741) and up 64% on 2019 (5,219)."

The Royal College of Psychiatrists called on the then education secretary, Nadhim Zahawi MP, to make children and young people's mental health needs a top priority (Royal College of Psychiatrists, 2021).

The NHS's Mental Health of Children and Young People in England Survey, 2022, noted the following:

- In young people aged 17 to 19 years, rates of a probable mental disorder rose from 1 in 10 (10.1%) in 2017 to 1 in 6 (17.7%) in 2020. Rates were stable between 2020 and 2021, but then increased from 1 in 6 (17.4%) in 2021 to 1 in 4 (25.7%) in 2022.

- 11 to 16 year olds with a probable mental disorder were less likely to feel safe at school (61.2%) than those unlikely to have a mental disorder (89.2%). They were also less likely to report enjoyment of learning or having a friend they could turn to for support.

- 1 in 8 (12.6%) 11 to 16 year old social media users reported that they had been bullied online. This was more than 1 in 4 (29.4%) among those with a probable mental disorder.

- 11 to 16 year old social media users with a probable mental disorder were less likely to report feeling safe online (48.4%) than those unlikely to have a disorder (66.5%).
- 1 in 5 (19.9%) 7 to 16 year olds lived in households that experienced a reduction in household income in the past year. This was more than 1 in 4 (28.6%) among children with a probable mental disorder (NHS Digital, 2022).

Regarding family support, the *Mental Health of Children and Young People in England 2021 – wave 2 follow-up survey* found that "Children and young people (11 to 23 years) with a probable mental disorder had lower levels of family connectedness than those unlikely to have a mental disorder" (Newlove-Delgado et al., 2021).

Self-harm

Self-harm is commonly misunderstood as it's often wrongly classed as a mental health condition. In reality, it's a behaviour perceived as an unhealthy coping mechanism for emotional pain. Self-harm occurs when someone inflicts physical harm as a means to alleviate their emotional pain. This behaviour is often regarded as a distress signal, though in certain cases it may be associated with conditions such as depression. Individuals resort to self-harm when grappling with intense emotions and thoughts, particularly in response to overwhelming situations or distressing memories that they struggle to articulate. Due to the stigma around self-harm, young people tend to engage in these actions behind closed doors, making it harder for parents or teachers to detect and address.

Besides releasing emotional pain, there are various other reasons why people self-harm. These reasons include the desire to feel in control; a need to physically care for themselves; an impulse to punish themselves for their emotions or experiences (including feelings of guilt or self-loathing); a form of distraction; a sense of relief; a way to detach from life or an attempt to end emotional numbness. However, this often leads to feelings of guilt or shame, trapping young people in a vicious cycle.

The cycle of self-harm can be addictive, so it's crucial to handle it with care when helping a teen break free from it. This is to prevent the transfer of thoughts or actions onto something equally destructive, or even worse, such as suicide.

Methods of self-induced injury include pulling out hair, hitting body parts against a wall, cutting, burning, hitting oneself, excessive exercise, self-poisoning, seeking out fights where they know they can't win, eating disorders, and the misuse of drugs or alcohol.

Sadly, when a teen suffers from a mental health condition, they are more likely to attempt self-harm or attempt suicide compared to those that do not. Self-harm, while not necessarily an attempt of suicide, may serve as a way for a teen to express his suicidal thoughts and feelings without actually taking his own life.

In some situations, you may need to take immediate action. Initially, talk to your teen and then get help from the appropriate source, be it a GP or if necessary an A & E dept. There are many organisations online that you can talk to. You can also seek out a counsellor/therapist and depending on where you are in the country, you may be able to access free counselling via a charity.

"In 2017 in England, a quarter (25.5%) of 11 to 16-year-olds with a mental disorder had self-harmed or attempted suicide at some point, compared to 3.0% of those who were not diagnosed as having a mental disorder. In 17 to 19-year-olds with a mental disorder, nearly half (46.8%) had self-harmed or made a suicide attempt" (NHS Digital 2017).

(Self-harm) "It's not an act toward ending a life, even though it increases risk. If anything, it is kind of life affirming. It is a way to try to do something about a situation" (The Children's Society, 2023).

"409,347 children were referred in England for issues, such as self-harm between April and October 2021" (The Children's Society, 2022).

Suicide

We've all seen the Samaritans advert telling us that every 90 minutes someone in the UK dies by suicide. According to the Samaritans approximately 200 young people (those under the age of 20) die by suicide each year in England (personal communication, 2023).

Don't be afraid to broach the subject of suicide with your teen. The Samaritans encourage people to use the word 'suicide' in conversations as they've found it to be advantageous to the situation. Using the word often eliminates the elephant in the room, giving a sense of relief to the person suffering. If possible, it's always best to plan your conversations and strategies beforehand, as this helps you remain calm and gives your teen confidence that you know what you are talking about. Furthermore, it shows your teen that he has options.

Anxiety

"*While they may seem tough and sturdy on the outside, inside, teens are still young and often fearful of both our words and our actions, and the connotations that they bring. So, tread lightly with your words and speak as much as you can from your heart.*"

Anxiety, the most common mental health complaint, is a natural reaction to various situations that we all experience at times. Often, it's felt throughout our body as well as in our mind. It's when anxiety becomes constant, overwhelming, or out of proportion to the situation that we need to take action as it can cripple us by eating away at our self-esteem and self-confidence. When we suffer from anxiety, we may also experience panic attacks, which are intense responses to the anxiety. It's not the anxiety itself that hurts us; it's our reactions when we respond to the thoughts and feelings that causes us pain. It can be very helpful to teach our teens that when feelings of anxiety arise, they don't have to 'fix' them by searching for solutions, they can simply acknowledge them without the need to make them go away.

Even before Covid-19, society was struggling with anxiety. In 2020, The Guardian newspaper published an article titled *UK has experienced 'explosion' in anxiety since 2008, study finds*. The start of Covid-19 lockdowns in 2020 brought significant increases in the number of sufferers, in adults and teens alike, and for previous sufferers, Covid-19 was the catalyst to triggering something more sinister. Although we are a few years down the line since the onset of Covid-19, teens are still struggling with anxiety, along with self-harm, loneliness, isolation, and demands from school, including the need to catch up with missed lessons and homework after all the lockdowns (The Guardian, 2020).

In some instances, anxiety can be hard to spot. As with adults, teens don't normally let on that they are suffering, which is another reason why we need to get to know and understand our teens by observing, listening and communicating with them. When broaching the subject with your teen, a good approach is to normalise his thoughts and behaviours so that he knows that he isn't alone, and that anxiety is a common issue amongst everyone.

Experts suggest that anxiety should be acknowledged but not fed. While supporting your teen, don't make excuses for his anxiety nor treat him any differently, otherwise he will become all-consumed by it. Instead, let his anxiety sit beside him, without dominating him. To illustrate, consider anxiety as a passenger in a car, not the driver. Work with your teen to reduce or eliminate his anxiety, gently guiding and showing that life must carry on. In the interim, keep an eye on him and seek help when needed.

On a positive note, I have seen many teens successfully conquer or reduce their anxiety to a much more manageable level. You will know if your teen is capable of tackling anxiety on his own or whether he will need external support. If he refuses support, you may not have any option other than to help him yourself or allow him to work through his issues alone. If he doesn't need intervention, to empower him, support his transition from being a victim to being in control. The sheer act of overcoming, or at least facing, anxiety head on will raise self-esteem and provide valuable life tools. If he isn't capable of managing it himself, which is understandable, then contact your GP, therapist or look online for suitable organisations. Additionally, consider seeking support for yourself too, so you are better equipped to help your teen.

To help our teens tackle their fears, we can encourage baby steps. Breaking down tasks into bite size pieces allows them to return to a task a day or two later to continue onto the next step. It's also useful to talk through situations or use role play to act out scenarios such as dealing with peer pressure, making career decisions, or sitting a test or exam at school. Often, when we are fearful, it can help if we arm ourselves with information. In this context, your teen may want to read up on official data on subjects such as climate control, career advice or exam techniques. True stories told by other anxiety sufferers, especially famous people, depicting how they overcame, or are living with anxiety can go a long way in putting your teen's mind at rest.

For teens dealing with anxiety, even a minor setback can feel like their entire day has been ruined or turned into a total disaster. If your teen experiences this, you may witness him struggling to concentrate on anything else for the rest of the day. In such moments, offer him support to help him recognise the positives in his day and share examples from your own experiences, explaining how things did not go to plan, but still turned out enjoyable.

Signs of Anxiety

Please note, as with all lists of 'signs to watch out for' in this book, some may overlap with other conditions that may be present in your teen, whether they are mental health conditions or other challenges. For this reason, it's best to ensure that there is more than one sign from each list and recognise that the severity will differ person to person. It's also advisable to seek medical advice when you see fit.

Below is a non-exhaustive list of Signs of Anxiety:

- Always feeling 'on edge'.
- Anxious when interacting with strangers.
- Avoidance of new situations.
- Avoiding socialising.
- Avoiding eye contact.
- Chest pains.
- Difficulty in breathing.
- Difficulty relaxing.
- Easily tired.
- Excess worrying about things.
- Extreme self-criticism.
- Extreme low self-esteem.

- Fidgeting.
- Irregular or thumping heartbeat.
- Irritable.
- Light headed or dizzy.
- Nausea.
- Nervous twitching.
- OCD.
- Over/under eating.
- Pins and needles.
- Restlessness.
- Stomach churning/cramps/pains.
- Tense muscles.
- Trembling hands.
- Trouble concentrating.
- Trouble getting to sleep or staying asleep.
- Unable to make decisions.
- Wanting to stay at home and not venture out.

Below are some tips to support teens who are experiencing anxiety. When reading, it's best to avoid being judgemental and to remove yourself from the equation:

- Ask him to describe his anxiety, he can explain, talk, write a word cloud, or draw etc.
- Connect with nature.
- Connect with your teen to understand him and therefore his anxiety.
- Encourage regular exercise.
- Explain about the critical inner voice we all have and teach him how to recognise it.
- Explain that he isn't alone and that anxiety is very common.
- Either together or on your own, use a journal to see when it's most prominent and look for patterns.
- Help him to slowly step out of his comfort zone.
- Help him to find a buddy or a teacher he can turn to at school.
- Listen to your teen and let him be heard.
- Look at ways to raise his self-esteem such as setting small, achievable and measurable tasks.
- See if you can work out together the causes of his anxiety.

- Set up an app that sends out daily, positive messages to uplift him.
- Set aside daily 'worry time', same time each day.
- Suggest that he writes a diary or starts journaling to allow his thoughts to move from head to paper. (You don't need to see it unless he offers.)
- Teach him to be kinder to himself – including using forgiveness.
- Teach him to say 'No' to pressures from friends and others by setting boundaries.
- To truly understand what he's going through, ask him to break down how he feels, step by step.
- Use relaxing techniques, such as take a long shower/hot bath, watch a funny film, listen to uplifting music, use breathing exercises, use the 5-4-3-2-1 grounding technique, connect with family or friends, in person or virtually, or play a board game.
- Work out the triggers.

Below is a list of phrases that you can use to calm your teen if he suffers from anxiety.

- 'Don't forget you are really good at ...'
- 'How big is your worry?'

NEUROLOGICAL, BIOLOGICAL, AND PSYCHOLOGICAL CHALLENGES

- 'How can I help?'
- 'I'm here for you.'
- 'If you could talk to your worry, what would you say?'
- 'I get anxious sometimes too. It's not much fun, is it?'
- 'I know things are difficult for you right now, but they will change, and you won't always feel this way.'
- 'It's O.K. to find things difficult. We all do at times. It means that you are learning and growing, which is positive.'
- 'It's normal to grieve about this loss. It will get easier in time.'
- 'I think most people would feel the same as you about this.'
- 'Remember, you got through......' (a previous challenge he overcame).'
- 'Tell me what you need from me?'
- 'This feeling will pass.'
- 'We will get through this together.'
- 'What do you think will happen next?'
- 'You are safe.'

Depression

Depression affects approximately 5% of the worldwide population, preventing many from living their everyday lives fully. Research indicates that depressive episodes in teenagers impair both cognitive and executive functions. Suggesting, teens suffering from depression are unable to function in the same manner as those that aren't suffering, so we need to manage our expectations.

During Covid-19, teens were severely impacted by depression and levels rose dramatically. Since the signs for depression aren't always obvious, and as teens rarely offer up information about their problems nor are forthcoming with their feelings, it can make it difficult for parents to recognise its presence. Which is why it's usually someone else who notices when something is out of the ordinary. To complicate matters, sufferers often struggle to accept help, even from their loved ones, as they feel that they are beyond hope. If your teen is suffering from depression, or signs of depression, then I urge you to seek help, sooner rather than later.

One way to detect whether your teen has depression, as opposed to 'a few bad days', is to look at the intensity, the time period, and the effect. If the intensity of his emotions is far worse than usual or if the depressive feelings are permanently present, then these may be signs of depression. If the behaviour carries on for longer than 2 weeks, or goes away and returns on a regular basis, then once again it's less likely to be normal behaviour. You will also need to consider how it's affecting his daily life. Is his school work being affected? Have his general enjoyment levels dropped by much? Are his relationships with others being affected and if so by how much and how so? Your answers should give you clues to whether or not he's depressed. Please don't take your decision lightly. If you have any doubts, seek expert advice, handling the situation with care to avoid placing further stress upon him. As with all mental health conditions, it's best to err on the side of caution because if spotted early, depression can be addressed and treated before it escalates.

"According to data, it is seen that the risk of depression increases in adolescence. The main reason for the rise in depression in children is the non-cooperation and support of mothers and fathers. The risk of depression decreases in children whose mothers and fathers are cooperative and supportive" (Lanjekar et al., 2022).

Common Signs of Depression

Below is a non-exhaustive list of the common signs of depression. Please note, some signs can overlap with other conditions or challenges. For this reason, it's best to make sure that there is more than one sign that you recognise from the list below and if in doubt, consult your local GP.

- Agitation or irritation.
- Difficulty concentrating (new or increased).

NEUROLOGICAL, BIOLOGICAL, AND PSYCHOLOGICAL CHALLENGES

- Constant low mood.
- Withdrawal or disengagement from life, people, or previously enjoyed activities.
- Dizziness.
- Drastic changes in sleep patterns.
- Drop in grades or changes in attitude towards school work.
- Feeling isolated or unable to relate to others.
- Feelings of guilt or worthlessness.
- Feelings of hopelessness or despair.
- Feeling numb or empty.
- Loss of pleasure in previously enjoyed activities.
- Panic attacks.
- Pins and needles.
- Sadness.
- Self-harming.
- Signs of anxiety.
- Sudden anger or aggression.
- Tearfulness.
- Tiredness or lethargy.

- Sense of unreality.
- Verbal or written comments or thoughts about suicide.

MENTAL HEALTH AND EDUCATION

"In 2023, more children completing our annual survey were unhappy with school than any other aspect of their lives they were asked about, but there is huge potential for schools to support and protect children's wellbeing" (The Children's Society, 2023). One year later, in the 2024 Report, 'school' was still at the top of the list for unhappiness (The Children's Society, 2024).

With our teens spending more than a third of their waking hours each week either attending school or completing homework, it's important that we look at the education system and see how it's supporting them. There is a plethora of information online about pressures placed on teenagers by education authorities, with many believing the focus should shift from being results-driven to well-being driven. Although there are countless amazing staff members within the system, we must acknowledge that schools are underfunded and overstretched. However, we must ask ourselves whether schools are prioritising their results and their popularity over the welfare of their students. It's well documented that the happier a child is at school, the more successful they will be, which in turn leads to a more successful school.

The Department for Education's NFER Teacher Voice Omnibus Research report, 2017, claims that only 40% of teachers believe they are equipped to teach pupils that are suffering from mental health conditions. Considering that, statistically, teachers are often the first line of support for their pupils, these figures highlight the urgent need to support teachers so that they can, in turn, support their pupils.

"Ground-breaking research by the Centre for Economic Performance (CEP) has shown that the influence of individual teachers on pupils' mental health is as significant as their influence on academic test scores" (Lowry et al., 2022).

Recently, I had a conversation with a retired headmaster and Ofsted inspector regarding the (2014) change in school curriculum. When posing the question "What's your opinion of the new curriculum?", he retorted, "It has killed off any creativity." Although we cannot do anything about this shift, we can encourage our teens to participate in creative activities, as we can't rely on an already overburdened system.

In 2023, The Public Health Evidence & Intelligence Team at Hertfordshire's County Council, carried out its annual Young People's Health and Wellbeing Survey (YPHWS) in schools, capturing information from 16,300 students (44.4% males) aged 11 to 19 years. When questioned on their 'Top worries', the males answered:

1st Future prospects.

2nd Schoolwork.

3rd Their appearance.

4th Feeling lonely.

5th Mental health.

(Hertfordshire County Council, 2023).

“In 2022, more children were unhappy with school than any other aspect of life.” With the lowest score obtained under the heading of "Being listened to" (The Children’s Society, 2022).

“School is also the place where most children spend most of their time, and, as such, has the greatest capacity to identify the issues children are facing and be part of the solution” (The Children’s Society, 2022).

The Good Childhood Report 2022 indicates that young peoples’ happiness in the areas such as life as a whole, friends, appearances and school is significantly lower than it was 10 years ago, which is rather disturbing. We know the importance of friends and when it comes to image, the pressures of social media. These findings raise the question of whether we have any say in how schools and local/national governments decide to support our children. We can campaign and lobby, but, in the meantime, we can take control as our children’s well-being should not be left in the hands of our school system, but in our own. I have spoken to many parents, who, on reflection, wished they had acted sooner and made their schools listen to them when their children were struggling to cope in school. Children, whose lives had been severely impacted by poor mental health. Some of these parents ended up pulling their children out of the school system altogether and others left them in, only to regret it later.

It's not a teacher's job to be a counsellor, thus there is a real need for permanent on-site counsellors and mentors at every school, college and university for students and teachers to access in times of need. Not only at crucial times, such as exams, but year-round. Someone that teens can vent to or someone that can help them unravel their feelings and work through issues. We can't rely on overstretched and underfunded services such as CYPMHS, (Children and Young People's Mental Health Service), as too many children slip through the net whilst waiting, with their health deteriorating in the meantime.

"We believe that a paid counsellor should be available in every secondary school, academy and FE college in England" (BACP, n.d.).

With so much to juggle during the Covid-19 pandemic, schools were financially overstretched and often struggled to meet their staffing needs. But how did the students fare? Evidence shows that, during the first lockdown in 2020, schools faced challenges delivering either offline or online lessons. There was no uniformity throughout the country, with some pupils receiving several lessons, others as few as 1 or 2 a day, and some receiving no lessons at all. However, there is also evidence to the contrary, some schools overloaded their students with work, giving them more schoolwork and homework than usual, which only added to the already present pressures of life. Furthermore, many schools were unable to mark or provide feedback to their students, nor help or encourage them, which would have impacted their motivation. Nationwide, large numbers of pupils had no contact with either their teachers or form tutors, which must have been incredibly frustrating for both teachers and students alike. Teachers also faced the mammoth task of carrying out their vital roles while managing their own families. While we all experienced the difficult situation that schools and pupils faced, the evidence clearly shows that many schools were not capable of supporting their students' mental health during the lockdowns.

SLEEP

"Sleep is essential as it contributes to virtually every function of the body."

Sleep is essential for our survival as it restores and rejuvenates our bodies. So why do we underestimate our need for sleep and why do we often feel guilty when indulging in this essential activity? Surely, we are doing ourselves a disservice by denying ourselves the amount of sleep we need in order to function properly? Sleep isn't a luxury; it's a necessity. For their health and well-being, our teens need between 8 and 10 hours of high-quality sleep a night, about an hour more than they needed when they were around 10 years old. During adolescence, their circadian rhythms, the 24-hr clock that regulates hormones, resets, making it harder to fall asleep. As a result, they often struggle to fall asleep until much later than they used to. This leaves them feeling tired during the daytime, explaining why they can easily fall asleep in the classroom.

Sleep deprivation is rife amongst teens, with many obstacles preventing them from getting the number of hours needed. With major demands on their time, such as homework, chores, extracurricular activities or babysitting younger siblings, their bedtime ends up being pushed back or their wake time brought forward, which doesn't leave much time for downtime, let alone sleep. Then there is often a long list of weekend activities. For older teens, it's the need to find a job to gain more independence and much-needed money, either for themselves or for their families. On top of that, the all-important time needed to catch up with family and friends.

Not enough sleep makes us grumpy and irritable, adults and teens alike. Being tired at school or home, unable to concentrate, especially when making decisions, is difficult for our teens, particularly if they haven't had to make similar decisions before, which is often the case. Have you noticed that when you are sleep deprived you feel more anxious and you worry about the smallest of things, yet when you aren't tired these same worries are simply shrugged off without much thought?

It's imperative that we work together with our teens to aid their sleep and constantly revisit the situation to improve both quality and quantity. Have a chat with your teen to find out what he thinks would work for him. If he's sleep deprived, be flexible and open to his suggestions, and to avoid making matters worse, don't make it an issue or label it as a problem. Getting to bed earlier doesn't necessarily mean that your teen will get more sleep, as often isn't the case. It's not a sign of wanting to abuse the situation if your teen suggests a later bedtime, it may simply be that he's fed up with laying wide awake for hours before he's able to sleep and wants to retire later, so he can fall asleep faster.

Sleep routines are beneficial because they train our bodies to know what to expect. Getting up at the same time each morning and going to bed at the same time each evening helps our sleep pattern. By following this, after a week or so, you should naturally wake up/fall asleep at the same time each day.

When it comes to sleep patterns, teens are easily caught in a Catch-22 situation. Conditions such as depression and anxiety can surface due to a lack of sleep, which in turn, can disrupt their sleep, causing a vicious circle. If your teen suffers from poor sleep or insomnia, share the following tips with him, noting that once he's found the ones that work best for him, he should stick to them religiously.

Sleep Tips:

- Eat enough during the daytime so you aren't hungry during the night.
- Avoid large/heavy meals just before bedtime. It's better to fill up during the day with food as opposed to eating too close to bedtime.
- Try gentle breathing exercises just before bedtime.
- Spend some time in nature each day to ground and calm your mind e.g. in a garden or park.
- Find some quiet time during the day or early evening to process your thoughts and calm your mind as this avoids lying awake worrying.
- Ensure the home environment is calm and not hectic or stressful before bedtime.
- Wind down 1-1.5 hours before sleep with reading, music, meditation, or a warm bath/shower.
- Take baths at least an hour before bedtime, as they raise body temperature and may delay sleep. If taken in the evening, warm is better than hot.
- Turn off blue screen devices 2-3 hours before bedtime.

- Ensure the bedroom is cool, dark, and comfortable, and use heavy curtains to block out the light.
- If you like a quiet bedroom, consider a white noise machine.
- To help circadian rhythms, be active daily during the day and get plenty of fresh air and exposure to sunlight, ideally before midday.
- Exercise is great during the daytime but best avoided 1-2 hours before bedtime, especially vigorous exercise.
- Think of 3 things that you are grateful for as you climb into bed.
- Limit naps to 20 minutes and, if possible, avoid them.
- Avoid stimulants such as sugar, caffeine and chocolate along with foods rich in fat in the evenings. Caffeine takes up to 10 hours to fully leave our bloodstream.
- Drink plenty of liquids during the day, avoiding too much too close to bedtime to prevent trips to the toilet during the night.
- Go to bed at the same time every night.
- Wake up at the same time every morning.
- Don't try too hard to sleep. Instead, trick yourself into sleeping by telling yourself you are just going to rest, if you fall asleep then that's a bonus. Changing your attitude helps ease the pressure to fall asleep.

- Only use your bed for sleeping, not for watching T.V. or talking to friends or doing homework.
- Make sure that you are sleepy when you go to bed, if not stay up a little longer.
- If you can't sleep after 30 minutes, get up and do something to calm your mind, such as tidy a messy area or hang up clothes in the wardrobe. Don't return to bed until you are sleepy-tired.
- Don't clock-watch as it can wind you up.
- Plan something enjoyable for when you first rise, such as a favourite breakfast or activity.
- Keep a notebook and pen by your bed to jot down thoughts, helping to move thoughts from head to paper to empty your mind.
- Reading can help you fall asleep or get back to sleep if you've woken during the night.
- Use the most supportive and comfortable mattress that you can afford.
- Journaling can be a form of therapy, quieting the mind.
- Have patience...it can take a while to catch up on sleep.

Sleep deprivation affects so many areas of our teens' lives including food choices, attention span, memory, reaction time, decision making, safety, including driving ability, and school grades, as poor grades are often due to lack of concentration and understanding. Not forgetting how the body follows the mind, so if something is worrying our teens, it will most likely affect their sleep, making them feel nervous or even hyperactive.

"A confluence of biological and environmental factors leads to short and ill-timed sleep among adolescents. Given the importance of sleep for cognitive, emotional, and physical health in adolescence, the high prevalence of sleep loss in this population represents a public health issue" (Tarokh et al., 2019).

Most parents, at some time or another, have suffered from sleep deprivation. Making them feel tired, irritable, anxious, over emotional or even exhausted the next day. Overreacting to situations, being incapable of making wise choices, feeling headachy, suffering from muddled thinking, and generally feeling fed up with life are all par for the course. So, if this is how we feel, we have to ask: how must our teens feel, constantly unable to fulfil their sleep quota?

Studies have shown that approximately 90% of American teenagers are sleep deprived, as are nearly 50% of all UK citizens, including adults. "Sleep deprivation is a very real and very serious issue affecting a far greater number of both primary and secondary school students than we think." "19% felt satisfied with their sleep every night, 34% said they had an extremely hard time falling asleep almost every night and 50% said they felt tired or dragged out nearly every day" (Sleep Action, 2022). The Guardian newspaper published an article titled *Children's lack of sleep is hidden health crisis*, which further proves that, as a nation, we don't tend to take the lack of sleep seriously (The Guardian, 2018).

I'm sure you have seen in the media, discussions of whether school start times should be later to allow teens to get a decent night's sleep, helping them get through the day. From a school's perspective, this would enable students to concentrate and function more effectively.

Long-term sleep deprivation can be disastrous for the body. It can cause depression, weaken the immune system, and lead to mood changes, paranoia, hallucinations, weight gain, a rise in blood pressure, heart rate, and heart disease. So, it's no wonder that teens have melancholy thoughts and often end up with depression due to long-term sleep issues.

Meditation is a valuable tool in aiding teens in dropping off to sleep, and early clinical trials on the effects of meditation on aggressive teenagers show some promising results, noting that as little as 5 minutes a day can be highly beneficial.

The Sleep-Wake Cycle

Although research is still emerging in the area of the sleep-wake cycle, we've learnt that this cycle is regulated by two biological mechanisms which interact and balance each other. One is our sleep homeostatic process, the other is our circadian rhythms. According to chronobiologists, as sleep is homeostatically regulated, we need both of these mechanisms to work together.

Circadian rhythms (CR) are our mental, physical, and behavioural changes that occur naturally. Circadian means 'around a day' and refers to biological rhythms that last approximately 24 hours, although they can vary slightly from person to person. Keeping our sleep-wake cycle in balance, they regulate when we feel awake or sleepy, with exposure to light and darkness acting as the key factor in resetting them.

CR are controlled by a combination of our internal biological clock system and other factors, such as age, seasons of the year, air temperature, genes, lifestyle: including stress levels, work shifts or exposure to jet lag, medication, mental health conditions, meal times, exercise times and being awake for too long. With light being the strongest influence. For teens, hormonal changes cause major disruptions to their CRs, along with lifestyle factors such as being very stressed or staying awake when they are sleepy.

The sleep homeostatic process (SHP) regulates sleep intensity, or our 'drive for sleep', whilst CR regulates the timing of sleep and levels of alertness. After a certain period of time, our SHP informs our body that it needs to sleep, and the longer we stay awake, the stronger the drive becomes for sleep, with a higher drive during illness.

When undergoing cognitively demanding or stimulating experiences, the drive for sleep becomes higher, which in turn, leads us to a longer and deeper night's sleep. In the morning, our SHP starts to build again. As with our CR, our SHP can be influenced by our genes.

It's thought that almost every cell in the human body contains its own circadian clock, which regulates daily biological rhythms. These cellular clocks are coordinated by a master clock in the brain called the suprachiasmatic nucleus (SCN). Located in the hypothalamus, the SCN is composed of approximately 20,000 neurons and plays a central role in regulating hormone production, sleep-wake cycles, body temperature, and metabolism. As light enters the eyes, it's detected by specialised photosensitive retinal ganglion cells and transmitted via the retinohypothalamic tract to the SCN, which uses this information to synchronise the body's internal clocks with the external light-dark cycle. Research led by Joseph S. Takahashi, Ph.D., Chair of the Department of Neuroscience at UT Southwestern Medical Center, suggests that the oscillation times of cells within our SCN vary widely, meaning they aren't all on a strict 24 hour cycle. This variability allows the cells to remain flexible and helps maintain synchronisation within the SCN, contributing to the adaptability of the circadian system (Shan et al., 2020).

When our teens were younger, their body clocks made them feel sleepy around 8-9pm, but now, being older, their sleep-wake patterns have shifted. On average, their natural sleepiness kicks in between 10 and 11pm. There are exceptions: some neurodevelopmental conditions, such as autism and ADHD, can affect the timing of when they become naturally sleepy. This natural shift, known as the sleep-phase-delay, is the body's tendency to shift its biological rhythms, including waking and sleeping times. A shift which is often difficult for both parents and teens, especially for parents who insist their teens stick to their previous, earlier bedtime, resulting in teens being sent to bed before they feel sleepy. With time and patience, our teens will recognise when they are tired and realise that there is no point lying in bed wide awake at 9pm if they know they won't fall asleep till 10.30pm. So, we just have to trust them. Problems can arise if they stay up too long and don't go to bed when they become tired as they will still need to get up early to go to school.

If our teens choose to ignore their 'sleepy' signals and party all night, their CR will be off kilter, leaving them feeling tired when they need to be awake and feeling wide-awake when they should be feeling sleepy. As the quality of our sleep affects how we feel the next day, with poor quality making us feel tired, we should encourage our teens not to go to bed late on weekends as they simply won't get enough sleep. Equally, it's unwise for them to have a long lie-in on the weekend as this can mess up their rhythms, making it very difficult for them to get up early on Monday mornings. Unfortunately, most teens don't realise the importance of sleep. They would prefer to be doing other things, as it differentiates them from younger siblings, and see staying up late as a treat or 'something that adults do'.

In the morning, between 10am and 1pm, teens' body temperatures rise, increasing their alertness. In the afternoon, between 2pm and 5pm, they may naturally experience a lull, in which case they will need their energy levels topped up with a snack. In adults, this lull naturally occurs a little earlier, between 1pm and 3pm.

NEUROTRANSMITTERS

Both neurotransmitters and hormones are chemical messengers, although they work differently. Generally, neurotransmitters are released by neurons in the brain (and nervous system) to transmit messages across a synapse, the tiny gap between neurons or between neurons and other target cells. Hormones, on the other hand, are secreted by endocrine glands directly into the bloodstream, which carries them to various tissues and organs throughout the body. Hormones regulate many basic bodily functions, such as growth, metabolism, and mood. However, the human body is complex, and some chemicals can act as both neurotransmitters and hormones. For example, dopamine and serotonin function primarily as neurotransmitters in the brain but can also act as hormones when released into the bloodstream, influencing bodily functions.

HORMONES

Hormones are chemicals that carry messages through our bloodstream to organs, muscles, skin and other tissues, helping to regulate and coordinate various bodily functions.

Historically, the teenage years have been a time associated with hormones, be it a rise or a fall, as they impact learning abilities, memory and food intake. While hormones have been blamed for teenage behaviours, shaping how they think, feel and act on a social, intellectual, physical and emotional level, recent research offers a different perspective. Experts now suggest that disruptive behaviour in adolescents is primarily due to an underdeveloped brain rather than just hormonal fluctuations. However, even if hormones play a smaller role than previously believed, their influence on emotions can still be significant, sometimes throwing even the most level-headed teen off balance.

"It is now known that hormones are not the only explanation for erratic adolescent behaviour; hence, investigators are now trying to establish the exact nature of the interrelationship between pubertal processes and adolescent Brain maturation" (Arain et al., 2013).

The paper titled *Adolescent Brain Development: Current Research and the Impact on Secondary School Counselling Programs* includes the following extracts:

"Recent advances in technology and research have led to the ability to 'see inside' the adolescent brain; these studies indicate that the brain, not hormones, is responsible for teens' thoughts, feelings, and behaviors."

"You can't change what's physically happening within a teen's brain, but you can use this information to change how you react and respond by developing a method for working with teens that'll help them rather than send them racing out the door."

"Their unpredictable behavior is really very normal" (Roaten & Roaten, 2023).

Hormonal fluctuations can cause both adults and teens to act out of character. For example, during the menopause, hormonal changes can leave women feeling rather volatile, triggering a tidal wave of uncontrollable emotions. This can lead to losing rational thinking and flying off the handle at even the smallest issues. If you spoke to a woman going through the menopause, you may be astounded by her thoughts and emotions. Another example is menstruation, where hormonal changes affect cognitive functions. From this, we can surmise that it's only natural for our teens to behave in ways that differ from what we believe is 'normal' behaviour.

Testosterone

When it comes to male teenagers, the androgen and steroid hormone testosterone is one of the most discussed hormones. It promotes sexual motivation and behaviour in both males and females and is instrumental in the development of muscle mass, bone density, and the deepening of the voice. Testosterone production is regulated by the pituitary gland through signals that stimulate its release. During puberty, testosterone levels increase about 20- to 30-fold, affecting the development of the sex organs and brain. Given these changes, it's no wonder that teenage behaviour can be erratic.

During adolescence, teenagers experience significant hormonal changes, including surges in their adrenal stress hormones, sex hormones, and growth hormones, which influence behaviour and brain development. While hormones are a major factor in behaviour, we need to take other factors into consideration such as natural temperament, and external factors like peers and family. Some theories suggest that these hormonal surges may contribute to teens seeking exciting, risk-taking activities. Parents often blame teenage aggression on the surge in testosterone during puberty, but research shows that this rise is not directly responsible for increased physical aggression.

Cortisol

Cortisol, a key hormone during adolescence, is a steroid hormone produced and released by the adrenal glands. It plays a central role in regulating the body's response to stress and danger. Affecting many organs and tissues, cortisol helps regulate blood pressure, blood sugar levels, metabolism, and acts as an anti-inflammatory agent. It also helps control the sleep-wake cycle, with levels typically lowest at night and peaking in the early morning before waking. With elevated levels potentially leading to health complications.

Melatonin

Another prominent hormone associated with adolescence is melatonin. A neurohormone, melatonin is our key sleep regulator that controls our body's internal clock, or CR. It is produced in the pineal gland, located deep inside the brain within the epithalamus, and is released primarily at night to help us fall asleep.

During the teenage years, melatonin is typically secreted around 11pm, a few hours later than in childhood or adulthood. Once released, melatonin levels stay fairly steady through the night, maintaining the ability to sleep. They tend to peak around 3 am. In adults, melatonin levels begin to drop off earlier in the morning, which helps adults wake up earlier and feel alert sooner. This difference explains why teens often struggle to get out of bed for school. Just as jet lag, certain illnesses and shift work affect our circadian rhythms by making them out of sync, so too does this shift of the release of melatonin. Which is why there is a natural tendency for teens to want to go to bed later and get up later, and why it's no surprise that when morning comes, and their alarm goes off, they are still tired as they haven't yet had the amount of sleep that their bodies need.

As Melatonin levels rise at night, it's very important to avoid blue or white light (white light includes blue light) in the evenings. This includes computer and mobile phone screens as they trigger photoreceptors in our retinas, sending a signal to suppress our melatonin levels and shift our circadian rhythms, making it harder to sleep. In the morning, sunlight enters our rooms and our body temperature rises, stimulating cortisol release, which in turn wakes us up. In the evening, as it becomes dark, melatonin levels increase and our body temperature decreases. To aid our teens, we can encourage plenty of exposure to natural sunlight, giving their bodies the cues needed to keep their body clock on track. Ideally, they should take in the morning sunlight soon after waking and stay outside or near a window for as long as possible during the day.

Dopamine

The neurohormone dopamine plays a critical role in several body functions, including movement and coordination, memory, mood, reinforcement learning, sleep, and the brain's reward system. It's often referred to as the 'feel-good' or 'pleasure' chemical, bringing the energetic 'rush' we sometimes experience. However, dopamine is involved in the anticipation and motivation toward rewarding experiences, rather than the experience of pleasure itself. Many of us have experienced this with food: we feel excited at the thought of eating something tempting, only to feel underwhelmed after the first bite if it doesn't live up to our expectations. Explaining how the brain is often more driven by the desire for reward than by the reward itself.

Elevated dopamine activity is linked to increased motivation for reward-seeking behaviours, which may explain its association with thrill-seeking and risk-taking in adolescents. Although much of the detailed research has been carried out in animal studies, growing evidence from human research suggests that the dopamine system undergoes significant changes during adolescence. Some studies indicate a hypersensitivity or heightened reactivity of this system in the teenage brain, which may increase the drive for sensation-seeking and contribute to impulsivity, mood swings, and difficulties with emotional regulation.

If our teens don't find positive ways to meet their brain's need for stimulation, they are more likely to be drawn to risky or potentially harmful behaviours as a substitute.

The dopamine reward system, a brain process that reinforces behaviours by linking actions to rewarding outcomes and supports habit formation, changes our brain and increases motivation to repeat enjoyable actions. Sometimes this has a positive effect, for example regularly exercising, and other times, in the case of overeating or drug and alcohol abuse, this has a negative effect. Problems start when the effects of our 'high' diminish over time, leading to cravings that drive addictive behaviour.

We can also connect this reward system with everyday behaviours, such as the constant urge to check our mobile phones, the challenge of encouraging our teens to stop playing their computer games, or the strong desire to have that second slice of cake. If you've ever been in love or simply walked past a bakery and enjoyed the smell of freshly baked bread wafting past, you have likely experienced dopamine's influence. While dopamine motivates the anticipation and pursuit of these rewarding experiences, especially during adolescence, the jury is still out on the exact relationship between risk-taking and this reward system. Several research papers I've read suggest a possible link, but they all seem to think that more evidence is needed.

Healthy activities to boost our teens 'feel good' factor could include taking on more responsibility at home, regularly helping others such as an elderly neighbour or relative, volunteering, or starting a new hobby or skill.

Serotonin

A precursor of melatonin synthesis, serotonin, otherwise known as 5-HT (5-hydroxytryptamine), is also a neurohormone and is classed as one of our 'happy hormones', helping us feel both happy and energised. Approximately 90-95% of serotonin is stored in our intestines with only about 5-10% found in the brain. Regulating digestive functions, including bowel function and appetite, it's involved in memory, circadian rhythms, body temperature, blood clotting and learning. Serotonin is a major player when it comes to regulating our moods. Low levels are thought to be associated with low mood, sleep problems, panic disorders, OCD, depression and anxiety, among others. High levels are referred to as serotonin syndrome and can be very dangerous. Serotonin is synthesised from the essential amino acid Tryptophan, via our food intake, although it's not easy to increase our levels via food.

Whilst dopamine influences the motivation and reward aspects of eating, serotonin generally suppresses feelings of hunger. Often, these two neurohormones work together to help regulate appetite and maintain balance in the body, though their interaction is complex and not simply a matter of one's imbalance causing overproduction of the other.

As far as brain research goes, there is limited information on serotonin, probably because measuring its levels in the brain is challenging.

You can help boost your teen's serotonin levels, which will lift his mood, by encouraging activities like walking or running, as well as getting enough exposure to sunlight, which is one of the best natural ways to increase serotonin levels. The good news here is that having a massage may help to raise levels of serotonin, so a great excuse to book yourself some 'Me' time!

HUNGER

The basic need for food on a regular basis is part and parcel of being human. But when this need isn't met, strange things can happen. We may become irritable or moody, struggle to think or even talk coherently, or feel fatigued or even dizzy. When your teen becomes hungry, his blood glucose levels drop, and his brain, the biggest consumer of glucose, may not receive the energy it needs to function optimally. This can impair concentration, memory, and cognitive performance. In response to low energy intake, the body may begin to slow down non-essential processes to conserve energy. As a result, learning new information or completing schoolwork can become significantly more difficult.

Yet teens don't always realise they are hungry. Transfixed on a piece of music they are listening to, captivated by a new online game, or engrossed in their homework, they may have an inkling but simply be too absorbed or too tired to bother to do anything about it. So, just be aware if your teen hasn't eaten for a while, or if it's near meal time, that his responses may be more dramatic or more abrupt than usual, so make allowances.

CHAPTER 3: COMMUNICATION – ENCOURAGING YOUR TEEN TO COMMUNICATE

CONNECT

"The bond connecting us to our teens ought to be forged with love, kindness, and compassion, with no bitterness or anger."

To *Connect* means:

- To be associated with (someone).
- To become joined or join together.
- To bridge a gap.
- To communicate.
- To deepen a relationship.
- To establish a rapport.
- To link.

CATCH UP TO KEEP UP

Ongoing connections with our sons are essential for maintaining healthy relationships. Not just participating in the odd conversation but connecting in a positive way on a regular basis to understand their hopes, desires, fears and limitations.

Unfortunately, for many, disconnection from their teens has become the norm. But that doesn't mean that we should add ourselves to the list and simply accept it. Arguably, the current generation of parents seem to connect better than previous ones, but we still have a long way to go. The teenage years can be challenging, so it's important that we support our teens both physically and mentally. If you have drifted too far apart, focus on bridging the gap. By reading this book and applying the principles, you will enrich your relationship and create a stronger, deeper bond with your teen.

As you start to regularly connect, you will gain a deeper understanding of your teen. You will begin to see who they truly are beyond the façade. For example, whether they are an introvert or an extrovert, naturally very stubborn or very easy going and so on. Once you know more about him you will be able to tailor your parenting to the style that he needs, tweaking it as he grows.

It's important to use every opportunity we can to connect and bond with our sons. As a minimum, we need to catch up on a daily basis. If we become complacent and let this slide, we will soon find ourselves not communicating at all. To facilitate communication, we may need to refuse requests from our teens, such as having meals in front of their computer screen or using electronic devices at the dinner table. We will also need to think twice about them spending hours alone in their bedrooms.

In many households, often due to the amount of homework, teens are holed up in their bedrooms studying. Although having their own space is important, it's far too easy to leave them upstairs without any connection for the entire evening. Being shut away from everyone else for long periods of time doesn't help with communication, so, if possible, move your teen to another room downstairs.

One way of tapping into your teen's life and lighting the fire of conversation is to show enthusiasm for something that's important to him. Something that he's passionate about, even if you're not. It may be his love of fashion, music, or sports. A friend of mine has a son who is really into sports cars, and although it isn't her thing, she is glad that it gives them an opportunity to talk. And her son is happy that she shows an interest in something that is important to him.

A while ago, my son wanted his bedroom painted. My initial thoughts were, 'When on earth would I get time to do this for him?' Then I realised that it would be fun and exciting to embark on a project together, and furthermore, I would be teaching him a useful life skill. Many ideas will present themselves over time if you are open to them, such as helping your teen polish his chess skills before a tournament, training for a sports event, proofreading an article for a competition he's entering or even assisting him with the odd piece of homework. Other ideas include talking to him whilst you are involving him in household chores, such as folding the laundry or writing the weekly shopping list, asking for his input when looking to buy a new electronic device such as a phone or laptop, including discussing budgets along with the pros and cons of various models. And when it comes to online gaming or the use of social media, no doubt he'll be happy to give you a few pointers on improving your skills.

Admittedly, male teenagers aren't as communicative generally as they were when they were younger. Yet, if you can just get used to being silent in your teen's presence, not always expecting or forcing him to talk, then you will both be happier. Sitting in silence allows our teens to talk when they feel comfortable and not feel pressured when they don't. *Contrary to popular belief, teens do want to talk to their parents, but often, we have to look for the signs and create the right atmosphere for this to happen.* So, if you find that your teen makes the effort to come and sit down or stand near you, don't feel pressured to talk about anything in particular. If possible, keep quiet until he speaks, allowing him the space to open up and tell you what's on his mind.

If the saying 'The way to a man's heart is through his stomach' is true, then let's use it to our advantage to connect with our teens. We could treat them to a meal at their favourite restaurant, order their favourite takeaway, cook their favourite foods at home, or even better still, cook with them. Sprucing up the kitchen table and serving an impressive meal using your best crockery will make them feel special.

There are lots of ways we can connect with our teens even if we are unable to speak face to face. Be it via a phone call, text message, sticky note, or email. We just need to keep the channels of communication open at all times.

Connection to each other is a core need and one which must be installed into the mindset of our teens at a time when, unfortunately, they naturally want to distance themselves from us. Achieving this connection quite possibly will be different for every family. Insisting on eating together once a day, going for an amble around the block after supper, or watching favourite sitcoms are common ways. Think outside the box and do whatever works for you.

As teens' thoughts and feelings often change, sometimes daily or even hourly, it's good practice to check-in with them on a regular basis. As an example, below is a story a colleague told me about the pitfalls of forgetting how easily teens change their minds.

"During the tail end of the Covid-19 lockdowns, I booked an 'experience day' for my teenage sons. I wanted to give them a treat and something positive to look forward to. But, a few months down the line my plan backfired. Initially, they showed interest in the event but as time went on, they realised the event wasn't for them. But because of my enthusiasm, my kids were too frightened to let me know that they were no longer interested. A few days before the event, they started to express justifiable fears about the trip. After a calm conversation, it transpired that they were too scared to tell me as they didn't want to let me down as I seemed rather excited about the event. It was rather ironic as I just wanted to create more joy in their lives, but it didn't dawn on me that, whilst I was busy creating this happy event for them, I hadn't checked in with them to make sure that they were still happy to take part."

SWITCH OFF TO CONNECT

"Technology can be a wonderful friend, but also a foe."

In today's age of technology, wherever we go and whatever we do, we are surrounded by smart gadgets. Yet to keep connected with our teens, we are constantly fighting these gadgets. Be it watching films or videos via their computers or smartphones, messaging or speaking to their friends, listening to podcasts or music on their headphones or using their earpods. Being plugged in not only blocks communication but also denies teens the mental space they need to think, reflect, and process their thoughts, feelings, and ideas. This is why downtime from technology is essential because it allows them space to think through questions and make decisions. If we are not careful, we risk losing our connection which will make it harder to reconnect later.

Admittedly, it's not just our teens that are guilty of these actions. It's far too convenient for everyone in the household to plug in to technology and unplug from human contact. But this prevents our teens from forming and understanding relationships both within the family unit and the wider world. By limiting technology, we encourage them to slow down, listen to their bodies, and face their feelings, however painful that may be. As well as experience being 'in the moment', which itself brings huge rewards.

We must be wise in managing both our teens' and our own use of technology. Even though it's very tempting to allow our teens to 'plug in' in order for us to relax, catch up on work, etc., technology isn't a teen-sitter and should never be used as such. The frightening thought is that the more teenagers engage with online gaming and social media the less they engage with real life. A by-product of this is that they are less likely to experience boredom, which in turn kills off imagination, creativity, and initiative.

From a physiological standpoint, when participating in online gaming, our brain believes that we are under attack, as it doesn't know the difference between online experiences and real-life ones. This is why our bodies experience a fight-or-flight response, at which point our heart rate increases, we become dizzy or start to shake, our respiration rate rises, our pupils dilate, our skin turns pale or flushed, we start to tremble, and our concentration goes out of the window. Maybe this is why this scenario is also known as the acute stress response.

Connecting to the Wider World

It's easy for our teens to become absorbed in the unrealistic world of computers, especially through gaming. To avoid missing out on vital life lessons needed for adulthood, we should encourage them to spend time with friends and family in the real world. To give a sense of purpose, we can motivate them to participate in projects or jobs within the family unit, or within their community. Holding down a job, whether paid or voluntary, instils good work ethics such as accountability and time management.

COMMUNICATION

"Communication is the key to all types of relationships."

Communication allows us to connect to each other. Being human, we are a social species that thrive on interactions, which is why communication is a vital aspect of our existence. Good communication strengthens our connections and enriches our lives. We love to gain and pass on knowledge, discuss ideas, and enjoy helping and sharing with like-minded people. Our desire to tell the world who we are and what we want in life is innate. If our channels of communication breakdown then we feel disconnected, sad, isolated and lonely, explaining why people that live alone easily experience loneliness. Another critical aspect of communication, vital in the relationship between parents and teens, is the inherent need to be heard. Without open channels of communication, our teens will struggle to express themselves, leaving us unaware of important things like whether they are feeling hungry, ill, or facing any safety concerns.

Talking is a key part of communication and is vital in building healthy relationships. By connecting us to others, it helps us to understand them. When we are exploring and developing ideas, talking enables us to process thoughts easier than mulling them over silently. The act of talking allows us to think more clearly and weigh up the pros and cons of a situation.

A wise friend, a retired headteacher, shared this great phrase of hers when she explained how children learn. Although it was told in the context of young children, it applies to all:

"Talking is external thinking, and thinking is internal talking."

This idea echoes the famous observation by Antoine Rivarol *that "Speech is external thought, and thought internal speech."*

COMMUNICATION – ENCOURAGING YOUR TEEN TO COMMUNICATE

During the teenage years, communication becomes even more important. When communication breaks down, the finger is often pointed at our teens. However, this doesn't always hold true, as the inability to communicate often stems from others, including parents. The good news is that this can be easily rectified.

Below is a list of common reasons why communication between parents and teens often fail:

- As they grow, teens naturally seek independence, often leading to some disconnection from their parents.
- Teens present parents with more complex challenges than previously, often demanding the need for more patience and understanding.
- Teens are on the path to working things out for themselves and often don't want parents to interfere.
- Teens are often tired, not interested, or just not in the mood to talk.
- Teens feel awkward at times talking about various topics.
- Many parents don’t understand the workings of the teenage brain.
- Parents easily forget the normal daily challenges their teens are facing.

- Parents aren't focused enough on their teens.
- Parents don't make the effort to listen properly.
- Parents don't make the effort to ask questions.
- Parents aren't receptive enough when dealing with their teen's changing moods.
- Parents aren't fully available for their teens.
- Parents' expectations may be unrealistic.
- Parents aren't mindful enough of how they converse with their teens, including the language they use.

FEELINGS

Do we all buy into the well-known fallacy that teenage boys don't like to openly show their feelings? If you have looked, or rather listened closely, to your teen's dialogue whilst playing an online game you would have witnessed just the opposite. Comments such as 'I'm scared the zombie/animal will catch me', or 'I'm worried that I won't get to X place in the game in time' are bantered around. Teens display emotions of anger, fear and distress, to name but a few, whilst gaming. Although in this example the airing of their feelings is to their friends, if we create the right environment we can also help them open up and share their feelings.

Furthermore, teens' emotions can unintentionally slip out when they feel angry, tired, upset, etc. By actively listening to our teens, we create opportunities for them to express their feelings, giving them clarity of thought and the ability to manage their emotions.

According to research led by Assistant Professor Erik Nook, a clinical psychologist at Princeton University, USA, teens often suffer from co-occurring emotions, such as feeling both anger and sadness at the same time, but they can't yet differentiate between them, inhibiting their ability to regulate their emotions. Whereas adults are able to distinguish between multiple emotions when they co-exist. This concept is discussed in the article titled *Negative emotions are murkier, less distinct in adolescence*, published by the Association for Psychological Science. The article refers to research led by Assistant Professor Nook, who explains:

"Children tend to report feeling only one emotion at a time, producing differentiated but sparse emotional experiences. Adolescents begin to co-experience emotions, but they are not well differentiated, and adults both co-experience and differentiate emotions."

"These findings suggest that the influx of co-experienced emotions in adolescence makes this a period of more murkiness in what emotions one is feeling" (Nook et al., 2018).

COMMUNICATION – ENCOURAGING YOUR TEEN TO COMMUNICATE

TRUE FOCUSED LISTENING

"The gift of being heard is extremely powerful. We all deserve to be fully heard."

The Merriam-Webster online dictionary defines the word 'Communicate' to mean: *to transmit information, thought, or feeling so that it is satisfactorily received or understood.* Note the word 'satisfactory' as it brings a whole new dimension to the sentence (Merriam-Webster, n.d.).

There are several key topics within the area of communication, one of the most important is the skill of listening. The main objectives behind talking to your teen are to give him the opportunity to speak, show that you are listening attentively, and help him feel heard.

From the time my son was born up until now, I have been in the habit of listening to every word that he has spoken. Each word has been precious to me, and I haven't wanted to miss any. I believe it's important to maintain this habit to keep the channels of communication open and to prevent miscommunication. It's easy to catch only part of a sentence, only to realise later that we misunderstood the message.

"By listening, you are giving two of your greatest gifts: your time and your love."

Effective listening is a skill that requires patience, practice, and time. But once mastered, can strengthen and deepen our bond with our teens, transforming our relationship. To gain valuable insight into how our teens are feeling, we should pay attention to their choice of words, as well as their speed, pitch, and tone. When engaging in dialogue with our teens, it's important to take a step back to observe their actions, including their body language, as they can provide valuable insights. For example, noticing how physically close they are to us can indicate how comfortable they are with the conversation. Similarly, if they raise their voice or appear timid. If they decide to walk out of the room, don't assume the worst, it could simply be that they feel the need to flee to protect themselves as they can't cope with the situation. Keep in mind, just because they are physically strong doesn't mean they are mentally equipped to handle every situation.

While listening, it's important to be non-judgemental, so you hear what your teen is saying and *not what you think he's saying*, or what *you feel he should be saying*. Bear in mind that we often have preconceived ideas of what a person means or even how they think, but we are usually wrong. It's important to 'be present' when listening so we can observe our teens during conversations. For example, if we are unsure if the topic we want to discuss will be uncomfortable for our teens, or if the timing is right, we need to look out for signs to know whether to continue the conversation. If we see them holding a very defensive posture, such as crossing both arms and legs, we will either need to disarm them before continuing or pause the conversation and make a mental note to revisit it later.

COMMUNICATION – ENCOURAGING YOUR TEEN TO COMMUNICATE

"He that answereth a matter before he heareth it, it is folly and shame unto him." King James Bible, Proverbs 18:13.

The following information forms the effective approach that I have developed called *True Focused Listening*, designed to help parents effectively communicate with their teens.

When conversing with your teen, you will need to park your ego at the door and leave it there for the duration of the conversation. Bear in mind that sometimes a situation will call for you just to be silent and sit and just 'be', without the need to talk, which in itself can be very powerful.

The value of listening to someone should never be underestimated. A while ago, I attended a Samaritans training course on Suicide Prevention, and it was clear that the skills needed to support those with suicidal intentions evolved around effective listening skills. Listening skills that don't just use our ears, but our eyes too.

When you first start focusing on listening, you will come across many distractions, be it your mobile phone, other people, or just the constant chatter in your head. Try hard to ignore these distractions. Imagine hitting the pause button and freezing time, allowing everything in the world to come to a halt until your conversation has ended and you are ready to go back to your day.

COMMUNICATION – ENCOURAGING YOUR TEEN TO COMMUNICATE

During conversations, it's imperative that your teen is allowed to talk freely without any interruptions. So, wait until he's finished talking before you even think of speaking. By interrupting, you give out a message which reads 'What I've got to say is far more important that what you've got to say'. Even though you may love the sound of your own voice, or indeed unconsciously have a desire to talk to someone, now isn't the time. And no doubt your teen isn't the person to listen to you either, it's the other way around. Take note, if you continue to go down the route of interruptions, your teen will feel rejected and may not bother to talk to you again for some time as he won't feel that he can talk freely if he suspects that, at any given moment, you are likely to jump down his throat with your own input. Nor will he feel relaxed, which will make it difficult for him to open up. So just listen to what he has to say, answer his questions and take a pregnant pause before launching into what you want to say. If instead you speak first, be mindful that he may be so focused on what he wants to say that he won't be able to concentrate or listen attentively. We also need to consider the fact that our teens may not *want* us to *interfere but simply listen.*

When our teens were very young, it was easy to fall into the trap of either answering questions put to them or finishing their sentences for them. But now that they are teenagers, we must respect their need to answer questions themselves. They have their own voice, and it needs to be heard. And, chances are, we may get the wrong end of the stick. Also avoid having two different conversations at once on two different topics as they will only be able to process one at a time.

When your teen has finished talking, or has asked you a question and it's clear that it's okay to talk, consider his feelings, particularly if he's displaying signs of upset, anxiousness or annoyance. Firstly, give these feelings space to breathe and the chance to be fully heard. It's important that we teach our teens to acknowledge the truth behind their feelings, rather than allow them to be silenced, as this can move their feelings from a place of suppression to one where they are openly discussed and validated. Repeating back, shortening, or rephrasing their words are effective ways to do this. For example, 'You feel sad that you weren't told about the cinema trip your friends were organising.' Or 'You are angry that your friend treated you badly and ignored you.'

By repeating back just one single word that he's said, e.g., 'Tomorrow?', you encourage your teen to open up and talk, showing you have listened, heard what he's said, and understood it. You can also expand on this, using phrases such as 'So you don't want to go to the restaurant with us unless your friend comes along too?' Or 'Can I check that I have understood.....' Or 'You're saying that.....' which not only gives him an opportunity to clarify anything that you've misunderstood, but helps him to process his thoughts, bringing clarity as he hears his words out loud. As a bonus, he will feel grateful that you've taken the time out of your busy day to hear him. This method is often referred to as mirroring. Mirroring informs your teen that you have fully listened to him. It also helps him come up with his own answers as he hears his words out loud. When you mirror, you don't put words into someone's mouth but merely facilitate. Mirroring allows your teen to slow down his thoughts and stops you interrupting or interjecting with your own thoughts or feelings.

As parents, we naturally want to fix our teens' problems for them to give them a smoother ride, which is why we often find ourselves diving into conversations to rescue them. Through our innate desire to problem solve, we can initially find repeating their words or phrases difficult. But, with practice, we can master this technique.

Similar to mirroring their words is mirroring their actions. For example, if your teen looks rather worried and refuses to eat any breakfast one morning, you can gently say, 'I can see that you're not hungry this morning and your face looks rather anxious about something.' This gives your teen a chance to talk and respond in a non-threatening manner. If something at school is the issue, then you may try something along the lines of, 'I can see you are disappointed with your mark. Getting a low mark on your test can be frustrating, especially considering all the hard work you put into studying for it.' In both scenarios, once you've spoken, wait for his response. When you see that he just isn't interested in talking or opening up to you, you can quietly say, 'No problem, I'm always here if you need me or wish to talk.'

COMMUNICATION – ENCOURAGING YOUR TEEN TO COMMUNICATE

If you see something is up with your teen, but unsure what to do, repeat back his words to initiate a conversation, giving him the chance to expand or you the chance to further understand what's troubling him. For example, if he says something along the lines of, 'Mum, I'm really tired as I didn't sleep much last night.' You could reply, 'So, you didn't sleep much last night?' Resist the temptation of butting in with the line, 'Nor did I,' as it stops the flow of his conversation, belittles him, and disregards his feelings by immediately dismissing them, making him feel unheard.

Paraphrasing is a useful communication tool as it demonstrates that we've understood what has been said. Paraphrasing allows us to respond empathetically, using our own words to describe the other person's thoughts and feelings, beneficial in situations such as the onset of, or during, an argument. For example, if your teen shouts in anger, 'I'm not stupid,' you could calmly reply, 'I can see that you are annoyed and don't want me to think that you are stupid.' Or if they yell, 'I don't want to talk to you about it,' or 'It's not your business,' a good response is, 'I can see that you're angry and that you don't want to talk to me about it'. You could also expand on this sentence and say, 'I understand that you don't want to talk to me about this now. I'm always ready to listen if you want to talk another time.' If appropriate, you could further suggest, 'If you don't want to talk to me about this subject, if you prefer, we can discuss the idea of you talking to someone else.'

COMMUNICATION – ENCOURAGING YOUR TEEN TO COMMUNICATE

At times, your teen may think you have understood what he's thinking or saying, when in fact, you haven't. Without much information to go on, it's important not to make assumptions as you may be far off the mark. Instead, if he isn't telling you much, ask him to elucidate. Bear in mind that, if the topic is a sensitive one for him, he may struggle to do this for you. Although frustrating, if he doesn't want to talk, don't push for an answer as it's likely to cause him distress. Instead, offer to discuss it later with him, when he's ready. If he decides that he wants to talk, listen intently without interrupting.

"We shouldn't try to fix our teens' problems, instead we should validate their feelings."

If you need your teen's full attention when he's engrossed in an activity, it can help if you gently tap him on the shoulder, use his name, request that he looks away, or moves his chair so you are both fully engaged. This way you know your conversation won't fall on deaf ears.

Sometimes, it's appropriate to ask your teen if he wants you to respond to him when he talks to you about his problems or whether he just wants a listening ear. When we tell our teens what to do, without realising it, we are denying them their own feelings.

When it comes to using the phrase 'I understand, *but....*' it's important to avoid the word 'but' at the end as it disregards his feelings and dismisses the fact that you actually understand his situation. However silly or small they seem to us, we should never dismiss our teens' thoughts or feelings as they all deserve a place at the table.

Once your teen has opened up to you, use this as an opportunity to ask him if there is anything else that is worrying him. Try not to show it if he says something that shocks you, for he may be worried about opening up to you again if he fears your response.

Another trap that most people fall into at one time or another is talking over other people. Have you noticed that when you do so you can't actually hear what people are saying as you are too busy hearing what you are saying instead? Then, before you know it, you are disagreeing with them or worse still, arguing. Don't mistake listening for an opportunity to be on centre stage.

It's so easy to listen purely with the intent to reply, as opposed to listening with the intent to hear the other person. So much so that the vast majority of people act this way. To receive information from others we need to concentrate on what they are saying, making sure that we understand the content. Most of us are so busy *listening to what we are about to say* that we aren't actually listening to what *the other person is trying to tell us*. When we delve into this a little further, we see that this brings up various questions. Questions such as: Are we so *desperate* to talk that we don't want to listen? Do we really *want* to understand what the other person is saying? Do we think that *what we have to say is more important*? Are we *frightened that we would forget what we want to say?* We often use conversations as *a way for us to be heard* instead of *prioritising* the other person. Then there is the concept that we don't really *want to actually hear* others as we aren't open to their ideas. To really listen, we need to engage several of our senses. Our ears to hear, our eyes to see, and our mouth to respond, when suitable. Along with our sixth sense to pick up on signs that aren't visible or audible.

Avoid placing any blame on your teen whilst conversing, otherwise he will clamp up and shut down the conversation. Don't attack him with your words as you will lose the opportunity to talk, not just now but in the near future as he may not feel emotionally safe to open up again in a hurry if he feels that he will be berated.

With practice, listening will become easier and will feel more natural. If you persevere, you will find gold at the end of the rainbow as you start to reap the benefits of True Focused Listening. You will see that your teen actually wants to talk, and the more that he talks the more it becomes a habit for him. Experts believe that the more teens talk, the more they get used to hearing their own voice, with a knock-on effect that they are more likely to open up and talk more often.

It's crucial to give your teen a voice and opportunities to be heard. Besides, being heard helps avoid conflict. Teens need to be heard even if their opinion is a moan and groan session, otherwise they end up frustrated. If people aren't given a voice, they can end up suppressing their feelings, possibly causing an unhealthy cocktail of deep-seated emotions, conceivably leading to the onset of mental health conditions. Research has shown that the long-term consequences caused by a lack of being heard in childhood include unworthiness, self-harm, self-loathing, low self-esteem, and inferiority complexes.

When our feelings are affirmed, so too is our self-worth. I'm not suggesting that you cave in to your teen's gripes, but they do deserve the chance to express how they feel, even if you later choose to dismiss their ideas.

It's obvious that teens will have to keep schtum at times and not say what's on their minds. Such as when they are around authoritative figures like teachers as they won't be allowed to freely express their feelings, nor fight back against any unjust rules or decisions. Although this initially seems rather unfair, the upside is that it provides valuable lessons for the workplace. Even at home, there will be times when they may struggle to express their feelings, due to lack of wisdom and/or language skills when they feel that a situation is unjust. If you notice this happening, gently coax their emotions out of them.

When a situation arises that requires you to say 'No' to a request from your teen, it's good practice to hear him out first. Then, if you choose, you can discuss your decision by letting him know your thought pattern, including how and why you arrived at the conclusion.

When it comes to your own time constraints, instead of believing that you don't have time to listen, recognise that you don't have time *not to listen.* Imagine the energy and stress you could save yourself, and your teen, if you really enjoyed listening and he really enjoyed talking. When we are so caught up with our own thoughts and emotions, we should try to be a little more flexible and find some time for the *important* things in life. Thereby if your teen wants to talk and it's 11.30pm, your hair is wet and you want nothing more than to collapse into bed, just find an ounce of energy to listen, even if it's only for a few minutes. For, validating our teens thoughts and feelings is often all they truly want from us, especially as they grow older and prefer to make decisions for themselves.

"We need to invest both time and energy in our teens, for they are today's generation and tomorrow's leaders."

The following expressions are useful to show that you are actively listening, and that you genuinely care:

- 'I can see that you are really very angry/upset.'
- 'I too would feel that way about it.'
- 'This really sucks, doesn't it?'
- 'How can I help?'

COMMUNICATION – ENCOURAGING YOUR TEEN TO COMMUNICATE

- 'If that happened to me, I would be livid too.'
- 'Our brains don't work as well when we are angry so let's talk this through when you are feeling less angry.'
- 'Would you like to do x or y?'
- 'When it happened how did it make you feel?'
- 'Thank you for telling me about this. It must have been hard for you.'
- 'It's O.K. to get frustrated when we learn new things.'
- 'Thank you for sharing that with me.'
- 'What can I do to help you?'
- 'What do you need from me?'
- 'Let's think about what we can control here and what we can't.'
- 'I can see that you are a bit down. Is there anything I can do?'
- 'On a scale of 1 to 10 how strongly do you feel about this?'
- 'I wonder how you are feeling about this?'
- 'How about you have something to eat then we can finish talking about this as I can see you are really hungry.'

- 'What you have to say is very important to me so can I just finish my phone call, and we can talk about it in about 5 minutes?'
- 'I hear what you are saying...how can I best support you?'
- 'I wonder if you are feeling disappointed about...'.
- 'I'm curious to know whether...'.
- 'Wow, you got 70% correct in the test'.

We all lead busy lives, yet neglect at home, not even severe neglect, just busy parents that never make enough time for their teens or never listen properly to them, can make the most well-behaved teen misbehave. Because of their desperate need for attention at home, teens can play up and even get into trouble just to get their parents' attention. Even when parents become annoyed at them and shout, teens can feel that at least it (the attention) is better than nothing. But in a school setting, this misbehaviour can label a teen as 'badly behaved'. Leading even the brightest to be put down a set at school or to receive repeated detentions. The jury is still out whether this is fair, as not only will the teen's potential be compromised, along with their confidence and motivation, but they will be subjected to humiliation by their peers. Leaving them to decide whether they will change their attitude or face inner turmoil as a result of letting themself and/or their parents down.

COMMUNICATION – ENCOURAGING YOUR TEEN TO COMMUNICATE

On the odd occasion, you may have noticed your teen coming across a little aggressive when you have asked him to complete a chore. I'm not talking here about being outrightly rude, but just a little too assertive. Perhaps you've asked him to help you with something around the house or garden. It's so easy to read this behaviour as being disrespectful. It's also easy to forget that we don't necessarily know what's going through our teens' minds at any given moment. Like us, they too will have their own agendas. Your teen may have something urgent that he needs to do that you are unaware of, such as preparing for a test at school the next day or submitting some online homework in the next hour. In which case, this may need to take priority over your instruction to tidy his bedroom or help you unload the shopping from the car. If you listen carefully when he speaks you may hear the sense of urgency in his voice, and he may even sound panicky. In our own busyness, it's easy to forget the constant pressures our teens are under. Be it important exams such as GCSE's or A' Levels or their relevant mocks, or pressures from parents, family, friends or peers. When this behaviour arises, try not to get swept away by how his words come across, instead, step back and see the bigger picture. Please note that I'm not suggesting you give him a get out of jail card that he can use anytime he sees fit but am merely explaining the need to understand his actions.

The beauty of True Focused Listening is the ability to both hear and see the other person. Once in the habit of practising True Focused Listening on a regular basis, you will find your mindset starts to change. You will pick up on so many signs and clues that you would have previously missed out on, including the ability to see your teen's emotions and feelings for what they really are. As you begin to interpret your teen's words in a new light, you will realise what previously was conceived to be a disrespectful tone was instead an intensely emotional one, combined with his inability to see another's perspective, thanks to his immature brain. The emphasis here is on his emotions and his incapability to control them, rather than his intention to be rude. This lack of emotional control is a major obstacle for our teens, one that will persist for several years. However, given time, it will evolve from an over-emotional and demanding voice to a much calmer one.

The more you learn to relax when practising True Focused Listening, the less you will find a need to interject during conversations. Eventually, you should find that you end up hardly saying a word, until it's your turn to talk.

We've looked at how to apply True Focused Listening. Now let's see an example that doesn't consider this approach, one where we engage our voice before thinking about the consequences. The scenario below shows how simple words can carry many connotations. I'm sure by now you can think of a better response from the Mum.

Tom states, "Mum, I got soaked this morning at the bus stop because someone drove through a huge puddle next to me."

"Tom, why didn't you wait under the bus shelter? You must have realised that there were puddles everywhere." Mum replies.

Tom now feels stupid. He also doesn't understand why his mum doesn't know that he may miss the bus if he's under the shelter as the trees hide his vision. He's also a bit annoyed that his mum ignored his feelings, and she didn't even bother to ask if he was O.K. being soaked at school all day.

As we can see, even a simple exchange of words can leave our teens feeling unnecessarily annoyed or upset. Handled differently, the relationship between the two could have strengthened, not weakened.

TRAFFIC LIGHT LISTENING TOOL

"If we paid our teens half as much attention as we paid them when they were newborns, we'd have a far richer relationship."

The Traffic Light Listening Tool is part of the True Focused Listening approach and was designed to demonstrate the importance of clearing our minds before conversing with our teens.

TRAFFIC LIGHT LISTENING TOOL

RED means drop everything you are doing and get ready to listen.

ORANGE means put your own thoughts on hold and listen using True Focused Listening.

GREEN means the conversation has ended – time to go back to your busy-brain mode.

COMMUNICATION – ENCOURAGING YOUR TEEN TO COMMUNICATE

HOW TO ENCOURAGE YOUR TEEN TO TALK

Fred Rogers, the much-loved American TV host, minister and musician, believed that listening is one of the most important things we can do for each other.

As parents of teenagers, one of our main aims in life is to encourage our teens to talk and connect with not only ourselves but with others. For this to occur, we need to create a happy and positive environment, so they feel safe to talk freely. Where they will not only be heard but understood. If the environment around conversations is hostile, our teens are unlikely to open up. If we nag, are impatient or snappy, or give the impression that we are angry, they will hardly warm to us. Equally important is making sure we are available for them when it suits them, even when it's not always convenient for us. If they believe we are too busy for them then they won't feel welcome. Even the simple act of smiling can make a big difference.

The right environment not only aids the flow of conversation but also ensures that our teens feel secure enough to open up and express anything they want without being judged or criticised, including embarrassing or private thoughts. If there is a room at home where your teen feels relaxed, use that space to talk, just make sure that no siblings, relatives or neighbours are in earshot. Bear in mind, some teens aren't keen on their parents hanging out in their bedroom.

COMMUNICATION – ENCOURAGING YOUR TEEN TO COMMUNICATE

Our choice of words is extremely important and can make or break our relationship. When conversing, consider how you construct your sentences. For obvious reasons, avoid interrogation style questions that probe in an unfriendly manner. Instead, use neutral language. Avoid accusing or judgemental sentence openers such as 'Why', 'What', 'Obviously', 'Explain', as they tend to be more confrontational than others. Likewise, rather than using a direct and often aggressive form of questioning such as 'Haven't you finished your homework yet!?', try using an indirect and less aggressive approach such as 'Have you managed to finish your homework?' or 'How's the homework going, do you need a hand?' and when it comes to the hot topic of keeping their bedroom tidy, try asking, 'Can I presume that you forgot to clean your room today?' with a smile, rather than snapping, 'Why didn't you clean your room today!?' in an angry voice. You are more likely to get the answer you want and create the atmosphere you need to pursue the conversation.

Take care with your choice of words, as some carry more weight than we realise, especially when giving instructions. We need our teens to listen and follow through with our instructions, but there is no need for them to be fearful of us.

Your tone of voice is a crucial player in the art of conversation and reveals a large part of the story. In fact, your tone often speaks louder than your words, so choose it wisely. So, instead of hollering 'I need to know...!' in a demanding voice, replace it with 'It would be useful for me to know...' in a polite voice. Along with your tone, consider the pace of your words and avoid talking too fast otherwise your words will neither be heard nor understood.

Choosing when to talk to your teen is just as important as how you talk. Getting the timing right makes a huge difference and can change the result of many conversations. So the next time your teen walks through the front door after a long day at school, refrain from lecturing him on how he forgot once again to give you his dirty washing, or how he left his room in a mess, as he may well be tempted to turn around and walk back out of the door, I know I would. Also, it's best to avoid snapping at him first thing in the morning, when he's bleary eyed and struggling to wake up. Furthermore, if his head is glued to a screen or is immersed in a stressful activity, he won't be able to talk, however much he insists that he's listening.

Although teens love to voice their opinions, when it comes to being put on the spot they often struggle to converse. Ergo, instead of asking direct questions, it can be useful to take a different approach and talk about situations, real or fictional. For instance, 'I was talking to a friend about such and such', giving your teen an opportunity to chip into the conversation without being put in the spotlight. This approach alleviates pressure, relaxes teens, and encourages eager contribution to conversations.

When broaching a difficult subject, to avoid discomfort, use indirect questions and talk around the subject, such as discussing personal experiences, either your own or those of a friend. Social media can help as you can talk about a post seen on Facebook or other platforms. (Keeping people's personal details to yourself.) Gently touching on a subject can test the waters for future conversations. If you are struggling to start a conversation, to aid the natural flow of words, you can subtly weave topics into the dialogue.

Be conscious of how you are feeling during conversations, for example, if you are feeling angry, be mindful of taking your anger out on your teen. Remember, on a daily basis, you are modelling how to talk to others.

Many teenage boys prefer to talk whilst engaged in an activity, rather than sitting down face to face. The benefit is that it takes the pressure off a one-on-one conversation, making the approach feel more natural. To achieve this, choose an activity that suits you both, such as taking a walk, playing a sport, going to the gym, walking the dog or shopping. A helpful tip is to start the conversation with a light non-emotional topic such as talking about a fun upcoming event or something related to your teen's hobbies. This prevents the conversation from shutting down too soon, which can easily happen if the topic feels overwhelming from the start. Another tip is to ask your teen's advice, as seeking his perspective can initiate engaging conversations and strengthen your relationship by demonstrating respect for his opinion.

Avoid jumping in at the start of a conversation by voicing your opinions, as this stops the flow of conversation. Instead, answer or comment in a neutral manner. For example, 'That sounds interesting', instead of what you may really be thinking, which may be more along the lines of 'No way!' or 'That's a silly idea!'

The use of the phrase 'not yet' can be very powerful, emphasising that your teen isn't a failure and that there is plenty of time and opportunities to obtain victory. Using a positive spin, you can rephrase sentences using 'not yet'. For example, instead of stating, 'You didn't pass the test' or 'You didn't get into the football team', use: 'You haven't got into the football team yet; there are always next month's trials.' Or say, 'You haven't passed the test yet; perhaps next time you will pass.' You can also imply this positive message in the following sentence: 'You got 75% correct. Nice to see your hard work paid off,' in a positive, relaxed voice.

Open-ended questions make it easier for our teens to respond, encouraging them to open up and continue the conversation. In comparison, closed ones tend to shut down conversations fairly quickly. Below is a list of useful open-ended sentence openers:

COMMUNICATION – ENCOURAGING YOUR TEEN TO COMMUNICATE

- ‘Tell me more.’
- ‘I wonder…’
- ‘Please tell me what happened when…’
- ‘How did you…?’
- ‘Tell me about…’
- ‘Please can you expand on this for me.’
- ‘How did that happen?’
- ‘How were you feeling when that happened?’
- ‘I’m curious…’

Below is a list of useful expressions to use during your conversations to aid your teen in opening up:

- ‘I don't like seeing you like this.'
- ‘You know you can tell me anything.’
- ‘How do you feel about this?’
- ‘How do you think you should handle this?’
- ‘How can I support you?’
- ‘I wonder if you had a good day at school?’
- ‘I imagine you’re tired after a busy day.’

COMMUNICATION – ENCOURAGING YOUR TEEN TO COMMUNICATE

- 'I wonder how you are feeling about this?
- 'I'm curious what your friends might think about it.'
- 'I'm interested in hearing all about it.'
- 'I'd love to know what you think about our decision.'
- 'The best/worst part of my day was when... How about you?'
- 'Could you tell me one of the topics you talked about today in one of your lessons at school as I'd love to hear about it.'
- 'Do you know...'
- 'Can we discuss your thoughts with regards to going on the school trip?'
- 'Can you elaborate on this for me?'
- 'There's nothing so bad that we can't talk about it.'
- 'If you can't talk to me or dad/mum then we can find someone else for you to talk to.'
- 'Nothing is too trivial to talk about.'
- 'I wonder what your thoughts on .... are.'

We all need empathy and our teens are no exception. When used towards others, it shows that we care and that we've listened and understood their feelings. Using phrases such as 'That sounds very upsetting for you,' is a good place to start. An added beauty of empathy, especially if used on a regular basis, is that our teens should pick up on it and learn to use it themselves.

The following scenario puts the above points into practice: Your teen is trying to sell his new jacket to a friend. He makes a statement along the lines of 'My friend Samuel has finally agreed to buy my jacket but can only afford £40 instead of £50 now.' Rather than trying to fix the situation or putting in your pennyworth by waffling on about how you feel, firstly repeat back what he said so he knows you have listened. 'So, Samuel is going to buy your jacket but can afford only £40 not £50'. Give him a chance to add anything, then, using a non-judgemental voice, ask questions such as, 'What do you plan to do?', 'How do you feel about the fact he can only afford £40?', or 'How do you feel about lowering the asking price?' Allow your teen time to think, keeping the focus on what he wants and feels, as opposed to how it affects you. If necessary, grant him more time to come to a decision. If he asks you what you think, to enable him to make future judgements competently, steer the decision back to him.

Chipping into conversations, at suitable times, with a few words of encouragement can be a useful way to relax your teen. It's best to wait until either he asks you a question or when a pregnant pause presents itself, as you don't want to interrupt him.

If your teen is struggling long-term to talk to you or your partner and doesn't have a sibling of suitable age to confide in, then ask him if he has a friend that he can talk to, or better still, find him a suitable adult. Mentoring schemes available from various organisations including charities and local councils can be extremely beneficial.

At times, through no fault of their own, teens can be rather impatient. During conversations, don't be surprised if your teen demands an immediate response from you. This may not always be possible as you may need time to contemplate and work through your ideas or may need to enlist the help of a friend to ascertain the answer. When demands are placed upon us it can be challenging as our brains are busy multitasking, 24/7, so sometimes we simply can't take any more information on board. If this is the case, tell your teen that you will revisit his predicament and report back to him at a later date, in a few hours or in a few days. In the meantime, know that by waiting he's learning the art of patience. In the long run, it's better for him to wait than for you to change your mind later.

If your teen tells you something in confidence, keep it confidential unless he's in danger or something has happened that you need to report. Otherwise, he may feel betrayed and be reluctant to share information again in a hurry.

Sometimes, you will ask your teen a question and not like the answer. This doesn't mean that he's being rude or obnoxious. It may just mean that you had formulated your desired answer before he had even opened his mouth. In which case, don’t interrupt but allow him to finish speaking. Avoid jumping in to defend yourself or explain what you hoped he would say at any stage. Once he‘s finished talking, and you have finished biting your tongue, take a deep breath and in a calm voice allow yourself to speak. He’s more likely to listen to you, and hopefully agree, if you have allowed him to talk first.

When you need to raise a point and need your teen to listen, try at all costs not to turn it into an argument. There is no reason to upset him or to say things you don't mean. Although you may be annoyed, the likelihood is that you don't intend to upset him so bear this in mind during the conversation. Have your say but be very conscious of not letting your ego jump into the conversation to have the last word.

During conversations, don’t make situations worse by going on and on about a point just to make yourself feel good. You don’t want to make your teen feel so bad that he ends up getting upset, whether unintentionally or not.

When talking, be clear and concise. Avoid waffling. Long-winded sentences and drawn-out conversations are detrimental to all involved and confuse teenagers no end. Chances are, they won't remember the main points, only the confusion caused by the conversation. When conversations draw to a close, summarise what's been discussed, ensuring that any expected outcomes are clearly outlined.

COMMUNICATION – ENCOURAGING YOUR TEEN TO COMMUNICATE

One of the benefits of parents modelling good behaviour is that we teach our teens how to act in ways that benefit them, including how to talk about their feelings. If we regularly share our feelings during conversations, teens will see this as the norm and hopefully follow suit, though we should avoid being overly expressive or offload our own issues onto them.

Daily, we need to break down the invisible barriers and find a way to engage with our teens. Finding a mutually convenient time to catch up every day is a good place to start. Noting that timing is everything. Avoid striking up a conversation when they are grumpy, upset, angry, starving, restless, or are just about to get into bed. As with adults, also avoid talking if your teen is tired. And if you are in a rush to go out or need to do something urgently, don't launch into a conversation as this will not be a suitable time to talk.

It's so easy to let catching up daily fall by the wayside, but it's imperative not to let this slide. Some teens prefer to catch up with their parents during supper time, giving them more time to do other things in the evening, while others prefer it to be separate from the evening meal. You may want to catch up on a one-on-one basis, or you may prefer to catch up as a family. Do whatever works for you. Don't be surprised though if your teen isn't as keen as you as he may see this as 'interrogation time' if you're not careful. Equally, be cautious of bombarding your teen with lots of questions or a list of expectations as the main objective of these conversations is to give him a chance to air his views, get things off his chest, allow him to ask you anything he wants and answer a few of your questions. In the end, you may be pleasantly surprised as interesting or even deep and meaningful conversations can emerge.

If we don't have much to go on whilst communicating, we can easily misread a situation. We may think that our teen means one thing, only to find out later that he meant something completely different. I remember a friend trying to organise a visit to elderly relatives during Covid-19. Her teenage son wasn't keen on going. She initially thought he just didn't want to go on holiday with his parents any more as he was getting older, but it turned out that he was worried about going anywhere near his relatives in case he was a Covid-19 carrier without knowing it and just wanted to protect them.

To connect with your teen, you will need to make yourself fully available. Even if you have been met with vague murmurs or no responses from him, it doesn't mean you should follow suit and offer the same nonchalant replies. You want to avoid situations where your teen attempts to strike up a conversation with you, only to find your attention focused on a screen or buried in paperwork. Multitasking when your teen is trying to engage may prevent you from listening properly. The same applies if you are not in close proximity, as you might only catch part of what he's saying, which can lead to missed opportunities to talk or misunderstandings that could spark arguments.

Make full use of body language to show your teen that you are actively listening. For example, avoid having your back to him as he will realise that you aren't properly engaged and most likely won't fully hear what he's saying. Likewise, if you are holding your body in a defence posture, your teen may pick up on the negative vibes.

It's useful to use eye contact when talking to your teen to show that you are totally engaged. That said, some days he may not want to use it with you, especially if he's feeling rather low or the topic of conversation is difficult for him. This is fine as it gives you an indication of how he's feeling. If communication between you has broken down, then short bursts of eye contact are best, as they show that you are listening without adding pressure. When it comes to teenage boys, although some believe that eye contact should be avoided, you know your teen best. If you are not giving off vibes of anger, annoyance, hostility, or the like, then it's fine to use eye contact.

Although you may have a topic in mind when starting up a conversation, your teen may have a different one. You may not even get around to talking about your chosen topic, but that isn't important. Unless urgent, pencil it in for another time and be flexible and just go with the flow of the conversation, even if it ends up going in a completely different direction than planned. I often find that teens can shine a light on situations that we would otherwise have avoided, proving to be a delightful experience for all involved.

Sometimes, we are in a situation where our teen is talking but we don't know how to respond. For reasons unbeknown to us we just can't seem to find the right words, or words just don't seem appropriate. In which case, just keep maintaining eye contact and keep listening. Provided that you're not sitting there with a look of horror upon your face or gritting your teeth, then your love and support will be felt. You can, if appropriate, chip into the conversation with words such as 'Oh' or 'Ah', 'Okay', 'No kidding' or 'I see' as these keep the momentum going, allowing your teen to carry on talking, knowing that you are listening attentively.

ACKNOWLEDGE AND RESPOND RULE

The Acknowledge and Respond Rule is used to promote healthy conversations and is useful if your teen doesn't often respond after you have spoken.

Rule: When you are talking to your teen, he needs to acknowledge and respond to whatever you are saying. He doesn't necessarily need to agree or even go into details, but he needs to respect the fact that you have spoken. The acknowledgement can even be a simple 'Yes,' 'No' or 'Okay'.

To implement the rule, talk to your teen and explain that you, and other family members, will adhere to it too. That it's common decency to respond to others if they've tried to speak to you. Then have a chat with everyone else in the household to make sure that they are on the same page.

CONVERSING

"*To 'converse' means to talk with, to exchange ideas, to exchange opinions, and to engage in conversation. It doesn't mean to talk without listening, nor to ignore the other person's points of view.*"

At times, you will need to negotiate with your teen. As you put your case forward, you will need to respectfully consider his thoughts and desires before coming to a decision. Let's use the popular topic of bedtimes as an example. Imagine that your teen has repeatedly asked if his bedtime can be pushed back an hour or two. Your response may be along the lines of 'So, what I'm hearing from you is that you feel that at your age your bedtime should be later?' Be respectful and avoid using a tone that will lead to an argument. Next, hear out his answer then discuss how you feel and, if possible, come up with a solution that you are both happy with. If this isn't possible, at least he will have felt heard, even if he doesn't agree with the outcome.

COMMUNICATION – ENCOURAGING YOUR TEEN TO COMMUNICATE

If your teen is experiencing problems in areas that require your involvement, you will need to work together as a team. Take the school run for example. Imagine you are frustrated with the stressful morning rush, always arriving just in the nick of time. You could suggest that your teen prepares his packed lunch, bag, and clothes the night beforehand or that you both get up and leave a little earlier. Alternatively, if you know the delay is your fault, because you are trying to fit too much into the morning, be honest with him and work on getting more organised.

When it comes to male teenagers, research dictates that the majority don't often open up to their parents, but I believe this isn't clear cut and needs challenging. I believe that in the majority of cases they choose not to talk as the environment isn't inviting, or the resulting conversations aren't pleasant. With this in mind, when your teen initiates a conversation, make sure it becomes your top priority. If vegetating in front of the T.V., your teen walks in wanting to talk, either put the sound on mute or turn the T.V. off. If someone then walks into the room demanding your attention, politely ask them to wait, so that you can carry on talking. If the phone rings when you're engaged in conversation, make a mental note to return the call later. Try your hardest not to break the flow of conversation as these moments are important and precious to you both. Sometimes teens, on a subconscious level, use situations like this to test us out, to see if we are listening and are interested in what they are trying to tell us.

COMMUNICATION – ENCOURAGING YOUR TEEN TO COMMUNICATE

Let's relate the importance of dropping everything when your teen wants to talk to a work environment. Imagine a doctor on-call. When they receive a phone call from work and need go to the hospital, they don't tell their colleagues to call back later because they are busy on a shopping spree or engrossed in a football match. Instead, they focus on their *priorities* and commit themselves to their patients. At times, we will need to duplicate this, dropping or rearranging our plans if the occasion to talk rises. If we fail to rise to the challenge, we may miss out on the opportunity to talk, and our teens may feel rejected and think twice about opening up again. Keep in mind though, instead of understanding how busy we are or that we have plans in place, our teens will instead think that they aren't our main priority.

There are many ways in which we can connect with our teens, and conversation is just one of them. Sound, especially music, is another powerful tool. Listening to music together can help us better understand them. The kind of music they enjoy and the lyrics they relate to can offer valuable insights into how they are feeling at any given moment. Sad songs may reflect a melancholy mood, while upbeat tracks can suggest a more positive outlook. That said, teens also sometimes listen to cheerful music when they are feeling low, as a way to lift their mood. To bring you closer to your teen, consider compiling a holiday or in-car playlist together, or take turns sharing each other's favourite tracks.

Another tip is to avoid bombarding your teen with questions. Instead, ask one at a time and when the time is right. Sometimes, simple, direct questions can be overwhelming, stopping teens in their tracks as they aren't always able to switch from their current thoughts to a comprehensible understanding of what we are expecting.

BEDROOMS AND BEDTIME

Teens' bedrooms are their sanctuaries. Somewhere to feel safe, happy, and relaxed. At night, before your teen goes to sleep, keep the conversation light and positive. Ignore the urge to initiate a conversation with him as he's climbing into bed as he needs to be able to relax as soon as possible in order to sleep. Resist the temptation to use this time as an opportunity to get things off *your* chest as this would be unfair and rather selfish. You want to avoid conversations that play on his mind and keep him awake, so don't remind him about his homework or unfinished chores. Instead, utilise the daytime to catch up, even if it's only for a few minutes. That being said, if he strikes up a conversation or starts asking questions, he may have something on his mind, in which case, answer his questions and leave it at that. Don't start asking him lots of questions, nor use it as an excuse for a full-blown catch-up session, now is not the time.

COMMUNICATION – ENCOURAGING YOUR TEEN TO COMMUNICATE

WHEN 'NO' REALLY MEANS 'YES'

To better understand our teens, we need to pay closer attention to them. We need to listen to not only what they say, but also to what they don't, as their silence can sometimes reveal more than their words.

Teens may even change their answers to make things simpler for us or themselves, especially if they feel they don't want to be a bother or a burden to anyone. Meaning that a 'No' might actually mean a 'Yes', or vice versa. If this happens, we shouldn't assume they are trying to trick us as they may be feeling timid or worried that their response will upset or annoy us. To prevent this 'Yes means No' scenario, we need to be mindful of how we phrase our questions, so our teens don't feel pressured to give us an affirmative but inaccurate answer. By taking a more neutral stance with our questioning, we can create a space where they feel comfortable expressing their true thoughts and feelings.

Periodically, you may need your teen to agree to do something or to act in a certain way for his own good. But this doesn't mean he will cooperate. If you are met with strong resistance, and if it's possible, put the idea on hold. Then try asking the same question again after a few days or weeks, as he may well be in a different frame of mind. In the meantime, you may also come up with a better way to rephrase your question. Your teen might even surprise you and give you a different answer, the one you were hoping for. However, If the action can't wait, you will have to decide whether to proceed. Keep in mind, this isn't a tactic to bully your teen into doing something they have a valid reason to resist, but merely another approach if you need to make a decision for his own good.

SPEAKETH AND THOU SHALT BE HEARD

Not long ago, whilst in my kitchen, I gazed at the ever-increasing pile of washing up. It was a depressing sight. I then glanced at the dishwasher. That too needed sorting. I felt disgruntled. I moaned and groaned to myself and felt the urge to stomp my feet like a frustrated young child. However, a few moments later, after I ceased moaning, I felt a wonderful sense of calm sweep over me. Even though I was alone, I had been heard as I had given myself the opportunity to safely express my feelings, without being interrupted or ridiculed, albeit only in my head. Then a strange thing happened. I felt a sense of relief and I immediately accepted the task at hand. The mental struggle had ceased. This event serves as a reminder of the significance of listening to our teens so that their fundamental need to express themselves freely, in a safe setting, is met. It further demonstrates the ability to accept tasks, even when we are reluctant, if we are simply allowed to be heard.

WORRIES

As parents, our minds are constantly being bombarded with information, some of which will inevitably slip through the net. If you are worried about a particular problem relating to your teen, without them knowing, consider keeping a note of things that they say in case you need to refer back to it. I'm not suggesting that you record every conversation as that would be immoral, only if you have a real worry. For example, depression, self-harm, eating disorders, bullying, etc. If you see an unhealthy pattern emerge, you will need to address it. Firstly, with your teen and then, if necessary, with a professional.

PUSH AND PULL

At times, it can be hard to know whether a teen is naturally pulling away from his parents, in order to spread his wings, or whether there is an underlying issue at hand. In this situation, it's best to listen to your gut. If you think there is something wrong, then investigate it. To complicate matters further, if your teen is hurting, feeling very unhappy or insecure, he may, subconsciously, decide to test you. In which case, he may be pushing you away to see if you are going to come back. People tend to push others away to avoid getting hurt, rejected, or disappointed. If this is the case for your teen, reassure him by telling him that no matter how hard things get and how much he pushes, you will always come back. Make sure he knows that you will *always* love him *no matter what* he says or does.

THEY JUST DON'T KNOW

Often, due to an immature brain, teens simply don't know what they want, and more often than not, don't know what they need. As parents, it's our responsibility to support them in addressing these questions, and when necessary, to assume control, making decisions on their behalf.

Although your teen may be quite verbal at times, with a headstrong attitude and a forceful tone of voice telling you what he wants or needs, there will be times when he simply doesn't know the answer to your question. It may not be the case of him being awkward, but rather cognitive overload or an inability to fathom the answer, even if the question appears simple to you.

If you ask your teen a question and he replies, 'I don't know' and then starts to show signs of distress, don't hassle or press him for an answer, just rephrase the question. If you still don't get an answer, leave it at that. He may not know the answer. You will need to use your discretion here as clearly some questions will need your perseverance, whereas others won't. Another option is to give your teen a few of your own suggestions and let him choose the one that he feels most comfortable with. However, if your teen is repeatedly using the '*I don't know*' catchphrase every time you ask him a question, this will need addressing.

There are many reasons why teens use the phrase 'I don't know'. Below is a list of interpretations of what they actually mean:

- 'I'm not sure.'
- 'I'm not in the mood.'
- 'I'm too tired to think.'
- 'I really don't know.'
- 'I really don't care.'
- 'I don't understand the question/topic.'
- 'I feel too ashamed, angry, frightened, etc. to talk about it.'
- 'I've got more important things on my mind.'
- 'I'm confused by this.'
- 'If I tell you, you may react in a way that upsets me, angers me or frustrates me. Therefore, I will use this answer as my 'get out of jail free' card so you leave me alone.'
- 'I'm so engrossed in what I'm doing that I don't want to talk.'

- ‘Your tone of voice is too grumpy or angry and it makes me want to shut down.’
- ‘I actually feel rather depressed and can’t talk.’
- ‘If I say this then you will leave me alone.’
- ‘I don't actually know how to answer your question as I fear being told off.’
- ‘I fear my answer will upset someone.’
- ’The real answer would upset me too much.’
- ‘I’ve already answered this and the answer hasn't changed.’
- ‘This conversation is embarrassing me.’
- ‘I can't give you the answer you are looking for as I’m unable to do so.’
- ‘I have forgotten the topic and need reminding.’
- ‘I didn't hear what you said and don't want to ask you to repeat it as you may get angry.’
- ‘I don’t want to disappoint you.’
- ‘I’m feeling anxious/suffering from anxiety.’
- ‘Is there any point, you don’t listen to me/take my opinions on board.’

Check that your teen isn’t confused by your questioning, if he is, then clarify. You can dissect his thought pattern by asking him how far he got in his thinking, perhaps he was stuck or confused at some point. You can also use one of the following phrases to retain the flow of communication:

- ‘That's a good place to start.’
- ‘Let’s work it out together.’
- ‘Work with me here.’
- ‘I wonder what you would say if you knew.’
- ‘Have a guess.’
- ‘What don’t you know?’
- ‘Imagine all the possible answers, which one do you think is right/feels right?’
- ‘O.K. no pressure, just come back to me when you do know.’
- ‘I understand that you don't know the answer but where/how do you think we can find it?’
- ‘Perhaps you need some more time to think this over. Let's catch up again later today/tomorrow.’
- ‘There is no right or wrong answer, I would just like your opinion.’
- ‘Maybe now isn’t a convenient time to talk. Would you prefer to pick up the conversation later today?’
- ‘Do you want me to explain what I mean further?’

- 'Does my question make sense to you?'
- 'Let me rephrase this...'
- 'I can see that this is upsetting for you. Are you able to continue the conversation?'

You can probe further and ask if he's interested in continuing the conversation. If he says, or indicates, that he is, suggest he thinks on it for a moment, keeping quiet whilst waiting for his reply. If he clearly isn't going to answer, then you can reply, 'I can see that you may need a little more time to think on this,' or 'It's not urgent, so let's return to this conversation tonight/tomorrow,' or 'When can you let me know your thoughts on this?' Explain that you want to discuss the topic, as it's important to you, but be open to his suggestions on when to talk, even if you have to tweak your schedule slightly.

If appropriate, gently ask if the topic is a sensitive one. If it is, then this would explain why he doesn't want to talk about it. Tell him that the conversation will be confidential and that you can delay talking about it if he currently isn't up to it. Avoid putting him on the spot or interrogating him, making him feel uncomfortable. You will need to use your intuition and common sense here as you may get so far and realise that the topic needs to be dropped as it's inappropriate, or that you are asking too much from him.

COMMUNICATION – ENCOURAGING YOUR TEEN TO COMMUNICATE

An Adult's Perspective on the 'I Don't Know' Response

As an adult, I know that if I'm mentally overloaded, with too many thoughts racing through my mind, I need to take time out to give myself some space. Space to process my thoughts and see how they sit with me. If I don't, then I know I can end up struggling when making even the simplest of decisions, and can even, on the odd occasion, find myself responding to internal questions with the 'I don't know' answer, which is further exacerbated when I'm tired. Therefore, if adults experience this, there is no reason why our teens wouldn't as well.

NOT IN FRONT OF THE CHILDREN

We've all had bad days where we've just wanted to go home and vent to someone, such as a partner, to get things off our chest. Unfortunately, if there is no one at home, or if they are too tired or busy to listen, it makes our teens prime targets for our angst. But we should avoid speaking to them when we have pent up anger or grievances, instead, we should wait until we feel calmer. In the meantime, we can distract ourselves, take a hot bath or relaxing shower or have a breather in the garden until we feel a bit more relaxed.

Occasionally, we find ourselves snapping at our teens without good reason. When this occurs, we need to stop and analyse our thoughts. Perhaps we are mad at ourselves or at someone else. Perhaps it's the bad driver who cut us up a few hours earlier, or the rude customer services person we spoke to on the phone. We need to work out a way to leave our anger at the front door or at least deal with it when we are on our own.

INSTRUCTIONS

Avoid making the common mistake of giving several instructions to your teen at once. Ideally, only give one, but if totally necessary, two. Due to the complex cognitive processes involved, too many instructions overwhelm them, causing some teens to rebel. Even adults feel stressed when they are given too many instructions at once. It's good practice to ask your teen to repeat back your instruction, as this ensures he has both heard and understood it, helping avoid future arguments.

SCHOOL LIFE

We've left the conversations held at the school gates behind us, and if not careful, can easily become distant from school life. Although having limited access can be frustrating, there is no excuse to ignore this major part of their lives. To maintain these links, we can connect with other parents, our teens or their friends, although we may need to employ a degree of subtlety as some teens aren't keen on their parents talking to their friends, and their friends may not enjoy being interrogated. Other avenues include parents' evening or parent teacher association events, social media groups (ours not theirs) and school teachers.

CHAPTER 4: EGO

"We don't want to learn from our children. Our ego won't allow it."

Although the above is rather a harsh statement, in many cases, it's true. Often, it's *only* our ego that prevents us from having a good relationship with our teens. Thus, if we can control our ego, we can improve our family's lives and pave the way for a deeper, richer, and more loving relationship. Controlling our ego is a process that brings endless rewards, shaping us into more grounded individuals and more mindful parents. So let's learn to challenge our ego, so we can truly listen, connect, and understand, not just our teens, but ourselves too.

WHAT IS OUR EGO?

"Be the person you want them to be."

The ego is a fascinating topic. For the most part, it's our enemy, creeping in and taking over our thoughts and actions, without us even realising. Existing in our conscious mind, the ego is a justification of who we are and how we are seen in the world, shaped by the conditioning of our life experiences. Never at peace, it's constantly searching for a better existence. Some refer to the ego as our 'false self', the sense of 'I' that we all have, yet it differs for each of us. It's through our ego that we perceive our own thoughts, emotions, awareness, and physical body. The way we live, including the decisions we make, are based on our own personal ego. If controlled, we can eliminate the need to justify ourselves to others and to ourselves, which can help diminish our fears. When we strip away our ego's layers, ditching our false persona, we metamorphose into our authentic self.

We can't completely eliminate our ego as it's vital for our protection. Part of our survival mechanisms, it helps us process information from our own unique standpoint, while also enhancing our self-esteem and fostering a sense of personal worth.

STEPS TO CONTROL OUR EGO

"One of the major stumbling blocks in parenting is that parents are not empathetic, compassionate, nor respectful enough towards their teens. More often than not, their ego looms larger than their teen."

The journey to controlling our ego requires self-reflection, a willingness to be open and honest with ourselves, and an acceptance of our shortcomings and imperfections, without reservation. Although painful and embarrassing, it's nonetheless worthwhile as the more we understand ourselves the more we can help our sons.

If we neglect the opportunity to work on our ego, thus allowing it to dominate us, our discontentment may well continue as an inflated ego readily kills off compassion and empathy, repels others, and affects relationships. Disrupting a calm mind in the mad rush to be better than others, it stunts spiritual growth and prevents us from moving forward in life. Cleverly, our ego can camouflage our true selves and disconnect us from our own hearts, costing us our happiness. Alternatively, if we aim for a balanced and healthy ego, with little internal conflict, we can live the life we were destined to live.

Below is a list of points to consider when embarking on a pathway to *Control your Ego*:

- Be open to learning and growing.
- Accept that you will make mistakes and that you aren't perfect.
- Be open to learning from others, no matter who they are or how old or young they may be.
- Practice forgiveness. Forgiving both yourself and others makes you stronger and more capable of moving on in your life.
- Be more open and accepting of others. Listen to what they have to say before passing judgement. Only then can you decide to take on board their ideas or dismiss them. There is no right or wrong when it comes to your decision, only the willingness to be open to listening in the first place. When we become open and non-judgemental then we worry less about how others see us.

- Learn to let go. You don't always need to be in control, even if your ego is telling you so.
- Face your fears head-on. Fear is part of our ego; it's always waiting for things to go wrong. Your ego loves to use fear to control you and limit your experiences in life. Yet, in most cases, our fears are unwarranted.
- Instead of fearing how others see you, ask yourself, 'Does it really matter?' We all know that we can't change what others think, because we can't control them. But if we reach a place where we are happy in our own skin, then what others think shouldn't matter.

EGO BOOSTING

"If we let it, our ego can come between us and our teen."

Admittedly, the strong bond between mother and child can make it challenging for us to see our child as a separate entity, yet, to avoid projecting ourselves onto our teens, it's important to see this separateness as our teens aren't an extension of us but individuals in their own right. We gave birth to them, but they aren't part of us. They may inherit some of our genes and no doubt traits, both positive and negative, and we may want to instil our own virtues into them, but they have the right to form their own. Our teens don't exist simply to fulfil our unmet needs, including any carried over from childhood.

To avoid their own humiliation, parents often embarrass their teens in front of others. They make unkind comments in the vein of how lazy they are, how illegible their handwriting is, or how badly they did on their last maths test, which is unhelpful for all and does more harm than good.

There will be times when we look to impress others, look to gain recognition or a pat on the back. Yet, if this recognition, otherwise known as 'ego boosting', isn't forthcoming and we don't receive the praise we so crave, then we start to act rather childishly, feeling angry and deflated. If your teen is around when you feel this way, don't expect him to respond in the same way as an adult would. He won't magically step in and praise you as he won't necessarily be on the same wavelength. Instead, to avoid taking your anger or disappointment out on your teen, praise yourself.

OUR CHILDREN BECOME OUR TEACHERS

"Hardly a week goes by when my teenage son doesn't teach me a thing or two. Not learnt through school but through life, and just by being the person he's become."

As parents, we often see ourselves as our children's teachers, alongside their school teachers. Contrary to this, we must realise that our children can become *our* teachers. I can think of so many positive attributes that our teens can teach us: persistence, integrity, loyalty, resourcefulness, optimism, creativity, resilience, to name but a few. I know my own son has certainly taught me tenacity, patience, tolerance and forgiveness, amongst others. Grandparents, friends or teachers also instil traits in our teens, ones we may have forgotten about but could learn from again.

Put Aside Your Emotions

During the teenage years, our children are ambivalent in their feelings towards us. At times, they can be our ally and at others, our worst critic. In the case of the latter, they won't hesitate to point out our mistakes, from the tiniest errors to deep-seated psychological issues, even those we are unaware of. Their comments can really hit a nerve, especially if they touch on a sensitive subject, making us feel angry and leaving us wondering whether they are deliberately winding us up. But being unaware of the depth of our issues, they can't be blamed for how their words affect us. If we allow our ego to put up a wall, we will most likely end up arguing. Which is why taking our ego out of the equation is worthwhile. Therefore, if we allow them, our teens can become our teachers, helping us work through deeply buried issues. It's worth noting that if we lose control of our emotions, our teens may not understand the reason behind any outbursts.

Your teen may also bring up sensitive issues that you are aware of and are currently working on. Issues that you are not willing to discuss with him as it may not be age appropriate. Instead, you can make a mental note and address them later in private. Sometimes, it may be beneficial to be honest and admit to him that he's right, and that you will take his comments on board and work on a particular issue, especially if your actions are causing him distress. By taking this stance you are setting a good example, showing that you are willing to listen and learn from your mistakes. To avoid arguments, it's good practice to keep our emotions in check, as we don't want our own personal issues to be the cause of conflict.

While communicating, it may not always be our ego getting in the way and causing chaos, it could be other factors, such as our sensitive nature or going through a tough time, making us feel more vulnerable than usual. Or biological issues like hormonal fluctuations, making us feel on edge and quick to fly off the handle. Whatever the reason, we need to put our feelings aside and listen and act objectively.

If you have been at loggerheads with your teen for a while, try working on dissolving your pent-up feelings privately. Otherwise, they will continue to cloud your judgement and negatively affect your relationship with him.

Admit You Are Wrong

Admitting we are wrong isn't always easy, especially to our children as we fear humiliation or embarrassment. Maybe it's because we see ourselves as older and therefore wiser or worry that our boundaries will be jeopardised. Perhaps we fear that our teens will hold it against us, as sometimes they do. That being said, it's still better to teach by example, and, in most cases, admit when we are wrong.

When making decisions, parents rely on evidence available at a given moment. In hindsight, we sometimes realise that we could have made a better choice. The challenge here is that our teens don't always understand this process, which can make them feel frustrated as they believe we should have initially chosen the better option.

SEND THEM OFF WITH A SMILE

When your teen leaves the house in the morning, send him off with a smile. Not only for his sake, but for yours too. You don't want to spend the rest of the day worrying or feeling guilty until you see him again, hours later. Besides, your teen will have enough on his mind and doesn't need anything else to ruminate over during his day.

GUILT

Many of us carry far too much unhealthy guilt around, including our teens. If we dig deeper, we often find that most of this guilt is unnecessary. Guilt drains us, weighs us down, keeps us stuck, and can lead to emotional distress. When we feel guilty, it's common to subtly mention it to others, sometimes unintentionally, as our subconscious seeks relief. However, if not careful, sharing these feelings with our teens can inadvertently burden them, which is unfair and potentially harmful. This is sometimes referred to as ‘parentification’, where children take on an inappropriate emotional or psychological role.

SHOW PRIDE THE DOOR

During the teenage years, we often have to bite our tongue while listening to words we may not want to hear. Words that hurt our feelings, bore us, upset us or annoy us to the point where we feel angry. But to understand our teens and grasp how they are feeling in any given moment, and to prevent further distress for either of us, we must overcome this and ride it out by keeping quiet and accepting it. When our teens have left the door of communication open, we mustn't allow pride to get in the way and use it as an excuse to ignore them or start an argument. If we close the door, our teens may not be in a hurry to open it up again for quite a while.

There is no shame in showing your vulnerable side and being totally honest with your teen. If he realises that you aren’t perfect, he can more readily accept the fact that he isn’t either. If you don't always have the answer to every scenario, e.g., what action to take or how to proceed, then that's ok, but let him know so he sees that he isn’t alone and that it's perfectly acceptable for adults to feel this way too.

I'm sure you've offered your teen many suggestions in the past that would have greatly benefited him. But due to his quest for independence, these may well have fallen on deaf ears. Some were probably shrugged off, while others may have been met with an objectionable response. You may even have found that a few days after making a suggestion your teen had a change of heart, deciding instead to take your idea on board, possibly because a friend had suggested the same idea or because he'd thought about it. Even if he forgot that it was your idea in the first place, refrain from giving him the 'I told you so' or 'Hey, that was my idea' lecture. Instead, just be glad he's taken your ideas on board and will benefit from them in the future. This allows him to modify his views without being judged, contributing to his tolerance levels.

Like adults, teens don't like being told what to do all the time. It makes them less receptive to the ideas of others, as humans naturally incline towards rebellion. Which is why, when appropriate, it's beneficial to let your teen come to his own conclusions. The following scenario expands on this:

'Mum, it's so cold outside,' Tony murmurs, bleary-eyed.

'Yes, perhaps you should wear your thicker coat?' Mum suggests.

'No, I don't want to because sometimes I get too hot in it,' Tony replies.

'Ok, but for the times you do get cold, isn't it better to have a warmer coat with you?' Mum asks.

'No,' Tony replies firmly.

Two minutes later.

'Mum, I think I'll take my thicker coat today,' Tony says casually.

'That's a good idea,' Mum says cheerfully.

When scenarios like this present themselves, we have a few options. We can respond with a smug look on our face and a 'That's what I suggested in the first place' type of response, which will put our teen's back up and inevitably shut down the conversation. Or we can remain quiet, content in the knowledge that we've achieved the desired result and encouraged them to follow their own thought process, strengthening their neural pathways. If Mum had insisted on Tony wearing his coat in the first place, he wouldn't have necessarily understood why and would probably refuse next time around.

BE SUPPORTIVE OF THEIR IDEAS

When your teen comes up with an idea which you can see he's sold on, but one which sounds rather nonsensical to you, bite your tongue. When he makes the effort to bring his ideas, hopes, and dreams to the table, it's important not to scoff at, dismiss, or ridicule them, but instead validate them. Even though his ideas may well be short lived and forgotten about in a few days or weeks' time, the important message here is 'Mum/Dad this is important to me so please let me go with it and give me your support.' Even if a little quirky, you may well be surprised at his ideas, and it's quite possible that there will be some mileage in them. Some may even teach you a thing or two.

We need to give the gift of possibility by encouraging our teens to dream big and aim high. Of course, you will need to use your discretion if you think an idea is in any way dangerous or immoral, and step in to explain why you can't allow it. But if it's harmless, then take a deep breath and remember it's all part of the learning process for all involved. If you are happy for him to proceed with an idea then encourage him to make a start. But if you need time to think, tell him that even though his idea isn't something you would necessarily have thought of or agreed to, you will take the time to think about it and get back to him. It's important to follow the conversation up at a later date, at a time that is convenient to both of you. If you choose not to return to the conversation, or forget, you run the risk of him believing that you didn't listen and instead were just fobbing him off, which is detrimental as it makes him think his ideas aren't valid.

The film 'Field of Dreams' beautifully depicts Kevin Costner's character's search to pursue his dream, even though others find the dream rather bizarre and even quite mad. It's a delightful film for many reasons, not just for how it portrays the importance of supporting loved ones, but for reaching for one's dreams, regardless of what others may think or how difficult they may be.

BEING OPEN TO LIFE'S LESSONS

Actions and consequences teach our teens invaluable lessons. However, we need to watch out for the occasions where it's the *parents* that need to learn instead. As tempting as it is to automatically hand lessons out to them, we must hold our hands up and admit that sometimes these lessons have our names on them.

I recall a lesson that I was taught years ago when I took a friend's son to his orthodontics appointment as part of his 2-year braces treatment. As he lay in the chair, I glanced down at him and noticed that his trousers were muddy in places. Without any thought, I exclaimed, 'Oh your trousers are dirty,' in a slightly shocked and embarrassed voice. The orthodontist immediately retorted, 'Oh it's due to this bad weather. It doesn't matter.' Later that day I reflected on this conversation, and although my comment was strangely out of character, I found it interesting to notice that my ego, disguised as embarrassment, had reared its ugly head. I surmised that I should have just kept quiet (or, ideally, not even had the thought in the first place) and instead silently glowed with pride as I witnessed this amazing young man lying still while his poor mouth was intruded upon, for the umpteenth time. This is a great example of the ego at work, and a reminder of how much we can learn from others, if we are open to learning. I'm grateful to the orthodontist for the lesson he taught me. Also, to my friend's son, as I know that I couldn't have endured so much pain for so long, and yet still be so patient and accepting.

RIGID THINKING

In the film 'Dragon', Bruce Lee raises the topic of water in a spiritual context, explaining that it's formless and shapeless. If humans were like water, we would be strong, powerful, flexible, and adaptable, and be able to overcome any obstacle placed on our path. And we would flow and move with life's changes. The reason why I reference this film is that, as parents, we can easily become too set in our ways, especially as we get older, creating rigid thinking patterns. But to support our teens in an ever-evolving world, we need to constantly think outside the box, challenge our thought patterns, and strive for flexibility.

Adults have strong opinions, beliefs, morals, values, and principles. For our teens to formulate their own, they need to work out what's important to them. Their decisions will be influenced by both their own experiences and other peoples'. As part of the process, our teens will test out their ideas on others including friends and family. As time goes by, some ideas will be concreted and others discarded, which may lead them to rejecting our advice, causing them to start an argument. But we shouldn't forget that even adults, when unsure of what to do, seek clarity by testing out their ideas on others to see how things sit with them. They do this by either asking for advice or by verbalising their own ideas, but rarely do we take this advice on board. You may notice your teen expressing his ideas using a forceful and emotional voice when he feels strongly about a topic, but this is usually down to an underdeveloped PFC.

Tunnel Vision

"*As the great Albert Einstein is often quoted as saying, 'We cannot solve our problems with the same thinking we used when we created them.*'"

At times, we all suffer from tunnel vision, especially when we have an idea and are hell-bent on pursuing it, come hell or high water, even to the detriment of the poor recipient. If you find yourself in this position, take a step back and instead of being cantankerous try to think rationally. Talk to a friend or partner before launching into a conversation and laying down the law at home, as others often see things in a different light. If you notice you are feeling this way when talking to your teen, and discover by his reactions, in the form of tears or anger, that the conversation is taking a nosedive, find the mental energy to put the brakes on and end the conversation.

At times, we all need to tell our teens off for either something they've done or something they haven't done. A word of advice is to make sure that when doing so you get the timing right. If you can see that your teen is struggling with issues and clearly can't deal with anything else, make a mental note to address it at a slightly later date. There is no benefit in pushing someone over the edge just to satisfy your own ego.

LEARNING FROM OUR PARENTS' MISTAKES

Although it's very admirable to learn from our parents' parenting mistakes, it's just as important to maintain perspective. In our attempt to avoid repeating their mistakes, we can end up overcompensating, causing the pendulum to swing too far in one direction. This prevents us from finding a balanced, healthy middle ground. Examples include permissive parenting, where the child takes centre stage and is overindulged, and authoritarian parenting, where parents are overly strict, neither of which are ideal. Which is why, we need to step back and learn from other's mistakes, while avoiding our own.

FOOD FOR THOUGHT

We've passed the stage of weaning our sons on broccoli. Yes, I did that. What a cruel mum my friends joked to me when I gave my son broccoli for breakfast. In my defence, he enjoyed it and who says a savoury nutritious breakfast isn't a great example to our kids? I'm happy to report, nearly two decades on, he still likes it. As our children are now much older and wiser, we need to respect their food choices. I'm not condoning that fast food is okay for every meal or that excess sugar, salt, or fat is the way to go, but it's so easy to get hung up on making every single meal perfectly balanced in terms of nutrition. In an ideal world, our teens would want to eat extremely healthily at each and every meal but with the power of marketing, the choices in supermarkets, and peer influences, there are too many unhealthy choices lurking around every corner tempting them.

In my own attempt to produce healthy meals, after a couple of attempts at offering my son seaweed I must admit I gave up in the hope that he would like it when he's an adult. Being a great fan of it and knowing its superpowers, I naturally thought he would love it too. I obviously needed a reality check!

Reflecting on my own childhood, I spent many an hour alone at our family table, long after everyone else had finished their meals and left. I had been told by my father that I couldn't leave the table until I finished every mouthful of fish. I can still picture it now, decades later. The fish was cold and hard, and it put me off eating fish for about 15 years. Ironically, although fish is good for you, it certainly wasn't good for my mental health at the time.

We shouldn't force any type of food down the necks of our teens. Force feeding is totally unacceptable and goes a long way in putting them off certain foods for life. Teens' palettes often change as they get older, so even if your teen currently consumes a limited range of foods, chances are that this will change. By teaching our teens nutrition and healthy eating habits, we equip them with valuable life tools, often broadening their food choices en-route. Involvement in tasks such as weekly menu planning, food shopping, or cooking prepares them for adulthood, and can be a fun way to connect.

SEEING THINGS DIFFERENTLY

We often expect our teens to be able to see things from our point of view, an adult's perspective. But caught in the void between childhood and adulthood, often this is not possible. Which is why it would be unfair to always expect them to be rational and able to think like adults. When explaining our views to our teens, we may be met with a headstrong or cantankerous response. But due to their limited deductive reasoning abilities, we must question whether they are truly capable of always understanding us. And when we factor in their quest for independence, it's no wonder that what we interpret as stubbornness is, in fact, normal behaviour.

If we refer to the work of the famous Swiss Psychologist Jean Piaget, a pioneer in developmental child psychology, we see that Piaget believed that children aren't miniature adults. That they think in a totally different way to adults and so their views of the world are entirely different.

YOUR PERSPECTIVE

There are numerous posts on social media, written by parents, moaning about how their children have changed for the worse over the years. How their sweet child has been replaced by an unloving, uncaring, monster. Yet, nothing has really changed since they were held as babies in their loving arms. They are still fundamentally the same person needing just as much love, support, and happiness. So perhaps it's their parents' expectations that have changed, or a lack of understanding of the adolescent journey, further highlighting the vital need to understand and listen to your teen.

CHAPTER 5: DON'T GROW UP

"In order to fly, you first need to stretch out your wings."

We are often fearful for our teens, frightened of letting them go as we won't be there to shield them from the dangers of life. However, for them to take flight, we need to instil confidence, trust, and responsibility to set them free. Free to fly and create a life for themselves, knowing that we are always here in the background, whenever they need us. Letting go isn't easy, as naturally we don't want our children to grow away from us. We want to hold them tight, make memories, bathe in golden moments, enjoy their laughter, their quirky little ways and their company, for as long as possible. But habits are hard to break, and after spending so many years raising our children it's difficult to pull back. Now, they no longer want us to see them as a child. The hugs and kisses and the 'I love You's', especially in public, are no longer welcome as these only lead to embarrassment.

For parents of older teens, especially houseparents who have devoted all their time to running the house and looking after the children, now will be a time of adjustment. An opportunity to reflect and decide on which direction their lives are now heading. Of course, we wish our teens a long, happy, healthy and accomplished future, but in the meantime, we want to hold them close and make the most of the brief period of childhood. If I'm honest, even though I want my son to soar and have a fulfilling life as an independent man, it does make me sad to think I won't see him every day. Thoughts of our teens leaving home stirs our imagination, bringing notions of detachment, empty nests, and no doubt thoughts of old age. This is the stage of our lives where we need to take stock to readjust our compass. The notion that we are being replaced by their partners and aren't needed nearly as much comes into play. But so too does the opportunity to finally put ourselves first and rekindle our dreams.

As our teens start to leave childhood behind and venture into adulthood, it's natural to go through a stage of mourning. Our relationship with them changes, and so too does the number of cuddles and the level of closeness that we once had. Our role changes from one of a carer, to one of a mentor. From someone that carried them to someone that walks a few paces behind them. This doesn't mean that the good times are behind us though. There are plenty more of these to come. Including, if we look close enough, the ones that are happening right now.

GROWING INTO A MAN

As male teens mature, the relationship with their mother changes. The closeness they experienced during childhood now doesn't feel appropriate. The natural tendency to pull away from their main female role model, on their journey towards manhood, now takes root. Their craving to belong to a group of likeminded males, and their need for male role models in order to navigate themselves in the world as male adults, contribute to their endeavour in becoming a man. This healthy 'pulling away' process initially began when they were around 7 years old, when their focus shifted away from their mother towards their father. However, it isn't until the teenage years that this focus on their father becomes so apparent. It also explains why our teens no longer want to be associated with, or seen as an extension of, their female parent, as they fear they will not be seen as a man.

From your teen's point of view, this is a gradual process, and one which he isn't likely to sit and analyse. Whereas, from a mother's point of view, she will noticeably recognise this shift in her son and miss the deep connection, leaving her feeling melancholy. But all is not lost. This shift doesn't mean that our teens don't love us. It just means that they've redefined our role in their eyes. They still need an authoritative female in their lives as it's their mother that will teach them about the fairer sex, showing them what makes us tick and how they should treat the females in their lives.

This shift highlights the importance of our teens hanging out with their male friends and peers and explains why we often hear them being macho or using forceful language when playing online or chatting, as this bantering is all part and parcel of their learning.

Some psychologists believe that one of the reasons why teenage boys argue with their mothers is that they need to assert their masculinity, whilst still keeping a close bond with her, and that arguments create the perfect scenario to do so. Although this may be true, this shouldn't be used as an excuse to give an argument the green light.

YOUR FEARS AREN'T THEIR FEARS

Our fears aren't our children's fears. Our teens will have their own fears which are unique to them, and which will change over time. Undoubtedly different from ours, and from the ones we had at their age. To avoid projecting our own fears onto our teens, we should be mindful of them. To help, we can consider confronting our fears in private. If not possible, we can consider addressing them in the future.

We shouldn't impose limitations upon our teens, even if they've had limitations placed upon them in the past as these restrictions may no longer be relevant and may serve no purpose. It's quite possible that our teens may have reduced or even eliminated some of their limitations without us knowing. From time to time, we need to reassess our perspective, as we could inadvertently be offering our teens an outdated, unhealthy crutch.

When it comes to the fears of today's teenagers, we can look to The Children's Society to glean an insight into their thoughts and feelings. Each year, The Children's Society charity produces The Good Childhood Report, a widely referenced review of trends and findings on young people's well-being, including analysis of contributing factors. The report investigates various aspects of young people's lives including home, family, school, friends, appearance, health, money, and their future. The report includes data from thousands of children aged 10 to 17 years. It's a highly respected document that has influenced many changes, improving the lives of many young people. The following citations are taken from their 2023 and 2024 reports:

"In 2022, the UK had the lowest average overall life satisfaction among 15-year-olds completing PISA across 27 European countries" (The Children's Society, 2023).

"Analysis of Understanding Society data showed the importance of positive family relationships for children's well-being, with children who did not feel supported by their family more than six times more likely to feel unhappy with their life as a whole (17.7%) as children who felt supported in most things (2.8%) by their family" (The Children's Society, 2023).

The final piece of information taken from the 2023 *The Good Childhood Report* relates to their participants' 'worries regarding their future'. Below is the list of their top 7 worries:

1st Having enough money.

2nd Finding a job.

3rd Getting good grades.

4th Finding somewhere to live.

5th Their mental health.

6th Going to university (if they wanted to).

7th Their physical health.

(The Children's Society, 2023).

From the 2024 *Good Childhood Report*, under the heading of 'Worries about society', participants, aged 10-17, said they were 'very' or 'quite' worried about:

1st Rising prices.

2nd Crime.

3rd Environment.

4th Online Safety.

5th Inequality.

6th New illness/pandemics.

7th Homelessness.

8th Refugee and migrant crisis.

9th Unemployment.

So not only were our teens deeply affected by Covid-19 and still are, but they are now worried about further pandemics.

"When asked about their experiences of their household's financial situation, almost one in five (18%) children and young people worried 'often' or 'always' about how much money their family had" (The Children's Society, 2024).

"11% of the children and young people who completed our survey in 2024 had low wellbeing" (The Children's Society, 2024).

TEACHING RESPONSIBILITY

"Being a parent to a teenager is like working in a circus without a safety net. We check that our teens have tightened their safety ropes, then watch as they proceed precariously across the tightropes of life, do a triple somersault, then continue onwards. Knowing that at any minute they might either land safely or fall."

As our teens grow towards adulthood, they will naturally want to be more involved in decision making. Being allowed to explore and experiment while still safely in the nest equips them with empowering decision-making tools such as critical thinking strategies, information gathering, and ethical and legal considerations, all of which will increase their ability to weigh up options, consider possible outcomes, and make choices, strengthening their neural pathways and developing their PFC. We will need to be patient while our teens grasp these concepts as they are still formulating their core values.

To aid our teens, we can coax them into taking charge of projects, events, or tasks. We can also encourage them to talk through their plans and ideas, using role play to build self-confidence, whilst avoiding drawing attention to their weaknesses. Whilst completing tasks, if things don't turn out as hoped, instead of jumping in to save the day, we should allow them additional time and space to weigh up their options. If your teen comes to you for help at the onset of a task, you can assist him by asking him questions whilst ensuring that he remains in control. The questions below will aid him in his decision-making process. As a last resort, you can give him some pointers and suggestions, making sure that the final decision is his.

- 'How do you plan to deal with the situation?'
- 'What do you need to do in order to reach a decision?'
- 'What do you think will be the reaction from others involved?'
- 'What steps will you take to get the result you want?'
- 'Do you plan to engage the help of others?'
- 'What sort of timeframe do you have in mind?'
- 'When do you plan to start on the project?'
- 'Can you see any pitfalls before you start?'
- 'Have you considered where the money for a budget will come from?'
- 'What's the outcome you are hoping to achieve?'
- 'What assumptions are you making?'

CHAPTER 6: GUILTY UNTIL PROVEN INNOCENT

"*He that is without sin amongst you, let him first cast a stone at her.*" *King James Bible, John. 8:7.*

TRUST AND MISTRUST

"*Many teens feel that if you don't trust them then they shouldn't trust you, as they believe trust works both ways.*"

Sometimes, it's hard to know whether someone is guilty of something or not, and our teens are no exception. If you find yourself in this situation, and no danger is involved, pause before you cast the first stone. Failure to do so could harm your relationship, as well as his self-esteem and self-respect. By giving our teens the chance to talk, we offer an opportunity to prove their innocence.

Mistrusting our teens can remove their incentive to behave as they see no point if they aren't going to be believed. Additionally, by eliminating their sense of moral responsibility to be honest, our distrust can leave them feeling unworthy and can lead to negative behaviour patterns such as lying, stealing, or cheating. It creates a chicken-and-egg situation: if we don't trust our teens, how will they learn to become trustworthy?

To maintain a trust continuum, it's vital not to break promises we've made to our teens unless absolutely necessary. If we consistently back out of our promises, they will no longer believe that we will 'show up' for them in the future. By the same token, if we are constantly unavailable when they need us, they may start to question whether they can trust us, which can leave them feeling insecure.

Lying

There are many reasons why teens feel the need to lie. They may fear telling the truth and lie to protect themselves, especially if they are fearful of facing consequences for their inappropriate behaviour, which is often the case with very strict or over-controlling parents. Teens also lie to avoid hearing someone blaming them for their actions. Or because they can't face being ashamed or embarrassed. Some lie because they can't handle the fact that they've let their parents down. Others may lie to protect other people, including friends and family. Similarly, they may lie to keep their parents from knowing their private life, to establish autonomy. Other reasons include the desperate need to gain attention or to impress others, such as their peers.

Then there are times when teens simply can't face telling their parents about a painful experience, so lie to protect themselves. They twist the truth to avoid talking about certain topics. In this fashion, when asking your teen about a recent event, such as an exam or a party he attended, don't be surprised if, due to his underlying fears, he tries to avoid the subject by talking about other things. He may end up telling you part of the story but not the whole story as it's just too difficult. Perhaps the party was rather disastrous for him or the exam a total washout. If you are led to believe that everything was fine, when in fact things didn't go to plan, when the truth reveals itself later you may feel like you have been lied to.

Misunderstandings can easily occur as it's easy to misconstrue something we've heard. If you or your teen mishears each other, you can easily end up believing something that wasn't intended and later interpret it as a lie.

There may be times when we think our teens have lied to us but have merely passed on information that they believed to be true. We may not believe the information is correct, but this doesn't mean they've lied as there is no intention to do so. Teens, especially young ones, often believe that information found on the internet is the gospel truth. As they are still very impressionable, they may repeat this information without realising it's untrue. Not forgetting, teens think very differently from us and understand much less than we do.

If you think your teen has lied, talk to him to find out why. This will help you understand him and his world. Then, reinforce or set new rules and establish consequences, if appropriate.

WHY DOES SOCIETY GIVE TEENAGERS SUCH A HARD TIME?

When pondering how society perceives teenagers, it's easy to believe that people feel scared or even threatened by them as the general consensus seems to be that we should be cautious of these 'hooded, antisocial creatures.'

One of the major stumbling blocks for people who don't understanding teenagers is that they don't know what to expect from them. By nature, if we don't understand something we tend to fear it, and in the case of teens, this gives rise to a fostering of public fear. Scarily, there is even a word in the dictionary to describe this fear: 'ephebiphobia'. As a result, society unjustifiably labels them, giving them bad press. So, it comes as no surprise that these young people are blamed for issues such as poor behaviour, bad attitude, laziness, and crime, to name but a few. This raises the question: what incentives do today's youth have to behave in an orderly manner, when they carry such labels and constantly feel the need to prove themselves to society at large? Admittedly, some teens commit horrendous injustices, but the majority don't. They are fine, upstanding young citizens, just trying to get through the maze of adolescence.

There are a host of reasons why society labels teens as 'troublemakers', 'lost causes', or 'problems', including the following:

1. *The public is afraid of teenagers.*

- Teenagers are misunderstood as not everyone has experienced raising or working with them.
- People who are frightened by teenagers assume the worst about their thoughts and actions.
- We misconceive the idea that teenagers deliberately act in certain ways just to infuriate or intimidate us.
- It's easier to put blame and shame onto others instead of taking the time to truly understand them.

2. A *lack of compassion or empathy for their tough path, from childhood to adulthood.*

3. *Forgetting what it was like when people were their age.*

For the majority of adults, it's been a long time since there were teenagers, so they've forgotten how they acted and how they felt.

4. *Little understanding of the issues that today's teenagers face and the pressures that these issues bring, compared to the ones that previous generations faced.*

Today's teenagers are facing very different issues than those of previous generations. All the same, how many people take the time to mull this over?

5. *Teenagers' behaviours can be very different from adults and children.*

We see these differences but aren't willing to accept them, so class them as 'irrational' or 'irresponsible' without challenging our own thoughts.

6. *Teens that are provoked by others can exhibit unhealthy behaviours.*

Innocent teens that are influenced by others can fall into bad habits. They can be exploited by peers or adults and forced to carry out illegal or immoral acts.

7. No *understanding of teenage brain development and its cognitive limitations.*

A large proportion of the public, including many parents, don't understand the cognitive challenges that are taking place during adolescence. Thus, teenagers' behaviours are seen as 'unacceptable', instead of 'normal'.

8. *Bad parenting.*

Parenting styles will affect how teenagers behave.

9. *They are victims of unfortunate circumstances.*

Teenagers may live in poverty, have parents that are alcohol- or drug- dependent, or involved in crime. They may suffer from sexual, physical, or verbal abuse, all of which can shape or change teenagers' behaviour.

10. *The media love to portray teenagers and adolescents in a bad light.*

Eye-catching news sells.

The following is an example of a misconception of teenagers:

CONCEPT: *Teens are loud and aggressive, and their moods change rapidly.*

Teens often tend to engage their feelings when they communicate as their rational thinking is still under construction. As a result, they may be unaware that they are raising their voices or choosing words that are more forceful than others.

When it comes to mood swings, it's true that teens' moods change rapidly. Just as it‘s true of many adults, including menstruating and menopausal women, manipulators who deliberately switch back and forth to control others, or those that are struggling with certain mental health conditions.

When it comes to playing loud music, don't we all love to get lost in music at times? Love to forget about our day and switch off? Perhaps on the odd occasion, to look and feel good, and maybe to impress others, we turn up the volume in the car. Clinically speaking, loud music releases endorphins in the brain, making us feel good, so perhaps that‘s another reason why they do this.

We also need to remember that people are naturally afraid of those who are physically larger than them. (This usually relates to their height.) Overall, in the western world, our teens are taller than previous generations, thus creating an innate fear.

Hoodies

After writing the above section, I started to wonder about hoodies as they are a common piece of clothing in most teens' wardrobes, and many adults' too, and are often given bad press. I wondered what the psychological reasons were behind the wearing of this garment. So, I reflected on this and conducted online research. My findings included many interesting results, not just the obvious ones such as feeling cold.

Reasons for the wearing of Hoodies:

- Helps to avoid worries about body image.
- Protects against UV radiation.
- Provides feelings of cosiness and warmth like a comforter, making teens feel safe.
- Offers a form of protection and shelter, especially for those suffering from social anxiety, anxiety or depression.
- Conceals injuries caused by self-harm or physical abuse.
- Deemed an item of fashion.
- Provides useful pockets for phones, etc.
- Keeps hands warm.
- Avoids criticism as a hoodie is a universal piece of clothing.

- Keeps teens dry in wet weather.
- Makes decision making easy if teens are too tired to decide what to wear.
- Hides a bad haircut or the need for a haircut.
- Helps teens that are uncomfortable with their gender as it's gender neutral.
- Matches most outfits.

Interestingly, hoodies can be traced back to mediaeval Europe when they were worn by monks. In England, the first garment which had a hood can be traced back as far as the 12th Century. In the 1930s, American warehouse workers wore hoodies to keep themselves warm against the bitter winters. During the 70s, hoodies became a popular fashion item, and by the 90s its popularity had grown enormously.

YOU KNOW YOUR CHILD

It's far too easy to jump down our teens' throats and hold them accountable for something they didn't do. When our day hasn't gone to plan, our thoughts can easily become rather negative, distorting our judgement of others, with a knock-on effect on conversations at home. If we find ourselves in this situation and want to blame our teen for something they've done, we first need to stop and ask ourselves whether their perceived actions are out of character. If they are, chances are we've looked at the situation through a skewed lens. If we truly know and understand our teens, the likelihood is that we will know the answer before we've even asked the question. At which point, we should calmly ask them to explain what happened. This approach helps defuse situations before they start to ignite. The following story, related to me by a colleague, serves as an example of this.

Sally had made her son his school packed lunch. When he returned home after school, she was rather annoyed that it was only half eaten. She had woken up early to make it, had made the bread the day before, and had even popped into her local store specially to pick up one of the ingredients the night before. Seeing half of it left in the box looking rather sad was enough to make her blood boil. Although she was tempted to shout in horror, she decided not to. Instead, in a neutral voice, she calmly asked him why he'd disregarded half of his lunch, pausing to give him the opportunity to talk whilst she listened. He explained that the crust, which made up a large percentage of the slice, got stuck in his braces and he'd spent ages trying to eat it. As for the lettuce, he simply didn't see it. She then proposed that the lettuce could have got caught in the lid and been missed. It was at this point that she saw the distraught expression on his face and straight away realised how genuinely sorry he was. She then listened to the 'judge' inside her head telling her that her child was someone that always told the truth. Immediately, she told him not to worry, explaining that the next loaf of bread would be much easier for him to eat. Then, in a non-criticising voice, she asked him to regularly check to make sure that there was no food left before putting it back into his school bag.

We can see in this example how easy it would have been for the mum to scold her son and for the conversation to turn sour.

This second scenario takes a different approach.

I was recently talking to a friend who told me that her young teenage son had woken her up early that morning. Typically, it was a day that she had planned a lie-in. Unfortunately, her son had other ideas, and she was woken to the sound of him practising his guitar. She went downstairs and abruptly told him that she wasn't impressed as she wanted another hour's sleep. She confessed to me that she had felt guilty at raising her voice to him so early in the morning and before his school day had even begun. She asked for my advice. I suggested that she speaks to her son using True Focused Listening, doesn't assume anything, and gives him a chance to explain. So that same evening, after he had eaten and relaxed for a while, she talked to him. After listening, and gently probing further, she realised that he was rather worried about his upcoming guitar exam and had laid awake in the early hours worrying about it. He had quietly gone downstairs and shut the door before starting to practise, thinking that no one would be able to hear. He had no idea how much sound travelled in their house.

It's too easy to assume that a tired, early woken mother must be in the right. However, this is not always the case.

It's clear that her son made the effort to close the door, but didn't realise how far sound travels, which isn't surprising as teens' thoughts are often insular.

Similar to this story, I have heard of teens that, unbeknown to their parents, have set their alarms an hour or so earlier in order to wake up and revise for next day school exams. So next time you are awoken from your slumber by noises made by your teen, find out why they did so before you wrongfully make assumptions.

This next scenario, related to me by a friend, reiterates the importance of thinking before acting on impulse.

A while ago, a friend gave herself the day off and went out for the day. On returning home, feeling happy but tired, she took one look at the bombsite of a kitchen and instantly her elated mood dropped. Her son had been at home all day as it was half-term holidays. She didn't feel it was appropriate to tell him off as he had other chores elsewhere in the house. She did, however, express her disappointment at him. A few minutes later he explained that he had spent most of the day completing homework and then was so tired that he had fallen asleep. If she had taken a different stance, the outcome would have been very different, and most likely not very pleasant for either of them. To avoid harming our relationship with our teens, we need to make sure that we are correct in our assumptions before accusing them of anything.

This last scenario is a good example of being branded 'guilty' without having the chance to explain.

GUILTY UNTIL PROVEN INNOCENT

Not long ago, I was talking to a friend's teenage son. His mum had recently reprimanded him as he hadn't been in contact with her when he had travelled to meet some friends. He explained to me that she hadn't listened and had set harsh consequences which had made him mad. His journey was long and complicated and that it was the first time he'd travelled so far alone. During the trip, his mind was preoccupied as he was focusing on getting from A to B without getting too overwhelmed, which is why messaging her en-route had slipped his mind. Although it's only fair that our teens keep in contact if we ask, we need to listen and understand their thought processes before we set harsh consequences.

THE POSITIVE VS NEGATIVE CYCLES OF TRUST

Below are the Positive and Negative Cycles of Trust diagrams. They explain the importance of giving our teens the benefit of the doubt and show the damaging consequences that can arise when we fail to do so. They also serve as a useful reminder to think before we act.

POSITIVE CYCLE OF TRUST

Teen is given the benefit of the doubt.

Feels trusted and capable.

Self-esteem and confidence grow.

Wants to impress and act responsibly.

Positive behaviour is noted or rewarded .

NEGATIVE CYCLE OF TRUST

Teen is NOT given the benefit of the doubt.

↓

Not trusted or constantly doubted by parents.

↓

Feels distrusted and misunderstood.

↓

Self-esteem drops – he loses faith in himself.

↓

Feels his parents will never believe in him.

↓

Stops trying or being honest.

↓

Negative behaviour is noted by parents.

↓

Parents react with more doubt or criticism.

(↑ back to "Self-esteem drops – he loses faith in himself.")

CHAPTER 7: CONTROL

"As parents, our role carries responsibilities that should not be forgotten, especially when it comes to the use of control."

"Punishment is what we do *to* a child, but discipline is what we do *for* a child," says Brian Salazar-Prince, an American School Counsellor. This quote beautifully captures how our attitude shapes our approach to parenting. Just because we set boundaries and rules doesn't mean we have to exert control in an authoritarian manner. Punishment infers spitefulness and is a negative short-term solution that brings long-term issues. Whereas discipline, carried out in a firm but loving manner using expectations and consequences, is a positive alternative.

FRIEND OR PARENT?

"Our children need friends, but we should not count ourselves as one of them."

At times, there is a thin line between being a parent and being a friend. We need to understand where the line falls in order to stay on the right side of it. Being too much of a friend leaves our teens parentless, without anyone to turn to if we can't muster it. Our teens can pick from an array of friends, but they don't have that choice when it comes to parents. Being over friendly blurs the lines, making it harder to set rules, boundaries, and consequences. If we lean on or confide in them, we put unnecessary pressure upon them, especially since they aren't yet emotionally or intellectually mature enough to handle it, not that it would be fair to them. And as much as they want us to go along with and agree to their every wish, the responsibility can become burdensome, leaving them feeling insecure. This is another reason why it's important for us to be the authoritative figure, not them. Although, on the surface, it may seem easier for us to befriend our teens, it does them a disservice as it doesn't set them up for life. Pampering to their every whim falsely allows them to believe that others too will follow their every command. Similarly, in our quest to prioritise them over ourselves we negate our own existence, making it difficult to be taken seriously and be given the respect that we deserve and need to parent them.

Teens need strong and supportive parents that will protect them when the going gets tough. People that possess confidence. People they can trust and turn to for advice, guidance, and support. While they need to know that we come from a place of love and understanding, they also need to know that we will set boundaries and rules, and that we are sagacious, capable of weighing up situations and making decisions based on truth, not merely on a whim to please or pacify them.

"It's simply not true that if our children like us then we must be great parents."

As parents, we often have to make tough decisions. Ones which our teens won't always agree with or like. As a result, they may not like us, and may even hate us, but we just have to accept this and get used to it, even if it makes us feel uncomfortable. We aren't here to appease our children but to prepare them for adulthood.

Contrary to this, teens need a certain amount of autonomy in order to feel in control, without which they feel powerless. As they grow, so too will their levels of autonomy, which, providing it's not abused, should be respected. Issues, such as threats from them about their well-being and their behaviour, can start when no autonomy is given, as they feel constrained.

LACK OF SUFFICIENT CONTROL

By failing to exert adequate control, we pave the way for complications. Being too lazy, weak, or busy to monitor what our teens are doing or saying is imprudent. It's crucial to strike the right balance. By failing to take interest in our teens' day-to-day life, we give the impression that we don't have time for them, leading them to feel they are low on our list of priorities. This can cause them to question how much we really care.

Uninvolved or low-control parenting styles offer our teens more freedom, however, once the initial excitement fades, and with no boundaries in place, they are easily left feeling insecure. If we are not careful and allow out teens to get away with too much, we risk undermining our authority. If things slide for too long, situations can spiral out of control and intervention may become necessary.

As our teens grow older, we should loosen the reins to allow them to grow, although we still need be aware of what's happening in their lives so we can guide them and intervene when necessary.

EXCESSIVE CONTROL

"*It's the bully that uses their child as a punchbag, verbally or physically.*"

We all deserve to be loved unconditionally. But sadly, this right is often overlooked as far too many children are neglected. Some may be comfortably off, residing in large houses in affluent areas, and some may live an impoverished life. Wrongly, love can be used as a bargaining tool and the word itself can be bandied around far too easily. Phrases such as 'You wouldn't talk to me or act that way if you really loved me,' are a form of abuse and used by parents that usually exert too much control.

Parents that exert excessive control believe their offspring are inferior to them and fail to recognise that they are individuals in their own right. Research reveals that being excessively strict induces many drawbacks, including rebellion or compliance in a submissive way, neither of which is ideal. With a knock-on effect that they may replicate this behaviour in their relationships and look for dominating partners.

Authoritarian styles of parenting encourage teens to lie, stifle creativity, cause anxiety and lower self-esteem. It also stymies the child's efforts to carve out a distinct and unique identity within the family. Parents who follow this style often find communication more difficult as teens struggle to open up and confide in them, creating a rift between parent and teen. Teens raised this way are more likely to question whether they are loved, as they are constantly being told what to do and what to think.

By dominating our teens, we strip them of their intuition and sense of power needed to grow independent individuals with a strong sense of self-worth. We also rob them of the opportunity to make mistakes. During the teenage years, mistakes are par for the course and teens should be allowed to make small ones without being constantly reprimanded. Teens that are excessively controlled feel intimidated, are unable to express themselves, and often struggle to find their own path in life. Micromanagement also leads to a lack of understanding in thought processes such as decision making, option evaluating, and actions and consequences. Teens brought up this way often struggle to self- manage and self-regulate. They feel their spirit is being crushed, and their self-confidence and self-reliance are diminishing. Which is why we should avoid pestering and hovering over our teens as it will annoy them and make them feel anxious and less likely to open up and converse. We can let them know that we are around if they need us, but we need to keep our distance until then.

GUIDANCE VS CONTROL

"Teenwork – Parenting a teen is all about working with your teen and not against. Set rules and consequences but listen and understand too."

Since everyone is unique, each of our teens will have their own points of view, own ideas and preferences and should be encouraged to make their own assumptions and conclusions independently. We can offer guidance and suggestions, in their best interest, such as going to university, college or following a direction for their careers, but we don't have the right to insist on their route. Where you choose to draw the line between guidance and control is up to you, but our teens always need encouragement and support, and not just when it suits us.

THE TIMES ARE A CHANGIN'

No thanks to the internet, the idea of listening, learning and looking up to parents has changed. Teens nowadays are just as likely to seek guidance on navigating life online, picking and choosing from people they admire, as opposed to relying on their families. From a parent's point of view, this can be frustrating as we naturally want to share lessons learnt, guide them and do the best job that we can. Yet, if we are smart, we will accept this as a means of learning and advancing ourselves. Thereby, we can join forces with the internet to offer our teens a more rounded approach to learning, as in the African proverb, ‘It takes a village to raise a child'.

CHAPTER 8: CONFLICT

"It's easy to assume the worst when we don't understand other people's behaviour. In the case of our teens, this can lead us to believe that they are intentionally trying to challenge us, when in truth, their behaviour may be driven by feelings they don't yet know how to manage or communicate."

We readily accept the negative assumption that having a teenager means constantly facing a battle. We even justify to ourselves, and others, that we are going to spend a great deal of time arguing with them. Yet, this isn't true and is a rather naïve way of thinking, and one that needs challenging.

Admittedly, being human, conflict is part of our everyday lives. Some conflict is normal and necessary for teens' cognitive development. But by some, I mean arguments or disagreements that happen on the odd occasion, that are quickly resolved. In order to learn about life, our teens are at the point where they are questioning different points of views and challenging people's reasoning, so naturally they will push boundaries to see what happens. They need to comprehend that others won't always agree with their ideas or principles, which enables them to think outside the box.

Our teens are trying to find their inner voice, so they won't necessarily see eye to eye with us or even their friends all the time, just as we don't with our friends. But it's when conflict gets out of hand or becomes a regular feature of our week that problems arise. Yelling, arguing or swearing on a regular basis is very unhealthy and needs to be addressed.

It's no secret that regular family conflicts between parent and child affects the mental health of all involved. Contributing to conditions such as anxiety and depression, whilst increasing the risk of the use of coping mechanisms such as self-harm and substance abuse. For this reason, we need to avoid conflict with our teens as much as we can.

It's not our job, nor the job of others, to stop our teens from having emotions such as feelings of upset, anger, excitement, frustration, annoyance, and embarrassment, as this is all part and parcel of being human. It's our duty to explain that feelings are all part of the ebb and flow of life, and that it's perfectly normal to feel certain ways at certain times. By teaching our teens how to deal with their feelings, we empower them to take control of their emotions.

Anger, a human emotion, can cause outbursts in both adults and teens. It's unhealthy to suppress these feelings as all emotions need a safe outlet. To support our teens, we must equip them with tools that teach emotional regulation. Otherwise, they may build up unhealthy resentment, which can easily surface at the least appropriate moment. By recognising and understanding their own feelings, teens are better able to express them in healthy ways and gain a deeper understanding of who they are. This helps prevent them from getting drawn into confrontational situations.

Problems arise when parents fight against their teens' emotions, failing to see that it's not always about defiance but it's often about an inability to manage what they are feeling.

By helping our teens identify their emotional triggers, and by recognising those triggers ourselves, we can begin to move forward. If we demonstrate effective calming strategies we can help them defuse situations before they spiral. Discussing ways to develop healthy, readily available outlets for their anger, such as hitting a punch bag or special pillow, or grabbing their running shoes and heading out for a run, we empower them to take control. By being a good role model, we are reminded that actions often speak louder than words.

If things do get out of hand and our teens act in an unacceptable manner, we will need to address the situation, setting consequences as necessary. Once sorted, it's important for them to know that we love them unconditionally. That we will not hold their actions against them. And that it's their *behaviour* that we don't like, not *them* as a person.

Referring back to the earlier section on the prefrontal cortex, let's not forget that our teens often respond emotionally. So, it's natural for them to display their feelings using a 'no holds barred' approach, as opposed to a carefully considered response. With this in mind, when touching on delicate subjects don't be surprised if your teen displays tears or experiences emotional outbursts due to his inability to control his emotions. Explaining why it's so important to choose our words carefully to avoid hurting them.

Once we acknowledge the crucial fact that teens use a 'feelings' approach to their responses, as opposed to a 'thinking' approach, we reach a deeper understanding. This includes understanding why they can struggle to comprehend the consequences of their actions on others.

To support the growth of our teens' emotional intelligence, we must explain the importance of acknowledging our own feelings, along with the feelings of others, demonstrating the importance of empathy and compassion. Without making them feel guilty, we can explain why raising their voice isn't acceptable as a normal course of action. When they have stumbled, to help them make the necessary neural pathway connections, we can talk them through the consequences of their actions.

"Because adolescents rely heavily on the emotional regions of their brains, it can be challenging to make what adults consider logical and appropriate decisions" (Arain et al., 2013).

Although having an underdeveloped PFC can be challenging for all involved, there is a silver lining in that it provides us with a valuable insight into how our teens are feeling, both about themselves and about situations that have occurred. For example, if we hear a distressed or panicking undertone in their voice then we know that they are worried or anxious and can act accordingly to assist them. Conversely, if they are excited, we can pick up on that too.

THE 4 STEP MODEL

The following 4 Step Model was created to prevent conversations escalating into arguments. This technique allows us to *respond*, as opposed to *react*, to our teens' emotional outbursts. Further on in this book we will expand on responding vs reacting.

Step 1. Listen to your teen whilst mentally noting any unusual reactions.

Step 2. Silently decipher this information in order to understand how he's feeling around a certain topic and why he may be reacting this way.

Step 3. Communicate, query, and respond to him, aiding him as necessary.

Step 4. Once the conversation has ended, calmly explain what is and what isn't acceptable when it comes to communicating.

JEKYLL AND HYDE

At times, it can be difficult living with a teenager as we don't always know what to expect and often can't seem to win. Rather like living with a Jekyll and Hyde. One moment they are unusually clingy, and we are worried that they are feeling anxious and something is wrong, and the next they are headstrong, rather arrogant, refusing to listen to anything we have to say and refusing to reason with us. When this happens, try not to blow things out of proportion. These episodes, *which they've little control over*, are often short lived, so soon will pass. Chances are, the quicker *we* get over this episode then the easier it will be for the situation to get back to normal.

With ideas and beliefs changing frequently, their thoughts are often transient, habitually leaving them struggling with clarity of thought. When it comes to adults, we are certainly no angels either. When we get stressed, we can end up becoming rather unreasonable too, taking our moods out on other people and switching personalities.

As hard as you try, you will find that every so often, you can't reason with your teen. This can be down to several reasons. For example, your teen may:

- Struggle to understand other peoples' points of view or the reasoning behind these points of view.
- Feel too emotional to think.
- Not be in the mood to listen to you.

- Have other, more pressing things on his mind.
- Just not be interested in having a lecture from you.
- Be too tired or too hungry.

AVOIDING CONFLICT

"Every single minute we are making memories. So, let's make them good ones."

In most cases, a teen's parents are their next and only line of defence. Therefore, if we make our teens feel unsafe by shouting at them or mistreating them in any way, they will feel frightened and assume they've no one to protect them. The same applies if we shout at or abuse others whilst in their company, for in their eyes, the person who is supposed to protect them becomes someone that scares them. Our teens need a safe space, and we are that space.

The world is made up of all sorts of people. Some are as tough as nails, and some are the more sensitive type. And then there are those who fit in between. I'm sure you know where your teen sits on this scale, and it's important that you take this into account when you talk to him as it will help you formulate your sentences. With the right approach, you can ask your teen questions in a manner that doesn't upset, hurt, or annoy him, since *how* we communicate is just as important as *what we say*.

When it comes to emotions, teens don't always understand why they feel the way they do. This can be quite frightening for them as they may not know what to expect from one minute to the next. Caught between a rock and a hard place, unable to control their outbursts, yet unwilling to endure the tension of constant arguing.

Try to prevent conversations escalating into arguments when you're negotiating with your teen or giving them the opportunity to take the lead, as both are important aspects of their growth.

Timers are Your New Best Friend

It's reasonable behaviour to give our teens notice when we want them to do something. It would be unfair to expect them to abruptly drop everything when it suits us. For example, ending a phone call, stopping a homework assignment, or closing down an online game, all at a moment's notice. If we relate this to adults, imagine how you would feel if your partner/friend entered the room and said to you, 'O.K. we're going out now, turn off the T.V. and let's go, immediately.' Surely, this would come across as being rude and disrespectful? In which case, why should we treat our teens any differently?

A cheap digital timer can be an invaluable tool when our teens need assistance ending a task. Acting as an impartial judge, timers help reduce conflict by preventing disputes over things such as how much time has been spent studying or how much time is left to play online. Knowing that our silent friend is working on our behalf, they allow us to relax as they prevent us from nagging, pestering, or reminding every 10 minutes. To make the idea of using a timer more appealing to your teen, let him pick one out.

'I' Not 'You'

If, over a period of time, your teen is behaving in a manner that is stressful for you, then find a suitable time to have a chat. Don't blame him or make him feel guilty, instead talk about how *you* feel. Make the conversation about *you* as opposed to him. Using the 'I' and not 'You' approach can be beneficial as it takes the heat off the other person and avoids directed blame. It may take several attempts for him to respond as you wish, but if you persevere, you will see that you will both benefit. Being an adult, you are able to control your emotions, so use this to your advantage. For example, instead of, 'You are annoying me,' try saying 'I feel annoyed.'

At times, we all feel overstretched and under-appreciated. Which is where the 'I' not 'You' approach comes in handy. It's best to avoid saying phrases such as 'You don't appreciate everything I do for you.' Instead, gently say, 'I don't feel very appreciated and at times it can make me rather upset or annoyed.' Swap, 'I stay up late just to pick you up from sports practice and you don't even appreciate it,' to 'I don't think that you realise that I give up my evenings in order to pick you up from your sports activities.' Using a calm and kind tone of voice. Not only will this approach reduce conflict but will teach the power of empathy.

Tone of Voice

Our tone of voice speaks volumes and can be a major player when it comes to sparking arguments. Let's imagine a scenario where, much to your annoyance, your teen has woken you up early. Instead of using the knee jerk reaction of, 'You woke me up this morning, you were so noisy,' you can rephrase it to, 'Do you think it would be possible if you could be a little quieter in the mornings as I heard you today and it woke me up?' Initially, you may think you are being too polite to someone that woke you up, but chances are your teen didn't deliberately go out of his way to be noisy. Another way of looking at this is to ask yourself how you would phrase the question if it was a friend staying over that was noisy. I'm sure you would ask them in a kind and caring voice, which leads me to wonder why we should talk any differently to our teens.

If you Can't Stand the Heat

If you feel your blood is about to boil and foresee a situation turning into an argument, physically remove yourself from the setting. If possible, try one of the following to help you readjust your mindset: do some exercise to clear your head, (the endorphins will brighten your mood); grab some fresh air, (this will calm you down and provide a fresh perspective on the matter); head into the garden; or switch on the T.V. to distract you. Ideally, spend a few moments reflecting on your thoughts and feelings. By taking some form of action, you will most likely avoid an argument, helping yourself and those around you.

Don't Take it Personally

"When we are in pain, our initial response is often to feel upset or angry, or to place blame upon someone, indeed anyone, for causing the pain."

During an argument, your teen may well say some very hurtful and cruel things to you or about you. Although the words may be painful to hear, there may well be valid reasons behind them. In order to avoid conflict, you will need to detach yourself from the situation and not take his remarks personally. Admittedly, this can be extremely difficult at times, especially if he says things that shake you to your core. Ideally, and to help in the long run, you may just have to learn to grow a slightly thicker skin. Your teen is most likely hurting and is taking his anger out on his nearest and dearest. Being parents, this can easily happen as we are our teen's safe space.

If you find yourself knee deep in an argument, avoid falling into the trap of over-explaining yourself by justifying your actions in response to your teen's accusations, as once you go down that road it becomes a very slippery slope. When we, figuratively, lay our words out in front of them, it gives them the opportunity to pick them up to scrutinise and reject each one. As a consequence, this relinquishes our power, and we lose control of the conversation.

Alternatively, we can make the odd comment, but it should stop at that. Conflicting as it may seem, in addition to losing our power, if we justify our actions, we also create an excuse to play down our teen's own feelings, thus belittling him.

If you find that during a normal conversation, not an argument, your teen makes a comment about you, he isn't necessarily questioning you or having a go at you, he's just expressing a thought. If the comment hits a nerve, just give a nonchalant response acknowledging the fact that he's spoken, but at the same time don't take on board what he's said, nor get upset by it.

As a parent, you may be doing a great job but if you find yourself in a heated discussion, which you feel may turn into an argument, then now isn't the time to tell your teen how wonderful you are, nor how hard you try at being a parent. This is your ego speaking, and if you let it talk it will do more harm than good. What your teen needs now is for you to step back and listen attentively, enabling him to air his feelings and grievances.

During conversations, your teen may tell you that he isn't interested in opening up to you and he may even say that you are the last person in the world that he would talk to. If you play this out carefully, you will realise that he is, in fact, opening up to you, and you will hear, if you listen heedfully, his story unravelling. It's at this point, that once again, you will need to remove your ego as it's not about *you* and *him*, it's *just* about *him*.

Our teens don't always know what they are saying during the throes of an argument, even adults find it difficult to think straight when strong emotions are flying around the room. In fact, during arguments, due to the strange workings of the brain, we can suffer from dissociation and block out traumatic episodes, leading us to forget what we said a few moments earlier.

We know that our teens aren't yet capable of looking at situations from an adult's point of view. Nor can they always articulate themselves in a mature manner in order to avoid conflict. We generalise that they are incapable of communicating with us, but in the same breath, we say that they are always arguing. *If we put these two statements together then Eureka! The solution is simple: Often, our teens' attempt at quarrelling is their way of communicating with us. And they are giving us valuable signals that should not be ignored.* But we must put aside our own emotions so we can control situations by gently guiding them away from being argumentative, as things will only escalate into an argument if *we allow* this to happen.

Struggling to deal with day-to-day concerns, with emotions often running high, we can't expect our teens to always communicate in a calm and relaxed way. Therefore, what we perceive as arguments aren't necessarily arguments. They are opportunities to engage and communicate.

This poses many questions, such as, 'Are arguments really conversations turned sour because of our teens' inability to control their thoughts and feelings?' Which leads us wondering, who is responsible for turning these types of conversations into arguments? We know that, as adults, if we handle these conversations correctly, we are able to stop them escalating into arguments. But we have to consider: if we are unwilling to stop things in their tracks, aren't we partly to blame when they escalate?

When it comes to full blown arguments, where your teen is yelling his head off or using foul language, then a different stance will need to be taken, which is covered later on in the book.

Let's reflect on argumentative behaviour and compare this type of conduct to how babies behave. When our teens were babies, we would readily accept them screaming, even at the top of their lungs, as we knew that this was the only way they were capable of communicating. Yet, we didn't ignore or berate them for doing so as we understood their limitations. We also comprehended that there was a good reason for this behaviour, be it that they needed their nappy changing, were hungry, or had other basic needs. So, are our teens needs and behaviours so very different now?

By now, you may be questioning why you should make all the effort and why your teen can't make the effort themselves. The answer is simple. *They aren't yet fully capable.*

Pick your Battles Wisely

A few years ago, I started applying the phrase 'Pick your battles wisely' to my life. I'm sure you are familiar with this expression. By realising that not every argument or notion is worth arguing about, and by allowing some of them to slide without so much as a comment, we make our lives a little easier. This is common practice amongst most married/cohabiting adults. Life's too short and our energy too limited to worry about every little thing. I found that if I only queried, questioned or worried about the things that were important to me, then my life, and therefore my son's, would be smoother. Which points you decide to stick with and which ones you drop are entirely up to you.

By following this concept, when faced with a comment your teen has made it becomes easier to ignore it, if you so choose. If your teen has asked you something in a way that has rather got your back up and you're not sure what to do about it, weigh it up and ask yourself if it's something that you can put in the 'I'm going to let it slide' pile, or in the 'Now hang on, that's just not acceptable' pile. If in doubt, leave it out of the conversation, then, if at a later date you find it needs re-addressing you can do so. Just bear in mind that if you wait, the time may have passed, and it may no longer be suitable to revisit, in which case you will know for next time.

THE WHY'S OF ARGUMENTS

"It's important not to avoid communicating with your teen for fear of conflict as you will create a void, damaging your relationship further."

If we think about the cognitive differences between teenagers and adults, it's easy to see why teenagers struggle to fathom the fact that we have a different perspective to them. And it's often this difference that can trigger arguments.

Due to their egocentric manner, teens often think that they know more than their parents, an egocentrism that grows in line with the growth of their cognitive abilities. If not handled properly, their headstrong approach can easily lead to a difference of opinion, and ultimately an argument.

Arguments can start far too easily, and we can all fly off the handle far too quickly. If one person raises their voice, then the other person will naturally follow suit. If your teen is the first one to start shouting and you decide to retaliate by shouting back, it will put his back up, and he will easily become angry or scared. At this point, trying to calm the situation becomes arduous. And due to his inability to control his feelings, your teen may then shed a tear or cause a commotion. No matter the outcome, when it comes to arguments, there are no winners, just losers.

Teens that argue on a regular basis often have underlying issues. When I mean argue I mean act aggressively, creating an excuse to be loud or rude. Teens can use arguments as an SOS distress signal, telling you that they are hurting and suffering, and that something is wrong. If you witness this behaviour on a regular basis, you will need to stop the argument as soon as possible so as not to add fuel to the fire. You will then need to work out what is troubling your teen. Maybe it's a short-term problem that can easily be solved, for example, a disagreement with a sibling or friend. Or maybe a more prolonged issue such as one caused by a traumatic event that is only now surfacing, possibly needing professional intervention.

ARGUMENT ESCALATION CHART

The following chart shows just how easily arguments can start, and how easily they can be avoided.

ARGUMENT ESCALATION CHART

Adult and Teen speak.

↓

Adult and Teen respond.

Teen	**Adult**
	Adult copies Teen's behaviour as they think they have the right to do so.
Voices are raised.	Voices are raised.
Emotions are high.	Emotions are high.
Shouting or Yelling commences.	Shouting or Yelling commences.

Escalates into an Argument.

↓

Argument is impossible to stop.

↓

Tears, frustration, anger, regret, and resentment.

AVOIDING ARGUMENTS

"Remember, the fool carries on fighting, but the wise man walks away."

Arguments are like runaway trains. They tend to pick up speed without us knowing, and by the time we realise it's often too late.

When a conversation starts to turn into an argument, if we can assess the situation rationally, weighing up our teens' circumstances, then we can pacify the situation and avert a quarrel. Circumstances such as, it's a Friday evening and he's exhausted after a busy week at school; something unusual or unsettling has happened to him recently; you have been unreasonable with your demands; he's very hungry; there has been a simple misunderstanding that's been overlooked; you've interrupted him whilst he was in the middle of something that's important to him such as mid-conversation with a friend or whilst engrossed in homework. It's also worth checking that you aren't mad at someone else, including yourself, as this can lead you to subconsciously *look for an argument*.

On the odd occasion, we start off a conversation when we are still undecided about the approach we want to take with our teens. Be it standing our ground, meeting them halfway, or another route. When this occurs, it's important to make sure that you don't make any decisions *before* you have heard what he has to say.

Although difficult at times, ideally, we should go into every conversation open heartedly. We are the adults here, not our teens, and we may just have to step up.

During heated discussions, it's easy to get bogged down with the finer points, dissecting parts of the conversation. We need to avoid this distraction as our teens can use it as an opportunity to point out other options, ones that are more favourable to them. Instead, we need to keep to the main points that we are trying to put across.

If you are in the spotlight during a heated discussion and are feeling over emotional and struggling to think straight, put a stop to the conversation. You can say something along the lines of, 'I'm feeling rather upset by such and such and I can't think of the right words to explain how I'm feeling. Can I return to this issue with you later today/tomorrow?' By doing so, you stop the conversation escalating into an argument, whilst protecting yourself and your teen from saying things you may later regret. Even during emotional or heightened discussions, our role is still one of a listener. So listen with empathy. If you feel there is a need to express your feelings, wait until the situation has calmed down. We need to allow our teens the opportunity to express themselves in a safe environment, without hearing threatening responses which will either shut down conversations or escalate them into arguments.

There may be times when your teen clearly doesn't want to talk to you. He may make comments such as, 'I'm too angry to talk,' 'I've got too much on my mind now to talk,' 'I can't deal with this right now,' 'I'm too tired to talk/listen,' 'I need to be on my own right now,' or 'I'm too annoyed to speak to you.' In which case, there is no harm just repeating back his words or summarising them. He will know you have listened and understood. However hard it may be to hold back your frustrations, you need to respect his wishes. Then make a mental note to pick up the conversation at a later date.

When striving to maintain equilibrium, it's important to look out for triggers that can disrupt the calm seas, such as those sparked by our teens' thoughts or experiences. By identifying these triggers, we can support their thinking and help them manage their behaviour. To aid them further, each time their triggers appear, we can discuss our observations with them to raise their awareness.

Make 'em laugh

To defuse a situation that is heading towards an argument, try using humour, making sure it isn't aimed at your teen. Pulling a weird face or making a light pun might lead him to burst out laughing. Be aware though, that it could have the opposite effect too. It's worth a try if you think it might work, as only experience will tell you whether it deserves a place in your parental toolkit.

Loaded Words

"*Inside, they are hurting. They show it through their emotions, hurling insults at us. It's their pain that we need to connect with, understand, and begin to unravel.*"

At the onset of arguments, the use of the mirroring technique can help defuse situations. By repeating our teens' words back to them, we demonstrate that we are listening and understand how they are feeling. Below are a few examples:

Teen: 'You don't understand!'

Parent: 'Yes, you are right, I don't understand. Please help me to understand,' or 'Tell me more so I can understand.'

Teen: 'I hate you!'

Parent: 'You hate me. That's your prerogative.'

Teen: 'I'm not a child!'

Parent: 'I can see that you are angry, and you think that I treat you like a child.'

Teen: 'I bet you're going to tell dad about this.'

Parent: 'You are worried I will tell dad. I will only tell him if you want me to, otherwise our conversations are confidential.'

RESPONDING VS REACTING

To avoid conflict and improve our communications skills, it's important to understand the difference between responding and reacting.

When we *react* to people, we deprive ourselves of the time needed to think clearly and calmly, preventing us from connecting with our rational mind. Instead, we allow our natural knee-jerk response to take over, which, if not careful, can cause harm. As this approach is instantaneous, and guided by our emotions, it can be quite hostile. Which is why we often find ourselves saying or doing things we later regret.

Contrary to this approach, *responding* is something we do after a pregnant pause, as in the phrase 'count to ten before you act.' If we respond, it means that we've taken stock of our thoughts and feelings and have decided, in a calm manner, exactly how we want to reply, which avoids us going off half-cocked. The beauty of responding is that we do so from a place of empowerment and self-control.

THREATS

Adults use threats against their children as a weapon of power to exercise their authority over them. It's unkind to threaten anyone and is a form of bullying. Something said in annoyance can confuse, worry, or even frighten a teen. If your teen is shouting or being rude to you then this has to be handled properly and not used as an excuse for you to reciprocate, turning the situation into a battle. It's too easy to say something to our teens that we've no intention of carrying out and is totally unfair to them. Threats spoken in the heat of the moment can come back to bite us if not careful.

Instead of threatening our teens, we need to calmly explain why we are unhappy. It may be that they've behaved in an unacceptable manner and that we will set rules if similar behaviour continues, or that they will have to deal with a consequence. Moreover, if we want to teach our teens actions and consequences, then there is no point in shouting an ultimatum at them as it defeats the purpose.

Previously, I touched on the subject of tone of voice. Indirect threats are an example of why tone matters. Without realising it, we can imply a threat through the way we speak, causing our teens just as much distress as a direct threat might. For example, using a loud and commanding voice, you tell your teen that your friend's son isn't allowed his phone after 9.30pm. This can easily lead him to fear that you plan to take away his phone at 9.30pm too. Yet, if you had said the same words in a kind and caring voice, he would not have felt threatened.

YELLING

There are many reasons why people yell. A large percentage of the time, people do so when they are feeling overwhelmed, mentally exhausted, or out of control.

When we yell, we release the build-up of pressure caused by our frustrations. Some use yelling as a weapon to scare or torment others. People who suffer from mental health conditions such as PTSD (Post-Traumatic Stress Disorder), NPD (Narcissistic Personality Disorder), or BPD (Borderline Personality Disorder), often experience high levels of anxiety, which can lead to angry outbursts such as yelling. Then there are those that resort to it when they realise they are losing an argument.

In some cases, the underlying cause of people yelling is the simple fact that they don't feel heard. Maybe they've tried to get attention in an acceptable manner, which has fallen short, so they used it as a last resort, not that this is a valid excuse. Yelling can also be a warning sign as it's sometimes used as a stepping stone to physical abuse, especially if the person is aggressive by nature.

Yet, yelling scares children and affects them psychologically in the same way that physical abuse affects them. Yelling can also lead to depression and other mental health conditions. New evidence shows that if teens are shouted at regularly, their brain structures can change, causing long-term damage. As we know, the average adult dislikes yelling, or being yelled at, and is often frightened by it.

Teens that grow up in households where parents regularly shout at them believe this to be normal behaviour, and therefore acceptable. As they don't know any better, they repeat this behaviour and often carry it into adulthood. Yelling at our teens, or indeed anyone, is a negative, short-term solution and not a long-term positive one. It's also a form of bullying and psychological abuse. Parents that communicate this way to each other, and to their children, are asking for trouble. I have witnessed children shouting back at their parents as a natural way of mimicking them. Even as an adult, I found it rather upsetting to hear. Sometimes, these children take it one step further and add foul language to the mix. In doing so, everyone in earshot is affected, whether they know the people who are shouting or not.

If your teen yells it could be that he craves your attention. Or that he's caught in a whirlwind of emotions that he just can't handle. He may feel unwanted, confused, or his basic needs may not be met. His reactions could also be due to worries which have been playing on his mind, such as a situation at school or at home. Another reason why teens act out of the norm is when they are feeling insecure. And we shouldn't overlook the obvious here, that they may just be very tired or very hungry. If you find that your teen's anger increases and becomes a regular habit, or turns into violent episodes, verbal or physical, then it's time to seek professional help, such as a GP or counsellor/therapist.

When we shout during conversations, we encourage our teens to react. Either by raising their voice or by becoming fearful of us, neither of which we want to encourage. Letting emotions out can feel liberating, but also scary. When our teens mirror us and lose control, they can easily become frightened.

AFTER THE STORM

"Never let your anger be greater than your love for your child."

After an argument, give both yourself and your teen some time and space to cool off. This could be as little as 5 minutes or as long as several hours, some teens quickly move on whilst others stew on it. It can be useful to review the conversation in your head to avoid falling into the trap of labelling the argument as 'just another argument with my teen'. You can ask yourself questions such as, 'Did I give my teen a chance to speak and air his views? Or did I dominate the conversation, making no effort to listen to him?' Perhaps he steamrollered you and didn't give you a chance to listen and understand what he was saying. Maybe you pointed out that his tone of voice wasn't acceptable, causing him to react negatively. If he came across in a rude or offensive way, did he realise this and was it intentional? Or was he suffering from amygdala hijacking?

Following an argument, at the appropriate time, calmly explain to your teen any points you wanted to get across but weren't able to. Don't force him to talk if he appears perturbed as this can further isolate him, making him feel vulnerable. We all experience tunnel vision and limited thinking when we are stressed, and our teens are no exception. Depending on the situation, it may be appropriate to say something along the lines of 'I can see that you were telling me such and such, but I felt such and such, which is why I acted that way'. Don't use this time as an excuse to argue further but instead to explain and iron out any misunderstanding and misinterpretations. If your teen wants to talk more, take a deep breath and listen compassionately. Despite being at loggerheads only a few minutes earlier, these post-argument moments can lead to deep and meaningful conversations, bringing you closer. When the conversation draws to a close, try to end it on a positive note. Remember, teens *do* want to talk but at times *don't know how*. It's really important at this stage to let your teen know that you still love him, even if a few moments earlier he said some awful things to you. As parents, it may seem obvious to us that no matter what they say we still love them, but to them it's not so obvious.

It's important to avoid drawing out arguments, prolonging uncomfortable situations. We mustn't forget that arguing is no fun for our teens, even if it seems like they are eager to participate. Teens don't want to argue with their parents and are extremely vulnerable when they open up and expose their raw emotions. In truth, shouting at their parents can be quite scary for many of them. So, once you have put your argument and follow-up chat to bed, don't keep revisiting it as this will cause anger and humiliation to your teen, and won't do your blood pressure any favours either.

Teens often mull over conversations, affecting some for days, weeks, or even months, which is why we need to be careful how we speak to them. We need to be mindful of what we let slip as it's not fair to burden them with our own issues. They are not responsible for our emotional well-being, we are. Paradoxically, by placing our own problems on their shoulders, we not only cause them undue stress, but grant them control over our well-being, and consequently, over us.

We can avoid many arguments by remembering that teens don't always fully understand what we are saying, as conversations can easily fall prey to misunderstandings. Even adults misread situations, failing to comprehend what others are telling them. Similar to misreading texts or emails, where even well-meaning ones are misinterpreted.

Like finding gold at the end of a rainbow, in time, you will feel the urge to argue disappear, and you will start to enjoy harmonious conversations. Instead of giving your teen a 'piece of your mind' you will talk in a loving, thoughtful and constructive way. As you become more in tune with him, you will find that maintaining mental peace becomes easier.

The Silver Lining

We all hate arguing, especially with our children. Nonetheless, there can be a silver lining: we can uncover more about our teens, including past events that we were unaware of, giving insight to how our teens feel about certain matters. Arguments also allow our teens to gain a deeper understanding of life, such as realising that people have different points of view, and teach the need to take responsibility for their actions when they upset or annoy others. They may even realise that they want to avoid future arguments as these situations make them feel hurt, vulnerable, angry, or even frightened. But, due to their PFC still undergoing development, don't expect these lessons to be learnt in a hurry. *Please note that I'm not condoning the initiation of arguments, or suggesting that you allow them to persist, as they should be avoided.*

APPRECIATE

Compared to when they were young, we are now able to communicate with our children on a much deeper level. We know that life is short and that we are lucky to have these wonderful people in our lives, and that before we know it, they will have flown the nest and we won't have the luxury of seeing them on a daily basis. They will be off on new adventures, leading their own lives and no doubt will be busy adults, without much time for us. So, let's use this time wisely. Let's not argue, berate, or harass them. Instead, let's enjoy their company. So, on the odd occasion, when they've forgotten to empty half the dishwasher or have abandoned a pile of dirty laundry en-route to the linen basket, instead of shouting or moaning at them, we should be grateful for having them in our lives. And, as harsh as this sounds, when things get tough remember that our teens didn't ask to be born, we chose to have them.

TRAUMA IN CHILDHOOD

"Teenagers need love. True love. Not love that comes at a price."

Lack of Love

The results can be catastrophic when a child isn't shown any love by their parents. Even in a two-parent family, the absence of love from just one parent can lead to problems that continue well into adulthood. And when children reach adolescence, chances are, the same problems will still exist, either consciously or subconsciously. Also, a lack of love in childhood can lead to adults seeking partners that are incapable of giving love. These problems can manifest in various ways including the following:

A lack of love leads to a lack of:

- Self-confidence.
- Self-esteem.
- Self-love.
- Self-importance.
- Trust in others.
- Understanding of one's own emotions.
- Unworthiness.

It can also produce:

- Anger issues.
- Feelings of guilt or shame.
- Feelings of 'What's wrong with me?'

If teens don't receive the loving, caring, and nurturing support that they both crave and need from their parents, they are likely to look for it elsewhere. Be it in the arms of someone they are dating, approval from both positive and negative peers, seeking validation from gang members, or from attention by breaking rules or laws. They may look to numb their feelings with the aid of alcohol, tobacco products or illegal drugs. By not caring about themselves, and believing they don't deserve love, they may take on risky activities in an effort to self-destruct.

Turning Words into Thunder - Abusive Behaviour

I'm going to touch on the subject of domestic abuse in adults as it affects far more families than most people realise, and when a parent becomes a victim so too do their children. Domestic abuse is often referred to as a 'hidden crime' as it often goes unreported and frequently happens behind closed doors, and in many cases, is carried out without the victim realising. This is why, in the case of verbal or emotional abuse, both victims and researchers believe that this type of violence is just as harmful, if not more so, than physical abuse. Domestic abuse may be emotional or psychological abuse, physical abuse, sexual abuse, violent or threatening behaviour, controlling or coercive behaviour, economic abuse, or any other type of abuse including the witnessing of any type of abuse.

Research shows that 1 in 5 adults in England and Wales experience domestic abuse during their lifetime, including 1 in 4 women and 1 in 6–7 men (Office for National Statistics (ONS), 2022). Worryingly, according to the NSPCC (2022), "around 1 in 5 children have been exposed to domestic abuse. Children never just 'witness' domestic abuse, the law now recognises they can be victims. Exposure to domestic abuse is child abuse, and it can have a significant impact on a child's development, health and wellbeing."

According to the Office for National Statistics, around 2 million people aged 16 and over experienced domestic abuse in the year ending December 2024 (ONS, 2024).

Although various organisations have conducted research into this topic, the majority of victims are too afraid to come forward, so truly accurate figures aren't available.

With less than 20% of cases reported to the police, it's important that people are alerted to this crime. One that can happen at work, home, or out socialising. When behaviours associated with domestic abuse rear their ugly head, people often keep quiet in order to keep the peace. But by doing so they automatically give this behaviour the green light. In order to show our teens that it's not acceptable, we need to challenge it. If you find yourself in a situation where you or your teen's mental or physical health is being compromised, then seek help as soon as you can. There are many organisations online that give information and offer helplines.

Domestic Abuse and Teenagers

There is a big difference between a teen moaning or saying the odd word that annoys you and being full on abusive towards you. For teens that have witnessed domestic abuse in their own homes, or in homes of those close to them, it's imperative that they are taught to put a stop to arguments as soon as they start so that they don't accept it as the norm.

For teens that have picked up bad habits from witnessing domestic abuse, care needs to be taken as they can't necessarily be scolded for their behaviour if they've been taught by example. Instead, they need to be corrected. Admittedly, not an easy task and one which will take time. If you find yourself in this boat, sit your teen down and without naming any names, address it by calmly explaining why any type of abuse is totally unacceptable. Be cautious not to label his habits. Make sure he fully comprehends what constitutes abuse. Convey that he needs to respect you as a person, and that you also respect yourself. Explain how this type of behaviour makes you and other people feel, spelling out to him how others may be affected as a repercussion of his actions. Clarify that no matter what his underlying issues are, this type of behaviour isn't acceptable, and that future actions will have consequences.

Living with a family member that is abusive can be very complicated for our teens. Naturally, they will have an innate loyalty to the family member, although at the same time, may know that their behaviour isn't acceptable or justified, which can easily leave them feeling torn. Nonetheless, as parents, we need to teach our teens how they should be treated, that they deserve respect, and that abusive behaviour should not be tolerated. While sitting in a safe and comfortable space, ask your teen how he feels when he is in this scenario. Again, without naming any names, explain to him that any type of verbal (or physical) abuse is not acceptable, no matter who it comes from. Instead of pointing the finger, it's best to talk around the subject, especially if they are close to the person in question.

If you are unsure if your teen's behaviour is a result of an in-the-moment outburst, due to stress or worries, or whether it's a regular pattern learn from an abusive parent or family member, then trust your gut. You know your child better than anyone. Even if others just put this type of behaviour down to 'teenage angst', it doesn't mean that you have to accept this too. To help you decide, you can analyse your conversations with him, including any arguments. By diarising your findings, you will recognise any worrying patterns emerging. If necessary, to quash any patterns, seek professional support for your teen.

If at any time, your teen shouts or verbally lashes out at you then don't respond. Instead, calmly tell him that you will not listen and then walk out of the room. However tempting it may be to stay in the room, chances are that you will just add fuel to the fire and end up arguing, causing you both a lot of anguish. Alternatively, you may get upset which will leave him feeling insecure. This will teach him that his behaviour is totally unacceptable and will not be tolerated. Tell him you would like to talk but you aren't willing to have abuse hurled at you and if he tries to start an argument, you aren't going to play ball and argue with him. Your teen will be watching how you deal with this situation. If he sees you keeping your calm in turbulent times and notes your refusal to accept abuse to protect yourself, in turn, it will teach him not to accept it from others. He needs to learn that arguments aren't the only way to put his point across. The script that our teens inherit will carry them through life and will shape and mould them, affecting both them and those close to them. So, we need to make sure it's not a destructive one. To help dissolve arguments, we can teach our teens to agree to disagree.

We all know that we can't avoid stress, that it's part of life. Therefore, we need to equip our teens with the tools needed to handle situations in a less aggressive manner. Working together, we can support them in managing their emotions and conversations in less destructive ways, teaching them that as they grow older, unless they learn to control their anger, they will end up in hot water.

Psychologist Albert Bandura was interested in the field of social learning and in particular childhood aggression. He believed that people learn from modelling others and hypothesised that children learnt behaviours by observing and imitating adults, especially family members. In 1961 Bandura carried out the famous Bobo Doll experiment where participants, children aged 3-5 years, were given an inflatable doll named Bobo. At first, the children witnessed adults interacting with the doll. Then each child, individually, was given the doll themselves and allowed to play with it on their own. The findings showed that the group that saw an adult acting aggressively toward the doll also then acted aggressively. The group that had witnessed the adult being gentle with the doll showed either no signs or very little signs of aggression towards the doll. Bandura surmised that the violent behaviour of the adult models toward the dolls led the children to believe that such actions were acceptable.

CHAPTER 9: EXPECTATIONS

"We chastise our teens far too often. Most of the time, they are doing the best they can and that's all we can ask of them."

Are we expecting too much from our teens? According to research, expectations of children are typically far too high. Not just academic ones, but physical, mental and emotional ones too. One of the principles behind the Cognitive-Friendly Method is to base our expectations in reality. By putting our understanding of the teen brain into practice, we can tailor our expectations for each individual, taking their age and cognitive limitations into consideration, which is vital as every teen matures at their own pace. Without this consideration, we would risk setting both our teens and ourselves up for failure and disappointment. And when it comes to our teens' happiness, as well as ours, you only have to Google 'The psychology of expectations' to see how happiness is threatened when we set the bar too high.

To set fair expectations, we first need to ask how well we know our teens, as many parents don't truly understand who their teens are or who they are trying to be. We have to question whether we are truly aware of their strengths and weaknesses, whether we understand how they think, and appreciate why they behave the way they do. If we can't answer these questions, then how do we know what expectations we can place upon them?

We should tailor expectations to each individual, as they may differ depending on sex. It's well known that boys mature slightly later than girls, with some developmental milestones occurring about a year earlier for girls. However, this can vary greatly from individual to individual, and ultimately, both boys and girls reach similar levels of maturity, even if the timing differs. Furthermore, because of the rapid pace of change, we need to ensure our expectations are kept up to date.

Unwittingly, we impose many of our own characteristics onto our teens, including our values, interests and goals, as well as ideas about appearance and behaviour, often viewing them through the lens of our own experiences. We form ideas about how they should behave, in ways we consider acceptable. However, they rarely meet these expectations, which leads to frustration for both us and them. This quest for our teens to act *our way* results in the desire to change them. (Not their behaviour, but them as individuals.) But it's not up to us to change them. Nor is it our job to tell our teens what their passions should be or how they should see the world. They have their own unique personality, which may be very different from ours. And that is okay.

Balanced and well-thought-out expectations can greatly benefit our teens. They can install a healthy sense of value and give something to aim for, while gently pushing them towards achieving more than they realise was possible. Healthy expectations can also teach our teens how to handle defeat, while equipping them with the necessary tools needed when planning for their future. To be fully understood, expectations need to be specific, measurable, attainable, realistic, and, where relevant, time-based.

We need to accept that when our teens try their best, it's enough. Leave it at that. They may not be the next Monet or Mozart, or even Terence Tao, but we all have different abilities and talents. If we force them to excel in areas where they are not capable, it will demoralise them and work against us. For some parents, it may be the other way around: their teens are highly focused and self-motivated, yet the parents show little interest in their teen's life. This can deflate the teens and make them question their efforts.

If we think about our friends, we don't reject them just because they aren't experts at everything. They are not all cognitively gifted, elite athletes, and incredibly creative people all rolled into one. Nor do we question why a high-flying executive pal can't draw or play a musical instrument. Like us, they are only human. And as tempting as it is to tell our friends and colleagues about our teens' latest accomplishment, we need to recognise this for what it is, just an ego boost.

Fred Rogers, the beloved American Children's TV host, produced some truly wonderful sayings, a few of which are related to this topic. One describes the notion that no one could really grow unless he is loved for who he is and appreciated for what he is, as opposed to what he may become. If our teens know that they are accepted for who they are they will feel loved and supported and will flourish. And by accepting them as perfectly imperfect, we help them accept themselves.

We have to trust our teens to a certain extent. Our relationship with them is more important than forcing them to do something just to suit us. If we want them to try something new, such as an activity or hobby, we should give them a choice of ideas then sit back and listen. A slight nudge and some encouragement are fine, as long as there is some interest in the topic, since there will be times when they want to try something new but simply lack the confidence. There is no point forcing them to sign up for something that they've no interest in as it will only put them off trying things in the future. They are still young and no doubt will feel very uncomfortable in ways we fail to notice or appreciate.

Some parents use their children to live out their own unfulfilled dreams. Be it the career they wanted for themselves, or even the route that their own parents wanted for them. Our children aren't a substitute for pursuing a career that we did not fulfil. And it's not up to us to decide their future. We can advise them, but it must be in line with their own goals, needs, and values.

A study carried out by Thomas Curran, PhD, a world leading expert on perfectionism at LSE, London, links the rise of expectations and criticism to perfectionism in young people. "Perceptions of parental expectations and parental criticism not only positively correlate with perfectionism but also are rising over time among young people" (Curran & Hill, 2022).

"With increasing competitiveness, growing economic inequality, and escalating pressure to strive and achieve as the societal background, increases in parental expectations and parental criticism likely offer one of the most plausible explanations for rising perfectionism so far" (Curran & Hill, 2022).

NEVER COMPARE

An important aspect of parenting is the avoidance of comparing our child to others, including peers, siblings and teenagers in general. Not only do they hate being compared, but it's also totally unfair as it makes them feel inadequate and can create lifelong wounds. What's right for our friends' teens isn't necessarily right for ours. Being human, when comparing ourselves to others, we instinctively focus on the things that others excel at, which makes us feel inferior. So, for our teens, who are naturally less confident than us, this action is likely to bring unwanted attention to their shortcomings.

Another trap that is easy to fall into is comparing our teens to ourselves or other family members. In the same fashion, if we are a very goal oriented or highly academic person, we shouldn't expect our teens to follow suit. Equally, it's unhelpful to compare our teens to how they were when they were younger as they are constantly changing, and this can confuse or even make them feel insecure, especially if they don't measure up to their previous high achievements or even just their previous likes and dislikes.

Part of life's rich tapestry is that we are all different. Maybe it would be simpler if we were all the same and if we all looked and thought alike, although I think it would be a bit weird and rather boring. I'm not sure we would enjoy our friendships as much and I wonder how we would learn and grow from each other.

THE GREATEST SHOWMAN'S MESSAGE

The popular film, The Greatest Showman, beautifully touches on the subject of rejection. Especially in the film's anthem, the song 'This is Me'. The song's empowering message is one of self-acceptance and the belief that we all deserve to be loved and accepted for who we truly are, without needing to change, regardless of how different we may be to those around us.

As the song conveys, we should teach our teens that it's okay to be different and that they must always be true to themselves. We should also encourage them to embrace their flaws and uniqueness rather than hide from them. Parents can learn from this too as we often point out our teens' flaws and errors, forgetting that they are still growing and learning, and most importantly trying.

Often, society, including parents, want children to be perfect and conform to 'the norm'. But, when this doesn't transpire, parents are left feeling embarrassed and ashamed. Many point out their teen's flaws, not only to them, but to others, often in their teen's presence. By believing that we aren't good enough, we internalise rejection and shame, which can leave us with deep-seated emotional scars. So perhaps it's time to rethink the old rhyme 'Sticks and Stones may break my bones....'.

LIVING IN THE MOMENT

'STOP the world – I want to get off!' is one of my favourite sayings. (No doubt taken from the 1961 musical or book.) Life is too busy for us nowadays, and it's no better for our offspring. Even through the turmoil of Covid-19 lockdowns there was constant schoolwork and homework plus numerous other pressures. So perhaps now is the time to focus more on being a human BEing, and less on a human DOing. Leading by example, we can slow down our pace of life and highlight the importance of living in the moment and being present. For the present is all that we really have. The past has passed and if we spend too long planning the future we will never experience today. What I find fascinating is that young children seem to instinctively know this. They are often transfixed on something, totally unaware of their surroundings or of the passing of time, demonstrating how we should appreciate being in the here and now. This is truly living in the moment. You may have noticed that when you tell young teens that something is going to happen, they often expect it to happen immediately. They don't get out a diary and ask which date you have in mind. These are great examples of appreciating both time and life.

UNNECESSARY PRESSURES

Our teens don't need unnecessary pressures. Although most are yet to start full-time work, they still have important events going on in their lives such as school tests, exams, sports events, or incentives such as the Duke of Edinburgh Award. Which is why we need to go easy on them when they forget things such as their P.E. kit, part of their lunch or a school book, and not scold them but instead support them, just as we would a partner or friend.

Building on this, imagine that your partner has an important meeting at work. They rush out of the house in a flurry, stressed about getting to the office a little earlier for a presentation they have to give. In their mad dash, they forget their wallet. Five minutes later, you spot it sitting on the kitchen worktop. What do you think your first thought would be? My guess is, it's probably not going to be, 'Oh dear, Alex has left their wallet behind. Oh well, if they want any money for lunch or petrol that's tough. That will teach them a lesson, they won't forget it next time! They'll just have to starve until supper. Serves them right for dashing out and leaving the breakfast I prepared.' Instead, my guess is that you would think kindly and feel compassion for them. Therefore, if we treat other loved ones with kindness, there is no reason why we shouldn't treat our teens the same way.

Sometimes, I will leave myself a Post-it Note on my front door to read on my way out. Even then, I'm often in too much of a rush to actually read it! I've also been known to forget to pick up something that's right by the front door as I've been totally distracted by my own thoughts.

We all have our shortcomings, so we can't really expect our teens to be faultless either.

Not long after the first lockdown in the UK in 2020, I had an interesting encounter with a lady I met in town. Concerned about their mental health, I enquired how her children had managed throughout the lockdown. But I was rather dismayed by her response. She compared her six-year-old son's inability to attend school to skiving off a paid job, demonstrating a definite tone of disapproval and annoyance. She said that as he was completing less school work, his brain hadn't been working hard enough. Describing his brain as having 'gone to mush' because he wasn't learning or studying enough. I listened intently and made no comment. However, I couldn't help but think that the child was likely being creative during that time, perhaps helping in the kitchen or garden, doing some arts or crafts, or even learning about subjects outside the curriculum. If so, he would still be learning important life lessons. Furthermore, does the brain of a six-year-old really slow down, especially if they have older siblings, which he does? In which case, surely, they are constantly learning from them? I even thought, heaven forbid, that he could have had some much-needed downtime, or perhaps some enjoyable, and no doubt, well-deserved playtime. Is it really necessary to push our children so hard? As soon as school starts the pressure would be back on again anyway.

Jean Piaget believed that children take an active role in the learning process. That they have a natural desire to sense, experiment, explore, and eventually master new ideas and concepts. Piaget's research confirms that children are constantly learning, even without our intervention. Something you no doubt have witnessed whilst your own child was growing up.

The academic pressures start so young nowadays. I remember when my own son was in reception class. At 5 years old, he learnt the names for 10 sided shapes. I didn't even know some of the names myself. They are being stretched and tested at every opportunity. In some households, the pressure is on when they are still in nursery and can barely talk. With the addition in recent years of a hiked-up curriculum and popularity of tiger-mum style parenting, it's no surprise that kids are showing signs of anxiety much younger than previous generations.

Then, after infants' school, there is the pressure to get into a good Junior School, then umpteen pressures to get into a decent Secondary school, even with a tutor for the brightest kids. Once in these schools, there's the constant pressure to get top marks to make both the school and the parents look good. The list goes on: the best university, the highest paid jobs. Where does it all end?

Earlier we touched on how busy children are today. We know that at school they must keep to tight timetables and that at home they have huge amounts of homework to get through on a tight time frame, and although all this can be a learning curve for their working life, is there really such a rush for them to learn it? In contrast to their busy week, they need to be able to slow down and relax at the weekend. Unfortunately, it seems so fashionable to cram every moment of their waking hours, from Saturday morning to Sunday night, with activities. If we are not careful, we risk our teens turning into machines that never switch off or wind down. It's so important that they learn to slow down in our fast 'I want it now!' culture.

Connecting with nature grounds our teens and allows them much-needed quiet time to reflect on their day and process their thoughts and feelings. Downtime, especially before bedtime, helps them unwind so they can sleep more soundly and can reduce problems such as insomnia, depression, and anxiety.

It's not just our teens who need to reassess unnecessary pressures, parents do too. Recalling a conversation I had several years ago with my GP, who was about to retire, I asked how he felt about retiring. Reflecting on his career, he told me he regretted working so many hours and not spending enough time with his family.

DON'T HASSLE THEM

We should be wary of hassling our teens for help or advice. Asking them to give us a hand with something that they are good at, such as troubleshooting a computer or sorting out mobile phone issues, is fine on the odd occasion as it builds self-esteem. But if it becomes a daily or weekly habit, we risk overburdening them as they already have so much going on. If they help, that's great; otherwise, let's take advantage of today's technology and jump online to find answers and let them get on with their day.

When seeking information from our teens, we should avoid pestering them. For example, if they've recently taken exams or important tests at school and the results are imminent, then we need to be wary of interrogating them daily. And definitely not as they walk through the front door before they've even taken their shoes off. Chances are, once they've received their results, they will need some time to process them. They are their results and not ours, so will affect them a lot more than they will affect us. If they want to tell us straight away, then that's great. If not, we need to give them some space. If you broach the subject and sense some tension, just be a little patient. Receiving results is an emotional experience for our teens. Some are very hard on themselves, and no doubt would have compared their own results with those of their friends even before we are informed, which may have affected them negatively. They may also be fearful of our responses, which is why it's useful to equip ourselves with some supportive ones beforehand.

APOLOGISING

We all want and expect apologies from people that have made mistakes, whether unintentional or not. But apologising can be a double-edged sword. If not careful, by forcing our teens to apologise we automatically trick ourselves into thinking that they generally mean it and understand why they are doing so, when in reality, it may be a very different story. Sometimes, although it may not be forthcoming, they will intuitively know that they need to apologise. But other times, they won't realise. Therefore, we need to make sure that they understand why an apology is needed. We can do this by explaining and demonstrating. With practice, they will make the connections themselves and see the situation from someone else's point of view, instead of their own egocentric point of view.

SETTING THEM UP FOR A FALL

"Parents are the people who judge you, your whole life." Young person.

Do we set our teens up for a fall? Earlier on, I touched on how teens are under so much pressure. Be it from school, parents, social media, family members, etc. Along with the pressures that many put upon themselves, including fearing that they won't live up to their parents' expectations, nor their own. Which leads me wondering if we've set the bar too high for them in the first place.

By nurturing our teens, we encourage them to explore different talents in a kind and gentle way, which is far less detrimental than scolding them for their inabilities. If they need support with their studies or hobbies, then we can let them know that we are available, or if we are not able to assist, that we will find someone who can. They are far more likely to turn to us if they know that we trust them to do so, and that the onus is on them to request it. So, whilst we keep an eye on their grades, we mustn't forget that we are *working together with our teens* to get the best out of them.

Recently, I went for a walk, and I passed a family out for a stroll. The dad was quizzing his son of about 6 years in maths. The child seemed to be enjoying the questions, yet it made me wonder if perhaps it was his father's undivided attention, or even the welcomed praise, that he was enjoying and not the questions. When our teens were younger, many of us were guilty of doing this on the odd occasion. But we must question what the underlying reason for this action is, and ask if it's really necessary? Instead, shouldn't we be discussing the birds, flowers, or trees, or even better still, our thoughts and feelings? Surely these are just as important as maths? Have we forgotten how important life skills are in our rush to compete and compare our children's academic results?

CHAPTER 10: RULES, BOUNDARIES, AND CONSEQUENCES

RULES AND BOUNDARIES

"The setting of rules and boundaries creates a foundation for trust."

The Difference

There are subtle but important differences between rules and boundaries. Rules are instructions or explicit guidelines that define what is expected or allowed in a particular setting or situation and are often negatively implemented. Boundaries are limits that are set on behaviours, ensuring that individuals feel safe and understood. Different situations call for different approaches. Boundaries help us understand the needs and wants of both ourselves and others, fostering respect for all. Through boundaries, our teens can learn empathy, helping them become less egocentric. In comparison to rules, boundaries can often be a more positive approach. With a clear understanding of the consequences from the outset, the setting of boundaries can grant our teens autonomy while guiding them towards positive choices. In situations such as safety, boundaries may not be appropriate, and rules may need to be implemented.

The following are an example of both:

Rule: '*Don't get into a friend's car if the driver is under the influence of alcohol.*'

Boundary: '*I can't answer that right now. I need time to think about it.*'

Why Do We Need Rules and Boundaries?

"*If we regularly spoil our children, we do them a disservice.*"

Rules and boundaries are an integral part of life. Everyone must live with them. They are met at home, work, in our social life, and in life in general. For instance, in our quest to secure a family home we will need to be responsible for our rent, mortgage, and bills, with consequences if we don't pay on time. Rules and boundaries also provide our teens with useful obstacles to navigate, equipping them with essential tools for life. Although we often resist, structure is an important part of our lives. Rules and boundaries help to create this structure by providing predictability and assurance, making us feel both safe and secure. They also allow our children to grow in an environment that protects, teaches, and nurtures them. These limitations demonstrate that it's not acceptable to misbehave or break rules, and that consequences will be dished out if they don't toe the line. Children of all ages need to be told what to do at times; otherwise, the world can become a scary place. That's why, by setting limits, we show that we care. Our teens need to know that there is an authoritative figure in charge to shelter them. It would be cruel to step back and hand them the reins, expecting them to navigate decisions that are deemed more suitable for adults. Which is why we need to be firm but fair and place these limitations on our teens. As our teens grow, so too does the seriousness of their actions, and therefore the severity of their consequences. Naturally, our teens will test us by pushing boundaries to see how we respond, and paradoxically, if they do so it aids them on their journey towards independent adulthood. When our teens become adults, for them to flourish and feel happy, safe, and stable, they will need to set their own rules and boundaries for others to follow.

Whilst their brains are still under construction, these constraints support them in making sensible decisions. With limited life experiences, teens cannot yet fully comprehend the consequences of their actions. Rules can help regulate teens' emotions, which, through no fault of their own, can spiral out of control and even frighten them.

Failure to set these constraints leaves our teens uncertain of how to navigate life. Given the upper hand, life would be chaotic and quite possibly unsafe for them, rather like a deer caught in headlights. Being left to run amuck, their fun would soon end, and they would find themselves feeling insecure. Knowing they have to deal with limits at school, if there aren't any at home, they will notice the difference and may try to take advantage of it.

In the case of excessively controlling parents, where teens aren't allowed to make mistakes, or in the case of neglectful parents, where teens aren't given any rules or boundaries, consequences will not be experienced, so ultimately teens will miss out on valuable life lessons.

Although the setting of these limits is important, they should not be used as an opportunity for parents to manipulate their children, as children should not be fearful of their parents. We can set limits in a calm and thoughtful way, without needing to rule with an iron fist. Teens need to respect parental authority, with the proviso that they are respected and treated fairly.

If we allowed our teens to do as they pleased all the time they would grow up with a sense of entitlement and an unrealistic view of the world. Which would create an opportunity for them to become attention seekers. Attention seekers can easily become depressed and often suffer from isolation, alienating themselves from their friends. People with a sense of entitlement often struggle with self-control and patience and are usually inflexible. They find behaviour, such as making apologies, very difficult to carry out as they don't see the need. Rules and boundaries stop people from being self-centred as they teach us to consider others.

Without rules or boundaries, it becomes difficult for our teens to understand the world as they start to become more independent. When they learn to drive and start working, they will have to follow rules. If they are used to having things always on their own terms, it could be a shock that they may not be able to cope with when someone tells them what to do. This could easily lead to issues at work or indeed issues actually getting a job in the first place.

Although parents should have the last word, there is no harm in sitting down as a family to discuss the setting of rules and boundaries as it gives each member a chance to air their views and put across their own suggestions, allowing everyone to feel heard. This process empowers teens, makes them more agreeable to our decisions, and creates a foundation for trust. During discussions, it's best to explain why you can't always grant your teens their requests, especially if there are issues around safety. If you find that some decisions need further investigation, you can work together with your teen to find a solution. By explaining your thought process, your teen will see that you aren't just dismissing his ideas on a whim but are giving them careful thought. You can also take this opportunity to discuss emotional boundaries that your teen may want to set for his peers and friendship groups.

Your teen's suggestions may include, for example, not being intimidated in front of friends. So, if your teen says he doesn't want to be hugged, kissed, or hear the words 'I love you' in public, you should respect this. Sadly, most teenagers hate it when you try to give them a cuddle or quick peck on the cheek to say goodbye or goodnight, but that's their prerogative. For a loving and respectful relationship of any kind to work, we need to not only make our own boundaries clear, but we need to honour the ones that other people have set. Just because we are adults, it doesn't mean that we shouldn't respect the boundaries that our teens set for us too, providing that they aren't too outlandish or affect the ones we've set for them.

We don't need to create a huge list of rules and boundaries, just half a dozen or so that we can easily implement. Rules don't need to be set in stone; they can change from time to time and be regularly reviewed. They may be simple, for example, 'We don't shout at each other', 'Messages from parents will be answered as soon as we can', 'We let parents know where we are', 'We don't lie', or 'Screens are to be switched off by 9.30 pm.' Or they can be more complex, such as different curfew times for different days of the week.

Rules and boundaries should align with our own personal beliefs, not be copied from friends or things we've seen online, as these won't stand the test of time. We need to firmly believe in them, or they will be hard to enforce as our teens will see right through them, recognising they aren't in line with our true beliefs. Which will confuse or annoy them as they will think we are being hypocritical. It's also important to make sure that our behaviour is consistent. In two parent families, a united front should be provided. Parents should avoid setting separate limitations as this can be difficult to enforce. It also confuses teens and gives them the opportunity to play one parent off against the other.

For teens that are clearly in pain, due to traumatic events such as changing schools, the loss of a close family member or friend, or parents separating or divorcing, rules and boundaries will still need to be set whilst we help them work through the issues at hand. In these circumstances, it's totally normal for them to show their anger, grief or frustration, but by having rules and boundaries in place they will feel safer and more secure.

It's natural to reflect on our parents' and even grandparents' styles of parenting, copying rules and boundaries that they put into place. Yet, before we blindly follow where previous generations have trod, it's important for us to analyse their style of parenting to see how it sits with us. Some may choose not to follow previous generations' approaches, which is perfectly fine since the decades have rolled on, and so too have the styles of parenting for the masses. It used to be a case of 'seen and not heard' in our grandparents' era, and for our parents' era it was sadly often a case of being smacked and not heard. Although it still goes on behind closed doors, many parents have learned that any form of abuse towards a child is simply not acceptable and that there are far more positive ways to tackle the challenges of parenting. We can also mix and match our predecessors' behaviours, copying some and dropping others.

Contrary to this, we all know that rules are made to be broken, although not on a regular basis as this sends out confusing signals which can lead to arguments. If you decide to break a rule, then it's best to think it through beforehand, otherwise it may work in your teen's favour instead of yours. Let's look at an example of breaking a rule to work in your favour. Imagine that you need to take a confidential phone call and need to make sure that your teen doesn't overhear. You know that he's busy on his computer playing a game and glued to the screen, so not likely to surface for a while. Yet, it's time for him to stop the game as his timer is about to go off. So, without consulting him you 'accidentally' let him carry on playing, thus allowing you to carry on talking. Alternatively, you could tell him that he can carry on playing for a while as you're on the phone. The trouble with the latter approach is that it sends out mixed messages, which, if not careful, he may use against you in the future.

If your teen is being very rude or behaving in an unacceptable manner during a conversation, put the brakes on and remind him of the rules. Explain that a consequence will be set if he continues down the same path. Although it's vital to give your teen a chance to be heard and speak his mind, it's equally important not to allow him to be rude and disrespectful to you.

A fun way to understand the importance of rule and boundaries setting is to watch the 1963 film titled *A Child is Waiting* starring Judy Garland and Burt Lancaster. The film beautifully depicts the difference between mollycoddling or smothering a child and taking the tougher approach of setting of rules and boundaries. The film portrays how the overindulging approach takes away the child's sense of accomplishment and self-respect, whilst the more structured approach empowers them.

Rules, Boundaries, and Peers

Once your teen starts secondary school, it can be hard to get to know, or even meet, some of his friends. No more chatting at the school gates or inviting them over for a playdate. Instead, you have to find out about them from your teen, which isn't always easy. Alongside asking to be introduced to them, you can ask your teen what he plans to do whilst spending time with them. If you are worried that some of his peers may be leading him down the wrong path, then you can take steps to ensure that he acts responsibly and understands the pitfalls of following their actions. Don't put his peers down; instead discuss different scenarios to equip him with the knowledge of what can go wrong so he can understand at the onset. Although many teens choose a healthy set of peers, for several reasons, others don't. Even though you can't choose his friends for him, you can instil morals, rules and boundaries to guide him.

Problems at school can be the result of peer pressure as peers can cause teens to rebel against school and its rules. Including persuading innocent group members to bring tobacco, drugs, or alcohol into school for either their own consumption or for the teen's. Or engage members to be involved in petty crime. When it comes to their studies, innocent teens can stop trying for fear of appearing cleverer than their friends. Which is why we need to keep tabs on what's going on at school so we can jump on any problems that arise, sooner rather than later. We may also need to set rules that apply when they are at school, in addition to the ones school set.

After a Wrong Decision

As our teens are still learning, at times, they will make poor decisions. How we handle the conversations following on from this is important if we are to lessen these experiences. In a composed manner, we need to listen to what they have to say and then ask questions to help them understand their actions and make the necessary cognitive connections. For example, 'What other choices did you have available to you at the time?' 'How could these other choices have panned out?', or 'Can you see how these other options would have been a better choice?' Using a non-judgemental tone to avoid conversation shutdowns.

STRUGGLING TO PUT YOUR FOOT DOWN

Some parents find the setting of boundaries and rules difficult. They feel guilty or can't grapple with the idea that they are necessary in order to protect their teens. This is particularly true for highly empathetic parents, who may struggle to balance nurturing with enforcing limits due to their deep sensitivity to their teen's feelings. Yet, to rid ourselves of the unhealthy desire to constantly reason with them, this enforcement is necessary. For some parents, the word 'No' isn't in their vocabulary because they fear the consequences. Nonetheless, it's far braver to say 'No' to your teen than to keep running around after him. Avoiding the word may be the easy way out, but being mature and responsible parents, we can't always take this route.

For those that struggle to set rules and boundaries, they can take solace in the fact that our teens often don't know what they want to do, due to their underdeveloped PFC. By choosing not to set any limits, we may unknowingly take our frustrations out on others by complaining about our teens to everyone around us. But being mean or even playing the victim to our teens' actions won't help. Instead, what we really need to do is recognise the need to set limits in the first place.

It has been proven that parents with low self-esteem and low self-respect have trouble setting boundaries for their children. Having never set any boundaries for themselves, they find it strange because it goes against their nature. Not being able to stand up for themselves makes it difficult for them to put controls into place. This incapability can leave them feeling frustrated, and without realising, they can take this anger and frustration out on their teens by unfairly raising their voice, arguing, or setting harsh unexpected consequences. All because they failed to set a rule or boundary in the first place. For these parents, rule and boundary setting will become easier over time and can transform them from a place of weakness to a place of strength. Knowing that, the more we look after ourselves, including prioritising ourselves and working on self-empowerment and self-confidence, the easier it becomes to enforce rules and boundaries. After all, the more we respect ourselves the more others will too.

Parents that are living, or have lived, in an environment where they aren't treated as they should be by a partner, such as an abusive relationship, may find boundary and rule setting difficult. They've been taught that they don't count, and as a result, neither do their values. They tend to lack the courage to set rules and guidelines, even though they see the need for them. But this struggle can lead to inner turmoil. Parents in these situations can fear the reactions of their teens just as they fear the reactions of their abusers, leading to feelings of inadequacy, weakness, and insecurity. Thus, creating a vicious circle, as they can become an easy target for their teens to exploit.

Once you've put your foot down and feel justified that it's down for a good reason, don't budge. If you change your mind, or worse still go backwards and forwards with your decision, you are either going to confuse your teen or give him the opportunity to provoke you, undermining yourself in the process. If your teen knows he can keep pushing and you will eventually cave in, why would he stop?

Women, especially mothers, have a natural tendency to put other people's needs first. Nonetheless, in order for us to attend to our own needs, we have to set boundaries not only for our teens but also for everyone we encounter. A friend of mine wanted to teach her son respect, so she set a rule where he couldn't take a shower after 9pm as it would wake up his siblings. Failing to uphold your own boundaries invites others to overstep them, opening the door to disrespect.

BOUNDARIES: THE USE OF SOCIAL MEDIA AND THE INTERNET

"Like it or not, social media and the internet are here to stay. They will be lifelong bedfellows for our teens, so we need to equip them with tools to navigate them wisely."

To regularly escape from the pressures of life and maintain the equilibrium of a healthy life, we all need to occasionally switch off and relax, including our teens. For adults, it may be a glass of wine on the sofa, a chat with a friend, or a night out. For teens, it might be playing computer games or texting their friends. This is understandable and social media and the internet in short bursts are acceptable. However, if this becomes an obsession or addiction or blocks the channels of communication within the family, then the amount of time spent online needs addressing. As we all know, it's unhealthy for our teens to spend all day online. Overuse is detrimental to both body and mind, leading teens to miss out on the real world and the experiences they need for adulthood.

One of my favourite proverbs is 'Give a man a fish, and you feed him for a day. Teach a man to fish, and you feed him for a lifetime.' We can't always be by our teens side, watching and guiding. At some point, we need to loosen the reins and give our teens some control, knowing that they have the skills to navigate the pitfalls of the internet and social media. They need to develop the skills to use these tools safely, following guidelines set. We need to show them that we trust them while expecting them to rise to the challenge of being responsible. Without trust they've no incentive to act responsibly. This does not mean we should turn a blind eye to which sites and apps they use, or how long they are plugged in, as we can set rules around their usage while still checking in with them on a regular basis.

We then need to step back and have faith. We don't need to be constantly breathing down their necks. This isn't to say that we should ignore the situation completely as we know how addictive and dangerous the internet can be for some teens. Even the dopamine rush we receive from reading a social media post is addictive.

A popular tendency is for parents to hover over teens or ban mobile phones or internet usage unless they are in the room peering over their shoulders. Others perform spot checks on their devices or even secretly log into their social media accounts. I don't know about you, but I certainly am not happy executing any of these. Where does infringement of privacy and parental lack of trust come into this? Not to mention the added anger or anxiety it would place upon our teens. Chances are, they would end up hiding their devices or deleting some of their apps temporarily or resorting to texting their friends in secrecy in the middle of the night. Let's not forget we are working on our long-term relationship with our teens, and we may need to reassess our approach if it jeopardises it significantly. This isn't to say that if we see a red flag we should ignore it. On the contrary, we may have to demand access to all their screens.

When it comes to how much screen time they should be allowed, there are no clear-cut answers that fit every teen. Each parent has to consider their own teen's needs. Every child is different and will use their screens for different reasons. Some teens use their phone apps to help them relax and sleep, while others use it to learn a language. Life skills can be learnt from watching videos such as cookery classes or money matters. Apps like BBC Bitesize can help with understanding of homework, while meditation or exercise apps can support positive well-being. You may decide that it's okay for your teen to spend x amount of time online if he's conversing with his friends, but only half that time for online gaming. But what is important is that we model good behaviour. It will backfire if we tell our teens they can only spend half an hour a day on social media if we spend over three hours. Teens aren't stupid. They will notice the discrepancy and challenge it.

On the whole, today's teens are a lot more tech savvy than most parents. Schools teach online safety, and teenagers talk amongst themselves and read up online. As tempting as it is to bury our heads in the sand, the more knowledge we have around social media, apps, gaming and the internet in general, the better equipped we are to make decisions around limitations and contribute to worthwhile conversations with our teens. We need to understand the world that our teens are living in to understand its pitfalls.

There is a great deal of advice available for parents, ironically online, but first and foremost, it's about trusting our teens unless they show, through their behaviour or emotional well-being, that they need our support and guidance. If intervention becomes necessary, then rules may need to be reinforced, adjusted, or clearly re-established, with appropriate consequences applied to help keep them safe. However experienced professionals on the subject may be, it's still best to trust your gut as you know your child and their genuine needs. Not that I'm suggesting the professionals don't know their stuff, far from it. They are a great place to start, but in the end, you will know what feels right for your teen.

When deliberating over a scenario, before you cast the first stone, make sure that your teen is actually guilty. It's easy to accuse him of wasting time scrolling the internet only to find that he's carrying out a school related task.

Plenty of research is available regarding teenagers and the overuse of screens. When it comes to smartphones, professionals state that 1 to 2 hours a day is the maximum they should spend on them. They have linked the overuse of mobiles to both depression and loneliness. Dr Jean Twenge, Author and Professor of Psychology at San Diego State University, USA, has carried out extensive research and delivered an insightful TED talk on the subject. She coined the phrase 'iGen' in response to the generation's heavy use of electronic devices such as iPhones and iPads.

Studies have further proven that reducing the number of hours teenagers spend on online gaming leads to positive changes in their attitude and behaviour.

If you are unhappy with the amount of time your teen is spending online or with their replies to your questions around the subject, then talk to him. There may be deeper issues that you are unaware of, such as peer pressure, cyberbullying, or the fact that he finds it difficult to resist online temptations and may be internet-dependent. It's also possible that he just wants to rebel against your rules as he's annoyed at you.

I think it's safe to say that most people want their teens to cut down on screen time. Yet, this can be tricky when the majority of homework is now completed online. Even when paper versions of school workbooks are out in front of them, they still need to use screens to check or aid their homework. However, we can enforce screen breaks starting with a 10–15-minute break every hour and adjusting as necessary. Alternatively, when your teen is completing homework, you can ask him to take a break and step away from his screen after completing each task. Don't expect him to be happy about this, as he may be under pressure to finish the work or be in a rush to complete it so he can do something more enjoyable.

With regards to the addictiveness of screens, we've all experienced times when we've been engrossed in a film and have even ignored the call of nature until the last possible moment. So don't be in a rush to punish your teen if he doesn't have the ability to take breaks. Instead, use a timer.

Somewhat troubling is the easy access to so many concerning adverts online via our teens' screens. Several research papers on adolescence health have shown that advertisements for alcohol and cigarettes and those that include content of a sexual or violent nature, have led to increases in adolescent violence, a rise in the use of alcohol and cigarettes, and the onset of early sexual activity. Research has also shown that if teens start to drink early on in life, i.e. during adolescence, then they are more likely to rely on alcohol within the next decade and often end up being reliant on it during their lifetime, compared to teens that start to drink at a much older age.

The Positives of Social Media

We all know the pitfalls of social media, such as fraud, bullying, grooming, harm, FOMO, imposter syndrome, and invasion of privacy. In contrast, the dark web exposes teens to more severe dangers like illegal content, malware, and serious criminal activity, along with increased risk of psychological harm and exploitation by predators.

But, as with most things in life, we must strike a balance. And the use of social media is no exception. Although a contentious topic, there are numerous advantages to using it. Whilst I don't endorse any brand of apps, nor am I an advocate for social media, we can't dismiss the idea that, if used wisely, it brings many positive attributes.

Which is why it's important for us to know the pitfalls so we can decide whether it's suitable for our teens. You may decide that some apps are allowed but some are totally unsuitable. But remember, we gave them permission to use this technology in the first place.

Social media does have a lot of bad press, but before we write it off let's look at the benefits that it brings:

- Aids cognitive development of understanding other people's feelings.
- Allows a deeper understanding of the world by exploring its injustices and justices.
- Helps teens to keep up with school related tasks.
- Enables teens to absorb complex information in small chunks, as opposed to having long, difficult, conversations in real life.
- Apps that enable self-expression empowers teens.
- Apps that allow the creation of teens' own works of art, literature, or videos, help attract an audience needed for future projects and careers.
- Information learnt can aid their studies.
- Helps teens acquire new skills, often for free or at a low cost.

- Enables those with social anxiety or neurodiversity to connect to like-minded people and become part of a community.
- Empowers teens through exposure to thought-provoking ideologies.
- Future careers, along with the understanding of the world of work, can be kickstarted through networking via business apps. Providing both work experience and job opportunities.
- Groups formed can give teens a sense of belonging and acceptance.
- Helps forge new friendships.
- Helps teens understand other people's points of view.
- Keeps teens in the loop with what's going on in their circle of friends.
- Less confrontational than meeting people in real life.
- Provides the ability to block people, which isn't possible in real life.
- Services such as online therapy platforms can be accessed, often anonymously, providing support to teens who may not be able or willing to access elsewhere.
- Short-term use can help to reduce loneliness. (Although long-term use can increase loneliness.)

- Teenagers can find motivation and inspiration by emulating their favourite athletes, politicians, or performers.

There is plenty of online research to browse regarding this topic. One I found particularly interesting is titled *Benefits and Costs of Social Media in Adolescence*. Here is an excerpt:

"The literature on social media and adolescents, as well as more extensive studies of emerging adults, reveals associations between time spent using social media and increased self-esteem, increased social capital (resources accessed through one's social relationships), safe identity exploration, social support, and more opportunity for self-disclosure. These processes are all critical to healthy growth and identity development" (Uhls, Ellison, and Subrahmanyam, 2017).

"Youth use social media for impression management by attempting to use these media to control other people's perceptions of who they are and how they act. Such self-exploration can help youth to discover aspects of themselves" (Uhls, Ellison, and Subrahmanyam, 2017).

CONSEQUENCES

Actions And Consequences

"Whether we like it or not, every single choice we make brings a consequence."

Daily, we are bombarded with decisions. Each decision leads to an outcome, and each outcome leads to a consequence. Whether in physical or spoken form, they affect either ourselves, other people, or sometimes both. Some consequences happen immediately, while others appear much later. We can't avoid this pattern, so we need to be mindful of how we behave. Consequences are either imposed by others or occur naturally in life.

In certain situations, even when we don't take any action, there can still be consequences. For example, whilst driving, if we ignore the fact that we are down to our last few litres of petrol we may find ourselves stranded without being able to finish our journey. Or worse still, if our teens get into a car when they know the driver is under the influence of alcohol and say or do nothing then their inaction can have consequences too.

As parents, we need to teach our teens that their actions will always result in consequences. We need to show them the bigger picture whilst we lay responsibility down at their feet. Indeed, there are many positive consequences that can happen in life, but on the whole, the lessons that our teens need to learn are the negative ones.

If you drop a pebble into a pond, you will get ripples, and these ripples will eventually cross the whole pond. This is the ripple effect. This theory, made famous by the film Dragon: The Bruce Lee Story, is rather pertinent here as it demonstrates how interconnected human beings are, and explains how our actions, no matter how small, can affect so many, whether we are ever fully aware of it or not. We can't expect our teens to understand this natural law the first time around. Many need time before they realise that if they repeat the same mistakes, they will get the same results. When this happens it's usually advisable to let any natural repercussions play out before intervening. This helps prevent conflict as it demonstrates that it's not their parents laying down the law but simply the way that life works. It also aids us by hindering our need to jump in and rescue our teens. If necessary, at a later date, we can ask our teens to reflect on their behaviour. Using their own suggestions, we can discuss alternative ways which will bring more desirable outcomes. Making sure that during these conversations we reiterate to our teens that it's their *behaviour* that's unacceptable *not them.*

Our instinct is to protect our children from not only harm, but a bucketload of emotional discomfort too. Even so, it can be hard for us to witness our teens learning this way. All the same, we need to take a step back and allow them to stumble and fall in order to learn from their mistakes. Teens need to learn about both themselves and about life. Unfortunately, learning doesn't happen overnight. Their inability to make the correct decision each and every time can be due to several reasons, including a lack of life experiences, pressure from others, e.g. peers, or simply as a result of their unsophisticated brain. Meaning that *they will need to make mistakes in order to learn.*

As with the setting of boundaries, the careful giving of consequences teaches our teens to respect others. Without them, they would soon realise that they could push their luck. If we don't respond appropriately, this could give them too much power. Power they would most likely be happy to exercise.

To avoid unnecessary conflict, don't regularly tell your teen that you are teaching him valuable lessons by dishing out consequences, as this may insult or anger him. In his eyes, he's mature and knows just as much, if not more, than you.

It's good practice to warn your teen that you are going to set a consequence so he knows what to expect, as this can discourage any initial inappropriate behaviour.

When setting a consequence, it's important to be clear what it entails. To avoid confusion and future grief, give detailed information, including start and end dates or times. Ideas might include reducing an enjoyable activity such as computer gaming, changing a curfew, or assigning extra chores.

Some parents are willing to work together with their teens and make a list of consequences. Others aren't and just set them themselves. You can decide which works best for you. Take time to consider what you feel is acceptable. It may be that if he's rude, shouts, or swears, then extra chores are given, e.g. cleaning the bath, car, or patio, washing all the household clothes for a week, or putting the bins out. The consequence needs to be carried out sooner rather than later to be most effective. Even though it's common for parents to take away personal items, instead of taking this negative approach it's better to add something, such as a task or chore. In most circumstances, it's not a good idea to confiscate your teen's mobile phone as often this is the main way for him to communicate with his friends. He may also suffer from a sense of loss. Although you may be annoyed with him, it's important that he isn't cut off from his source of support. The purpose of consequences is to teach our teens life lessons. Akin to the use of rules and boundaries, it should not be used as an opportunity for us to regularly berate our offspring. So, instead of waiting till they've messed up, we should encourage them to behave, and, if appropriate, we should reward them for good behaviour.

After you have set a consequence, give your teen a chance to speak. Not so you can back down or change your mind, but to allow him to express his thoughts. Don't expect the conversation to go smoothly nor for him to jump for joy at the prospect of a consequence, but at least he will have had the chance to air his views, and you will have the chance to spot any early problems or roadblocks.

Beyond the consequences that we and others impose onto our teens, life itself will deliver its own, which some people refer to as karma. When this happens, we can be there to support and guide, but not to gloat or say, 'I told you so'.

In a previous chapter, we touched on how the brain can block out painful thoughts and memories. This is one reason why we should avoid shouting consequences at our teens, as there is a good chance they will block them out, learning nothing from the experience.

When it comes to teaching teens about the consequences of their actions, some parents believe in punishing them at any cost. Often before they've taken the time to understand what's behind the unacceptable behaviour. A better approach is to find out why our teens behaved so, before we get them to carry out any consequences.

The following scenarios show how expecting our teens to take responsibility for their own choices from the start can influence their actions:

- Roger has access to his dad's car and uses it regularly. His dad has noticed that Roger has stopped filling it up with petrol afterwards like he used to. So, Roger's dad gives him the choice of either filling up his car with petrol before he uses it each time or use the bus instead.

- Noah's room is constantly messy, which bothers his mum. She tells him that he can keep his room messy on a regular basis as long as he's willing to do all of his own clothes washing.

- Brandon doesn't complete his homework on a regular basis. Fed up, his parents insist that he can either choose to complete his homework each week or carry out a couple of hours housework instead.

- Theo constantly leaves his bike out in all weathers. His parents tell him that he can use his bike on the condition that he puts it away in the garage each time, otherwise he will have to walk.

Below is a summary of the benefits of setting rules, boundaries and consequences:

- Avoids egocentric behaviour.
- Can be a warning indicator or distress signal if teens constantly break rules.
- In some cases, removes responsibility from teens, thus avoiding unpleasant outcomes, including feelings of guilt or stress.
- Keeps teens safer.
- Makes teens feel safe and stable.
- Predictable parental behaviour reduces uncertainty and apprehension.
- Provides structure.
- Puts parents in control.
- Reduces conflict.
- Shows respect for others.
- Shows teens how the big wide world operates.
- Cultivates responsibility.
- Guides teens in understanding consequences.
- Helps teens appreciate other people's wants and needs.
- Encourages teens to be adaptable.

BE FLEXIBLE WITH CHANGE

We need to be flexible when setting rules, boundaries, and consequences. For example, at the start of Covid-19, some of my friends let their sons play on their computers for longer than they normally would because they believed that it was important for them to keep in touch with their friends. They considered the fact that it boosted their teens' morale as they weren't at school and therefore had no contact with them.

When our teens were very young their routines and limits changed every few months as they grew. Now older, often growing faster than we realise, their rules and boundaries will need to evolve as well. Regularly reviewing them helps ensure they remain appropriate for their development.

CHORES

"*As parents, our job is to guide our children towards adulthood and not do everything for them en-route.*"

As our teens grow, so too does their need for independence. Part of this independence involves taking on more responsibility at home. While it can be difficult juggling homework and revision, especially in the run up to important exams, we need to teach them that we aren't going to pick up the slack if they don't complete their allotted chores. By making excuses for them, we rob them of their sense of power, sense of achievement, and role as a member of the household. Although we may think we are being kind to them by letting them off the hook, by doing so we give out mixed signals, and risk the chance of begrudging them. It's important to stay strong while we teach responsibility, even if it means having to hear their odd moans and groans. When allocating chores, we need to find a balance as overloading them may mean getting to bed late or neglecting homework. They also need time to have fun and wind down.

When delegating chores, offer your teen a couple of options as this helps to empower him. And if you phrase it carefully, it can work even more in your favour. For example, ask him if he wants to empty the dishwasher now or take the bins out later. Like most adults, teens will usually opt for the 'later' task. So, phrase your options in a way that steers him towards the chore you would prefer. That way, you are giving him a choice but still keeping control.

Calmly and slowly give clear, simple instructions for what you want your teen to do, then let him get on with it. No point in nagging as it often causes teens to switch off. If your instructions aren't clear, he might do the task incorrectly, avoid it altogether for fear of getting it wrong, or feel so confused that he shelves the idea completely. If, after a while, he hasn't started or completed the task, step in and calmly explain what was expected of him. Hear him out before getting frustrated.

Let's face it, even adults moan about chores, even if it's to ourselves. So, we will be hard pressed to find a teen that doesn't moan. Personally, I've been known to moan at the thought of putting the rubbish out, especially when it's minus 2 degrees outside and I'm already in my pyjamas. Which is why I've concluded that the best way to handle this is to let them have their moans. Having said that, I'm talking about a small whinge and not a full-blown argument or a moaning session that goes on half the morning. Not that I encourage moaning, but by allowing it at least they are expressing themselves, which is something we need to promote. Perhaps what we perceive as 'moans and groans' are in fact, just our teens' honest thoughts and their attempt to communicate? As adults, how often have we wanted to moan and groan about a situation but felt we couldn't? Maybe because we think we are 'supposed to know better' or because we are not in the right company, where complaining might be seen as inappropriate. If so, then clearly our teens are just being open and honest and perhaps should be commended for doing so?

SEX, DRUGS, AND ALCOHOL

Some parents don't feel confident talking about sex, drugs, or alcohol with their teens as they get nervous or tongue-tied. Especially those whose parents struggled to discuss these important topics openly with them when they were growing up. Nonetheless, just because we aren't comfortable doesn't mean that we should sweep conversations under the carpet. Instead, we need to address them head on, even if it takes us outside of our comfort zone, or if it means that we need to do some research on the topics. Once conversations start, our fears will soon diminish. Although ideally, we would sit down and have a long, meaningful chat with our teens, realistically this may not work. Some teens may not feel comfortable talking to us about these topics, some are too embarrassed, and others can suffer from information overload, which can lead to confusion or stress. It could also be that they are simply not mature enough to handle these conversations. We also have to consider that our teens may be more advanced in their actions in these areas than we realise, and may not know how to tell us, or they might not want us to know.

In order to make conversations flow, look for opportunities to talk. For instance, when watching T.V., tap into the topic at hand and casually ask your teen for his opinion or make a comment that invites a discussion. If you can think of a recent scenario that you or a friend has experienced, then use this as a sentence opener. You can even use posts seen on social media, such as Facebook, to spark a discussion, although in both cases, for common decency, you don't need to name names. Comments posted online can be ice breakers too. Then, there is the popular use of car journeys, providing an opportunity to talk as there is no escaping, so privacy without embarrassment. You can also let your teen know your own values and experiences.

Without the need to lecture, you can have frank and open conversations explaining the pitfalls of drugs, the overuse of alcohol, sex, including pornography, STD's, consent and unplanned pregnancy, to name a few. Thanks to these subjects being taught in schools, you can turn the tables and ask your teen questions, even innocently, as opportunities may present themselves before you have had a chance to brush up on the subject. Showing him that even though your knowledge is limited, the topics are important and need to be discussed. This helps you understand how much he knows and what his thoughts are on each topic. However awkward it is to talk, and no matter what his response may be to your suggestions or rules, keep communicating.

When it comes to allowing teens access to alcohol, there are several schools of thought. Some parents believe that by allowing alcohol in small amounts, in a controlled environment such as the family home, it takes away their desires to drink from the forbidden cup and stops them sneaking around behind parents backs or going mad at parties. Others believe that no alcohol should be consumed until their children have moved out of the family home and are fully independent adults. Many aspects come into play here, including religious and moral ones, as well as the needs of younger siblings and any additional support the teens themselves might need.

CHAPTER 11: INSTALLING CONFIDENCE

"We need to believe in our teens, trust their abilities, and have faith in who they will become."

PRAISE

When used correctly, praise encourages our teens to be kind and helpful, boosts their confidence, and motivates them to strive towards greater goals. Although praise is often associated with something that has been successfully accomplished, for example a high mark on a test at school or a match won by their sports team, it's good practice to associate praise with 'acknowledgement' and apply it to our everyday lives. Regardless of the outcome, we should acknowledge our teens' efforts and progress, such as learning from their mistakes, showing persistence, or rising to a challenge, as well as their hard work or creativity. When they've put in a significant effort, whether it's preparing a meal or performing their personal best in a football match, we should praise them and turn a blind eye to the messy kitchen or the muddy clothes as any critical comments will deflate them and discourage future efforts.

They say that a little praise goes a long way, which is why our teens will benefit greatly if we point out their resilience, competence, and leadership skills, showing that even when they find themselves in difficult situations they have an important role to play.

But the word 'praise' should not be thrown around casually. We should avoid praising our teens for being naturally bright or talented, as this doesn't recognise effort or perseverance and can leave them believing they can accomplish things that might not always be possible, ultimately leaving them disillusioned when they fail. It can also stop them from developing resilience, as they think they can fall back on their natural abilities.

Praise should be used in moderation. If overdone, it has no effect, but if seldom practised, we aren't giving our teens the positive feedback they so crave.

DESCRIPTIVE AND EVALUATIVE PRAISE

Descriptive and evaluative praise are the two main types of praise. Below are explanations for both.

Descriptive Praise

Descriptive praise praises a person's efforts, as opposed to outcomes. It communicates that we've taken note of efforts made and demonstrates that we appreciate our teens' actions. Descriptive praise often raises teens' self-esteem and self-confidence and is the sincerest form of praise as it explains specifically what we appreciate instead of giving a blanket response.

Some common examples of descriptive praise include, 'I like how you've added fresh herbs to enhance the flavour and give the soup a decorative touch,' instead of, 'This soup is nice.' Or 'Thanks for texting me to let me know you missed the bus home. If you hadn't bothered, I would have worried as you were so late'. This method makes your teen feel good about his actions and also lets him know *exactly* what he did right and how it made you feel. For a teen that tidies up his bedroom without being asked you could say, 'I appreciate you tidying up your room before I even mentioned it. That's one less thing I have to worry about.' Other useful phrases include, 'I really liked how you organised your time this weekend. You finished all your homework without me even reminding you.' Hopefully, you will get to use this phrase, 'Thanks for washing up for me tonight, I really couldn't face it.'

Compared to evaluative praise, our tone of voice often differs when delivering this type of praise. Instead of an almost false 'well done' tone of voice, you will find yourself speaking more casually and sounding more natural.

Evaluative Praise

The alternative to descriptive praise is evaluative praise. This approach includes throwaway remarks such as 'Good job' or 'That's great' which doesn't actually show our teens what they've done and can lead them to believe that they don't actually deserve any praise. You can almost hear them muttering to themselves 'Yeah, mum always says that, but it doesn't really mean anything.' Teens often think that when you use evaluative praise you are saying things merely out of love for them.

Evaluative Praise can work against us as it can make a teen feel that even though they've made a huge effort, their efforts weren't enough. Making them question whether they can ever please us.

In my own experience, when a dinner guest has said to me that they've been impressed with my culinary skills, if they can be specific e.g. the lightness of the cake or the way the food was beautifully arranged on the serving dish, then I seem to be able to accept the compliment and believe that they aren't just saying it for the sake of saying it. If, however, they just remark that the food 'was nice', then I would think that they are just being polite.

DELAYED GRATIFICATION

Delayed gratification occurs when a reward is purposefully postponed. In some cases, the reward stays the same but is simply delayed. In other cases, a choice may be offered: a) have the reward now, or b) have a larger one later. The latter approach was made famous by Psychologist Walter Mischel, author of The Marshmallow Test. When it comes to willpower and self-control, we can abet our teens by using this strategy, which, if used responsibly, can potentially teach valuable life lessons.

As our teens will need to learn patience to handle whatever life throws their way, delayed gratification can be beneficial, as it teaches us that rewards are often sweeter when we are willing to wait for them. It's not that our teens are to blame for their impatient or impulsive behaviour, they are simply waiting for their PFC to develop in order to see the bigger picture.

Thanks to technology, we have the world at our fingertips. Teens living in today's fast culture of online gaming, constant phone checking, and the disengagement from the natural world, can efficiently perform multiple tasks simultaneously. Not that we help the situation by our own constant need to multitask. The problem with this is that it promotes restlessness. Perhaps this is why today's teens are sometimes referred to as the 'I Want It Now!' generation. Delayed gratification can support by teaching patience, which can be applied to several areas of their lives. Be it their health, diet, exercise routine, finances, or even leisure, including the management of electronic devices. Teens can learn that by putting in the hard work now, they will be rewarded later. For example, they could wait until after exercising before having that tempting slice of cake. Or by waiting for the sales to start, they can purchase the laptop they have their eye on at a lower cost. When they start working, they will need to wait until the end of the month to be paid, and if they are well rehearsed in self-control, their bank balance will benefit.

To help our teens understand delayed gratification, we can break larger goals into smaller, achievable steps, allowing them to see progress along the way. They can further divide each task into manageable parts to work steadily towards success. For example, if they want a new mobile phone, they can put money aside each month as watching their money grow adds excitement. Delayed gratification can also facilitate in decision-making, such as buying a car or saving up for a house deposit.

SELF-RESPECT

It's important to raise children that not only respect others but respect themselves too. By only respecting others, they may never truly be happy. They also need to avoid becoming people pleasers or falling into the trap of never saying 'no' as this diminishes self-esteem and self-respect.

It's good practice to regularly reflect on conversations held with our teens to ensure we've been respectful, as mulling over our words and tones keeps us in check. If we realise that our approach has been less than our best, we can rethink it for next time.

SELF-TALK

"You don't need permission to be yourself, so just go and be awesome!"

As soon as your teen is old enough to understand the topic of self-talk, have a chat about it. I'm talking about the voice we all have in our heads that can be both our friend and our enemy, often referred to as our inner gremlin, critical voice, or inner voice. Explain how our internal chatter can be detrimental, especially if it's negative. Encourage him to be positive and kind to himself by challenging this voice. More often than not, the messages we hear are self-limiting ones. It would be amazing if our teens started to learn to challenge the negative talk and fight their inner demons at such a young age, learning to avoid questions such as, 'What if I fail?', 'Am I good enough?', 'Is there something wrong with me?', or 'What if no one likes me?' Or statements that their inner voice may make such as 'You aren't good enough.' 'You are stupid.' Or 'You are lazy.' Although experts believe that we can never really get rid of the gremlins completely, they believe that they can be tamed.

SELF-ESTEEM & SELF-CONFIDENCE

"We should teach our teens to dream and soar, showing them that they can become anything they wish to be."

With the knowledge that their brains are still developing, our teens may feel empowered to view challenges as opportunities for growth rather than as fixed limitations, which can significantly boost their confidence. However, not all teens will respond in the same way. Some may find this idea encouraging, while others might dismiss it or feel uncomfortable being reminded that they're still developing. By understanding the teenage brain, parents can adopt the Cognitive-Friendly Method practices that align with their teen's developmental needs. An approach which encourages self-assurance and facilitates in building a positive sense of identity.

Self-confidence is the ability to trust in one's self, take on tasks, and rise to challenges, while being held responsible. It differs from self-esteem, which tells us how we feel about ourselves or about how we feel in relation to others, and is an emotional appraisal of our own self-worth. Our level of self-esteem is evident when it comes to the ability to forgive, both ourselves and others. Self-esteem and self-confidence don't go hand in hand. So, if someone has a great deal of self-confidence it doesn't necessarily mean that they also have strong self-esteem.

Teens live in an adult-dominated world, and for the start of their journey into adolescence they are physically smaller than most adults. This will naturally affect their self-esteem and jeopardise their confidence. Studies have shown that there is a correlation between height and happiness, with a historic tendency to be more prevalent in males.

We need to encourage our teens to have faith in themselves by demonstrating our faith in them. One approach is to assist them in completing a strengths and weaknesses list, reminding them of strengths that they didn't even realise they had. In time, we can aid them by moving items from the weakness list to the strengths one.

When a teen's self-esteem is constantly low it can lead to negative thoughts. Which, if left to manifest, can lead to serious mental health conditions. Lack of self-esteem makes teens vulnerable, in many ways. They are more likely to be picked on by peers and more susceptible to being a target of violence, of any type. If you spot low self-esteem or low confidence levels in your teen, try and work out the causes so you can start to build upon their beliefs, reaching out for help if necessary.

In today's world of technology, it's easy for shy teens to hide behind a screen. If your teen is this way inclined, encourage him to step out of his comfort zone. Find him a mentor to talk to, encourage him to take on new challenges such as building something from scratch, explore a new hobby, attend a drama class, join a gym, or find a self-defence class. These help bring him out of his shell, provide him with a sense of achievement and pride, and bring him closer to independence.

To build shy teens' confidence in social situations, they could be given small responsibilities such as running errands to the post office or local shops. They could also be encouraged to order food in a café or ask for help in a shop. For the teen that needs a bit more exercise, mowing the lawn for an elderly friend or washing the neighbour's car may be more suitable. Or, for ones that need to improve their culinary skills or broaden their palate, they could be asked to cook a meal once a week or plan the weekly menu, perhaps inviting a friend over to sample their dishes. Afterwards, just as you would thank a partner or friend, you can thank them for their efforts. Don't expect them to complete the task exactly the same way as you would, or even to your own high standard, but as long as they've put in 100% effort then that is good enough. These activities are designed to teach the value of contributing to the household, being responsible for their actions, following instructions, and learning how to run a home.

Becoming a mentor for a younger or less abled person can be a great way to build teens' skills and confidence. Just as lending a hand at a library or finding a buddy at school would help. To nurture their self-confidence and self-esteem, we can teach problem solving skills, while allowing them to explore their passions. Popular with many is the Duke of Edinburgh's Award (DofE) where they complete sections in volunteering, physical exercise, and skills, and take part in an expedition. Although not easy, this programme goes a long way towards developing life skills. Starting with the bronze award, it progresses onto the silver and finishes with the gold. Even during Covid-19, a total of around 180,000 young people across the UK started their awards, and in the year ending March 2023, 323,676 young people started their DofE (DofE, 2023).

Although responsibilities encourage growth in self-confidence, teens can sometimes feel overwhelmed by them. If your teen is experiencing difficulties, explain that you totally understand why he feels this way. Encourage him to talk through his ideas so that he can overcome any obstacles. Suggest to him that he breaks down tasks into smaller chunks and instead of fixing things for him, support him and spur him on by telling him what a great job he's doing.

A CHANCE TO BREATHE

Our teens' schedules are tightly packed during the week, so to relax and unwind they need opportunities to break away from this rigidity whenever possible. So, pencil in some down time for your teen and give him a chance to stop clock-watching or be watched by his parents or siblings. As adults, we enjoy the peace and quiet of our domestic sanctuary and teens also enjoy having the house to themselves for a while. In order to give your teen some space, you may want to occasionally arrange for the family to go out so that he can stay at home and enjoy his home on his own to relax. (Provided that he's mature enough.) If you can avoid it, don't set any tasks for him to do when you are out, but if you do, make sure that they are small ones that only take a few minutes. Giving him time alone shows that you trust him, and you respect his need for independence.

HOPE

"Hope propels us forward, enabling us to clarify our future."

It's easy to talk in a negative manner without even realising it. Before we know it, the odd comment or statement has slipped out, and its negative connotations have passed our lips and into the ears of our teens. The teenage years can be especially tough for our sons. During puberty, their self-esteem typically declines and their self-consciousness increases. That's why, it's critical to keep the candle of hope alight for them. Talking about life in a positive light, installing a healthy dose of hope, and pointing out the good things that are happening right now, however small, is a good place to start.

Young children naturally have hope in abundance. Unfortunately, as we get older, life can knock us about and our levels can diminish. But we need it to get through the tough times, to fend off depression, to give us something positive to look forward to, and to give us courage. Hope comforts us when we are down and restores our faith in ourselves and in humankind. It provides us with the inner strength needed to carry on and complete the tasks and duties we are struggling to finish or even begin. Hope can be found in many different places, such as through a friend or even a stranger.

Nowadays, teenagers are very sensitive to their environment. They often worry about issues such as the cost of living, war, climate change, money, and future pandemics. So we need to allay their fears by listening and validating them. By encouraging them to explore ideas and take action, we help ease their fears. For example, they can take part in a climate change awareness-raising activity, join a political party or learn how to budget and manage their own money, however small the pot.

PEERS AND PEER GROUPS

Being human, we have a psychological need to form friendships and spend time with other people. By joining groups, we satisfy this need. During adolescence, this need becomes greater, which is why our teens have a strong desire to belong, and be accepted, into their chosen groups. As teenagers' prefrontal cortex (PFC) is still developing, they have to rely more heavily on their amygdala, which drives the strong emotions linked to rejection and acceptance, making them especially sensitive to the fear of rejection. While their PFC helps them figure out how to behave to gain acceptance, its immaturity means teens often struggle to resist peer influence or consider alternative choices. As a result, they tend to default to following the group since their brains haven't yet fully developed the confidence to stand apart.

During the teenage years, parental influences decline and peer influences increase. Although parents continue to have the most impact, the support and comradery from their friends strengthens. Psychologist Leon Festinger's theory of Social Comparison suggests that being a group member allows us to evaluate our own attitudes and beliefs, explaining why peer groups can act as sounding boards in helping teens make decisions. Being part of a group facilitates individuals' understanding of their social roles in their quest for self-discovery, enabling them to transition from the focus of 'me' to a sense of 'us'. Group members can share knowledge, learn new skills, make each other feel safe, and gain invaluable insights into themselves. And by spurring each other on, they motivate one another and raise the bar, strengthening neural pathways.

Teens often try out different social groups to see if they fit in, helping them venture further down the path to self-discovery. For instance, by trying out the school debating society they may learn that they are good at debating, enjoy using their critical thinking skills, are a competitive person and are good at constructing an argument, either for or against. Alternatively, they may find it's not really their thing and may even understand why. Being a valid group member gives our teens a sense of pride. Aided by friends, they can work towards common goals which couldn't be achieved on their own. Ideas and notions can be tried out and adapted in a safe environment within their groups, before carrying them forward into the wider world.

So, we can see why being part of a group is so important for our teens. It may be the first time in their lives they feel confident and independent enough to do so, as previously they were dependent upon us. As adults, we know how important it is for our emotional and spiritual well-being to be around, and have the support of, like-minded people.

Another reason why it's so important for our teens to feel confident is because they are often very self-conscious and feel they are being watched and judged by others, including their peers.

Dr Niobe Way, Professor of Applied Psychology, New York University, USA, has extensively studied the role of close friendships in the mental and emotional development of adolescents. She emphasises the importance of helping teens build confidence by reassuring them that showing feelings and vulnerability is both healthy and natural. Way encourages young people to value emotional closeness in their friendships, even if it goes against traditional ideas about masculinity (Way, 2024).

It's too easy for society to stereotype boys as not needing the same emotional connections as girls, but this assumption does them a disservice as it denies them the experiences they crave (Way, 2024; Way, 2011).

As parents, we need to encourage connectedness in our teens to help them build strong networks of friends that will support them throughout their lives, not just when they are young. Rather than telling our teens to 'man up,' we need to ask ourselves why masculinity can't include forming close, non-sexual relationships with others.

According to the Institute for Public Policy Research, "Research indicates that British children spend more time in the company of peers, and less time with adults and parents, than young people in culturally similar countries. Recent MORI polls have shown children's concerns to include parents not always being there when needed and not making them feel loved and cared for. Changes to family structures are significant here" (Dixon et al., 2006).

SUPPORTING FRIENDS

We all want our teens to support their friends. But for very compassionate teens, emotional turmoil can be an issue. In trying to help by listening to and supporting their friends' dramas, they can expend a great deal of emotional energy. Feeling responsible for friends may seem admirable but taken too far it can cause distress. If your teen experiences this, stay calm and use True Focused Listening to allow him to release some of his burden. If he's finding it all a bit too much, tell him to turn off his phone and if need be, his other devices. Remind him that his friends have parents of their own that they can turn to, who are more experience and better equipped to help. Then help your teen set his own boundaries.

IDENTITY

German Psychoanalyst Erik Erikson believed that the searching question of 'Who am I?' is most prominent during adolescence. One that will cause a plethora of unease and confusion as teens navigate their tricky path to adulthood. No doubt you will have already witnessed your own teen trying out different identities and personas as he questions such topics as religion, moral beliefs, political views, and sexual orientation. He will also be trying to formulate ideas with regards to his future career.

When it comes to gender, today's teens are generally very good at being inclusive and avoiding assumptions, and it's even common for them to correct their parents, quite rightly so. The language of gender, identity and pronouns is rapidly evolving. According to one student I spoke to, new words are introduced every day at school, and she can barely keep up with them all.

Constantly exploring and questioning their own identity and gender must put them under pressure. Due to world prejudices, and scrutiny by peers and society, some teens find themselves in a real dilemma as they want to be true to themselves yet are afraid to accept who they truly are.

During the teenage years, our children are trying on different hats to see which ones fit best. Which is why they act differently around different people and can change personalities over a short period of time. As they draw on information from their past and present, they reflect on their hopes and dreams. Not an easy task, they need our full support through this phase of growth, especially when it comes to being open and accepting of any gender or identity they choose to adopt. Essayist and critic Logan Pearsall Smith (1865-1946) beautifully summed it up when he said, '*Don't laugh at a youth for his affectations; he is only trying on one face after another to find his own*'.

The following chart gives us a clearer view of our teens' inner chaos.

WHO AM I?

Do I want to go to college, university, or neither?
Who are my role models?
How do I feel about myself?
What are my strengths and weaknesses?
Where do I fit in the world?
What makes me happy or sad?
Do I follow my parents' religion or decide for myself?
Who are my real friends?
What are my responsibilities?
What is my sexuality?
What are my own morals?
What am I good at?
Am I normal - what is normal?
Do my parents really know anything?
How do I feel about sex?
What do I want for my future?
What jobs am I interested in?

DON'T MAKE CHILDHOOD AN EASY RIDE

Many years ago, I read that the best way to prepare your child for adulthood was to make sure that their childhood wasn't an easy ride. I must admit, my initial thoughts were that this seemed rather cruel. So, I spent some time analysing this and realised that it held a lot of truth. Noticing that, if we fail to equip our teens with tools and experiences needed, they will most likely struggle when out in the big wide world. I realised that it would be far crueller to wrap them in cotton wool before throwing them to the wolves of life. So, by allowing them to learn whilst still in the nest, we are there to help, advise, and console when things go wrong. And by learning lessons along the way, our teens will be far better equipped with tools such as resilience, self-confidence and self-empowerment. Resulting in adults who are focused, level headed, and strong, and ones that are more likely to succeed in all areas of life.

Hence, our need to let them stumble and fall, pick themselves up, and work things out for themselves. By understanding consequences, learning from their mistakes, experiencing both failures and triumphs, and taking ownership of their decisions, they mature. Putting them in good stead for adulthood, when they have to face larger, more serious, dilemmas. In order to build resilient adults, we must give our teens the freedom to overcome obstacles. Otherwise, if we allow them to shirk responsibilities, they will feel insecure and inadequate, turning to us every time they face difficulties.

We all want our teens to soar. See them take ideas and dreams and turn them into reality. But in order to achieve this, we need to instil confidence, tenacity, and a sense of commitment so they see projects through to fruition. We don't want them to sit on the sidelines watching the dreams of others come true knowing that they don't have the tools to make theirs happen. It's very rewarding to observe our teens take what initially seems like a mad idea and turn it into a great one, witnessing a passion evolve into reality.

It's a sad fact that many adults struggle with a lack of life skills. Unable to get back up on their own two feet due to the belief that someone will come and rescue them. The trouble is, often there isn't anyone around to help them. We don't want this for our teens, so we need to give them the tools to cope with the majority of situations that life will throw at them.

As parents, it's our duty to teach our teens responsibilities as they metamorphose into adults. They need to understand the importance of showing up and not letting people down. They must be accountable for themselves and their actions and know that it's not okay to mess people around. They also need to comprehend that missing work without a good reason is not acceptable.

FAIL BETTER

Many years ago, whilst studying marketing, I learnt about 3M's personal project scheme called '3Ms 15% culture', which is still in force today. 3M employees are encouraged to spend a portion of their work time cultivating and pursuing innovative ideas for creative projects for the good of the company. The company recognises that, in turn, new and innovative products are often created as a result of this entrepreneurial approach. What is so admirable is that this scheme allows people to comfortably make mistakes. It's great to know that, even at work, in order to succeed, you can fail several times. Think what a buzzing and creative atmosphere must prevail. That's the sort of company I'd like to work for! If we take this idea a little further, imagine how amazing it would be if schools used this approach. If they encouraged and even pencilled in some creative time into their timetables to explore pupils' ideas. Ideas that would encourage their fellow pupils. Perhaps the children would end up teaching not only their peers but their teachers too. Serving as a reminder that our teens are still young and aren't fully fledged, and that it's natural for them to make mistakes in order to learn.

In the early 1990's, there was a new word added to the American Heritage Dictionary. It was 'intrapreneur', which means a person who is acting like an entrepreneur whilst working in a large organisation. Isn't it great that 3M, along with other companies such as Google and Intel, invest in their staff so much that the staff feel valued? Admittedly, these companies benefit once a product is brought to market, although it has cost the company time and money. In fact, in recent years, other companies have followed suit and even offered cash prizes and paid time off work, helping those with a great business idea but no funds to launch a product.

We need to instil the ethos that getting it right first time isn't always important, and that it's okay to mess up, but also crucial to keep trying. Akin to Irish author Samuel Beckett's famous phrase, from his piece Worstward Ho, 'Ever tried. Ever failed...'. Interestingly, Beckett believed that failure was part of any artist's work.

ROUTINE

Routines not only help organise our days, weeks, and months, but bring us a sense of security, anchoring us in turbulent times. Ask anyone that's between jobs about daily structure and they will tell you that it's something that easily falls by the wayside. With too much time on their hands, they struggle to efficiently organise their time, leaving them feeling insecure and unmotivated. When it comes to our teens, routines can help prevent arguments over timetables or participation in activities. To empower them and prepare for their independence, we can let our teens plan and implement their own routines, teaching time management skills and the consideration of others during negotiations.

There are other types of routines, namely traditions, that give our teens something to look forward to, bringing joy and a sense of security. These are often related to food, for example, waffles on a Wednesday, takeaways on a Friday night, or pancakes on a Sunday. Or in the form of an activity such as Saturday nights for watching a film with friends, or Sunday for visiting family members. The beauty of traditions is that they provide a lifetime of happy memories.

CHAPTER 12: INTERVIEW WITH FORMER CUSTODIAL MANAGER AT HM PRISON & PROBATION SERVICE.

This Chapter comprises an interview held with Ashley Leenders. Ashley worked for HM Prison and Probation Service as a Custodial Manager in various prisons, including Feltham, Holloway and The Mount. (A Custodial Manager is the most senior uniformed officer in a prison and one step below a Prison Governor.) When it comes to working with Young Offenders, Ashley gained a wealth of experience during his 17 years of service.

Penny: How does an underdeveloped brain affect teenage behaviour?

Ashley: Thanks to their underdeveloped brain, teenagers are very spontaneous and are less empathetic than adults.

Age is often the key to making sensible decisions. This is especially true for teenagers as their brains don't fully develop until they are in their mid-20s. So, in the meantime, we have to be patient with them.

Penny: How does social media affect teenagers?

Ashley: When it comes to social media, teenagers have instant access to everything. Which, in one respect, makes life easier for them, especially if they are neurodiverse. For example, teenagers with ADHD can watch videos to obtain information and learn in a fashion more suited to their needs, instead of struggling to concentrate on reading long texts. But, in other respects, it makes things very confusing for them as they can access information which isn't necessarily age appropriate. Another downside is that they can lose their childhood far too early.

If we compare this to when I grew up, my generation had to learn from our parents as we went along. If we didn't understand a topic at the dinner table it would go over our heads and therefore not affect us. But teenagers today don't experience this as they have everything at their fingertips via social media.

To avoid our teenagers growing up too fast, restrictions can be put in place for the use of social media.

Penny: *What are some of the issues that young offenders face?*

Ashley: In the case of young offenders, about 80% of the time the dad isn't present in their upbringing. Although in many cases, neither parent is present as it's common for the mum to be a drug addict and the dad to be in jail.

When it comes to role models, there's a link between not having a role model and being a young offender. If the dad isn't present, then these single mums have to deal with difficult situations. They may have to work long hours, leaving early in the morning and not returning home till late at night. In which case, many have no alternative other than to leave their young child home alone. When these children get older, they start to go out onto the streets. And although these teenagers think they are independent, they don't have the cognitive know-how, so they find themselves in over their heads. They see a gang member as a role model. But the role model ends up exploiting them by involving them in crime, such as county lines.

Another common issue is that they don't experience being parented by a parent, but instead by a grandparent. Often because both parents are absent, either because they are behind bars or have died. Which is why they often end up living with their grandparent(s) who've taken them in to give them a roof over their head to avoid them going into care. Although they have their grandchild's best interest at heart, many are too old to cope, and with no one around to bridge the age gap they can easily end up struggling, causing many a child to run wild. These well-intentioned people find themselves in over their heads as they are trying to bring up a child in a different era to the one their own children grew up in. And a very different world to the one they were raised in, leaving them feeling rather baffled. Being advanced in their years, they are out of the loop in raising children and often end up being much softer than the child's parents would have been. And as some feel that they've 'done their bit' raising their own children, they now think that it's time for them to take a back seat and relax, which affects their 'parenting'.

INTERVIEW WITH FORMER CUSTODIAL MANAGER AT HM PRISON & PROBATION SERVICE

Penny: How important are the setting of boundaries for teenage boys?

Ashley: Boundaries make teenagers feel safe and they prevent parents from becoming too soft, which is why it's important for parents to set them in the first place. Even within the home, boundaries need to be set. There are no set boundaries that apply to teenagers as they will vary parent to parent. We need to teach our teens that they can't just do what they want. We know that parenting is a hard job, it's 24/7. We are constantly on top of our kids because we want to do what's right for them. Yet, some parents just can't be bothered to set boundaries and rules. They think that just because they are teenagers and are big they are capable of doing most things. When in fact, they aren't mature enough to handle most situations. Parents seem to want teenage boys to be men way too early, yet they are not (cognitively) ready to be men yet.

We can use boundaries to help us unleash parts of adulthood in a controlled manner, as opposed to fully exposing our teenagers to the big wide world before they are able to understand it.

Rules need to be set when teenagers go out and about with regards to keeping in touch with their parents. It's important for them to check in on a regular basis. I know many young people who finish their school day and don't return home till very late as they have been told that they don't need to be in until 10pm. But they should be going home and checking in with their parents in order to tell them where they are going, when they will be leaving, and when they will be home.

We should also set rules as to the places our teenagers can and cannot visit. Making sure that they are age appropriate.

Parents that have grown up in a different country to the one they are raising their teens in don't realise that the cultures are very different. And that their parenting styles may need to be altered. When their teens see how their friends are being raised, they notice the differences and can become disgruntled. Leading them to rebel. This is especially true in the case of very strict parents.

Penny: Any tips to help teens stay out of trouble?

Ashley: Parents should educate their teenagers as to the dangers they can get themselves into. For example, many parents don't realise that teens can end up in jail by being guilty by association. I think the media doesn't do enough to educate people in this area.

To keep themselves in check and to avoid getting into unhealthy situations, teenagers can regularly ask themselves questions such as 'Why am I here (in this place)?', 'What am I here for?', 'What is this friend offering me?' and 'Why am I speaking to this person?'

Many parents think that their teens will simply learn from their mistakes. But when it comes to drugs and gangs, it could be too late by then.

Teens that don't receive love crave it, and they look to achieve happiness from materialistic things such as trendy clothes, which makes them an easy target for groomers. Groomers nowadays tend to be young men in their twenties and not middle-aged men, as often perceived by the public.

Even though your background might be very different from the one you're raising your own teenager in, it's vital to teach them the importance of getting an education. Even for the teens that hate school. They need to know that they must get everything they can out of it so they can progress into work. Plus, school will give them structure and a sense of community.

If a teen is going off the rails, it's never too late for a parent to step in and help. The two main problems that teenagers face are drugs and gangs. And most of the time these two come together, each as life changing as the other. With boys, it tends to be gangs and with girls it tends to be drugs. And when they get into trouble with gangs, it's really difficult for their parents. Many end up paying off the gangs, as well as moving house.

Penny*: *What factors influence teenagers in a negative way?

Ashley: Bad influences from social media, the media, friends, and people in their network all contribute to teenage delinquencies. However, the number one factor though is not your intelligence but your neighbourhood.

A perfect household can still suffer if it's in the wrong area. Which is why it's important to teach your teenagers life skills, as those without any become weak and an easy target for criminals. Especially if they are not educated to deal with life and morally don't know what's right or wrong.

We are not born violent or aggressive, we learn it from what we see and where we've grown up.

Penny: What signs can parents look out for if they think their teen is in trouble?

Ashley: Parents need to understand their teens. Know how they think and what makes them tick. It's the huge amount of effort put in over the years which helps parents understand their teens. From the time they changed their nappies up to the present day. Although it's difficult for parents that have been out of the picture for half their teen's life, they still need to take the time to get to know and understand them. Instead of listening to the media, stop and take time to understand your teen.

If parents think that their teen may be in trouble, they should look out for anything that is out of the ordinary in their behaviour. Such as a change in their mood. From being loud to suddenly being quiet or vice versa. When this happens, parents shouldn't pass it off as 'just another phase'. It may be another phase, but parents need to understand why this phase is happening as it could be a trigger for something more serious. Also, if parents see new, expensive items suddenly appear then this could be a telltale sign. Or if they see something on their teenager's phone that alarms them then they'll need to investigate. The best way to deal with situations is to be upfront and speak to their teenagers. Teenagers respond to directness.

Penny: ***What are the common mistakes that parents make raising their teenagers?***

Ashley: Letting them grow up too quickly. Allowing boys to use social media too early. And giving them too much freedom.

All teenagers have mobile phones which parents rely on in order to keep an eye on them. But what if their teen turns their phone off because they don't want their parents to contact them? Or what if their phone is taken off of them? Or if they've switched them off to avoid parental contact? Even if parents have access to their teen's friends' numbers, their teen may tell them to ignore the phone if a parent rings. So, it's a mistake for parents to think they can always get hold of their teenager by phone.

Penny: ***Is it ever too late for parents to have a positive impact?***

Ashley: No, it's never too late for parents to have a positive impact on their teenagers. If a teenager has got himself into trouble with the law, the worst thing you can say to him is 'I told you so'. Instead, ask him what he's done. Then ask him how you can help sort it out and how you can stop him from doing it again. As parents, we don't want our teens to do certain things, but if they do, then we want them to tell us what they've done so we can figure out the best way to handle it. We may not be able to change situations, but we can make sure we have the right attitude to support them in sorting things out.

Unconditional love is the key here and so too is being non-judgmental. We've all made mistakes and done things when we've been told not to do.

Penny: How do you think the general public perceives teenagers?

Ashley: The general public views them negatively. Yes, the odd one is bad, but this gives a bad name to the rest of them. The media gives teenagers a bad name too.

A lot of people are scared of teenagers. They think they are no good. Especially if they are wearing hoodies. But when it's freezing cold, I put my hood up too! In fact, we've been wearing hoodies since the 1970s!

CHAPTER 13: INTERVIEW WITH LONDON-BASED SCHOOL TEACHER.

This Chapter comprises an interview held with Helen Trenoweth MA (CAA), ISAR CAP. Helen is a teacher, author, and lecturer. She brings over 30 years of teaching experience to her role, including significant positions such as Head of Year. Having taught at single sex, as well as co-ed schools, she estimates she has taught about 15,000 adolescent boys. Helen has also raised teenage sons.

Penny*: *Why do teenage boys exhibit unwelcome behaviour in the classroom?

Helen: There are plenty of reasons why teenage boys get into trouble at school. To begin with, their brains often develop a bit later than girls'. Then there's the risk-taking behaviour they engage in to impress their friends, often without considering the consequences, which can lead even good kids into trouble. Sitting in a classroom all day doesn't help either, nor do the high-energy drinks sold at every corner shop near every school I've worked at.

On top of all this, teenagers struggle with sleep. They stay up late because they can't fall asleep, but we still expect them to get up early for school. When they are tired, they reach for an energy drink or load up on sugar or caffeine, which only disrupts the class and messes with their circadian rhythm even more. I'm all for starting the school day later for teenagers so they can sleep in. This way, they don't have to wake up very early during the week and then spend all weekend catching up on sleep, which only throws off their internal clock.

Penny*: *What are the main differences between girls and boys when it comes to their attitude towards school and towards learning?

Helen: Girls can be chatty and sometimes get off task, but even when they do, they are still being creative. A little chatter isn't a bad thing as it actually helps build strong friendships in the classroom.

Academically, girls often outperform boys, even in traditionally male-dominated fields like maths and science. And let's not forget, all-girls schools consistently outshine all-boys schools. Girls are also much tougher on me with questions like, 'Why hasn't this been marked?' and 'Where's my grade?', which just shows their maturity level.

One thing I've noticed is that boys born in the summer tend to have poorer behaviour compared to the older boys in their year group. Another factor to consider is birth order within families, as whether a boy is the first, second, or third child can impact his behaviour at school.

Penny*: *How best can parents get involved in their teens' education?

Helen: Being involved in your teen's education is a habit that should be established early on. There are plenty of ways for parents to get involved, like attending parents' evenings, volunteering to teach a class, staying updated on the curriculum through the school's website, and being active in their teen's homework assignments. I'm a big fan of whole-family homework and projects as it brings everyone together.

When it comes to barriers like poverty, schools can't always tell what a child's situation is just by looking at them. A teen might appear well-put-together but could have been living in a bed and breakfast for the past two years. Of course, there are other signs that teachers look for when a child is in need, but parents need to communicate with the school if they are struggling as staying silent won't help their child. There might be a club or some other support that a teacher can offer to help.

Some parents don't show much interest in their teens' education, but it's vital to stay involved. Keeping tabs on grades, progress, and behaviour reports is important. Fostering good habits from the start makes a big difference. Parents should show interest in all areas of their children's lives, including their education.

My job is to keep your child safe and ensure they have access to the resources they need to succeed in their lessons. But I do believe we need more hands-on deck. I often tell parents that, next to their child's health, education should be their top priority. We should be making the most of their free education without putting too much pressure on teachers, who are often just trying to get through the day.

Penny: Do you have any tips on discussing sex and drugs at home, especially if teens aren't comfortable talking about them with their parents.

Helen: I think parents should ask themselves whether they'd rather their kids learn about sex from them or from some pornography site being passed around the playground, or from friends who likely know just as little. It's best to keep the conversations open and honest, focusing on love and relationships.

Don't be embarrassed. It doesn't have to be a complicated conversation, but it's better than saying nothing at all, especially since the topic of pornography is so common in schools and teens talk about it a lot. If you show your child that you're interested, they'll come back with questions. Try to remember what it was like when you were an adolescent, how you felt about dating, what you were thinking when you first considered having sex, and how awkward and embarrassing it all seemed.

Unfortunately, schools tend to focus on discouraging sex by talking about condoms and all the scary diseases you can catch. But if you start the conversation and it doesn't seem like the right time, you can always revisit it later. Use the news or articles as conversation starters as there are plenty of resources out there. Sure, teens are going to be embarrassed, and you might be too, but try not to show it. At least you'll have had the conversation together, and hopefully, your teen will see that you understand what they are going through.

Penny: What are your recommendations for raising teenage boys?

Helen: Within the home, even if parents have different expectations or values to each other, it's crucial for them to present a united front to their child.

The setting of boundaries is key for gradually building trust between parent and child. For instance, if a parent sets a 9 p.m. curfew, they can explain to their teen that while it might seem early, honouring it could lead to a discussion about extending it to 9:30 p.m. later on.

Single parents should also set boundaries for themselves, like being mindful of who they allow into their teen's life and ensuring those people share the same expectations and boundaries. When parents live apart, some parents worry that different rules between households might confuse their teens, but teens are actually quite capable of adapting to different sets of rules, just as they do at school with different teachers.

When it comes to freedom, parents can make it clear that they don't expect their teen to drink or do drugs, and, as long as they don't, they'll be allowed to hang out with friends who make similar choices.

It's important for teens to feel heard, especially when they have worries. Whether it's about a parent spending too much time at the pub or having a partner, these topics need to be openly discussed. Just as we worry about them, our children worry about us too. By understanding what's on their minds, parents can take steps to help them feel more secure.

Parents should encourage teens to have conversations about their day after school, rather than just going straight to their rooms for the evening. They shouldn't accept just a one-word "fine" when asked how school went, they should get filled in on what actually happened during the day. This is something parents often do well when kids are younger, but often it eases off as they get older. On rare occasions, teens can be excused from these conversations but should respectfully request this.

Penny: Do you think teenage boys want to communicate with their parents?

Helen: It really depends on the parents' relationship with their teen. I always advise parents not to let their boys shut them out. Establishing communication early on is key, and you can't just expect boys to start talking if you haven't been engaging with them their whole lives. This might sound old-fashioned, but eating together at the dinner table is important, even if it's not possible every night. Setting up a ritual, like a Friday night dinner or takeaway with the TV off and phones down can create space for real conversations.

It's not true that teenage boys can't express their emotions, especially when there are no girls around. I've seen how valuable drama is in all-boys schools, where it gives them a chance to get things off their chest. I've witnessed questions such as, 'I don't know how I'll feel about getting a job to support my family,' 'I'll be the man of the house, so how do I take care of my children if I've got to work?' and 'How do I get around gender identification issues?' When they cry in class, it's a powerful sign that they're genuinely feeling what they're expressing. Drama and music hold so much power; it's a shame that the arts are always the first to face budget cuts.

The first sign that your child isn't communicating should be a signal to dig deeper into what's going on in his life. Invite his friends over, focus conversations on what's happening at school, meet his friends' parents, and get involved. It doesn't just have to be about eating junk food and playing games with his friends as there's a lot more you can learn by being present.

CHAPTER 14: WISE WORDS FROM OUR PANEL OF EXPERT TEENAGERS

After interviewing Ashley and Helen, I wanted to speak with more experts. So, to gather further insights into their world, I conducted one-to-one interviews with several teenagers aged between 13 and 18 years. Here is a summary of the findings.

1) *"For you, what are the best things about being a teenager?"*

The majority of teenagers felt that the best things about being a teenager were "friends," "less stress than when I'm older," "freedom," and "not having too many responsibilities yet." Others replied:

- "Having lots of energy."
- "Less parental involvement."
- "No bills to pay."
- "Not too much pressure."
- "Fun experiences you may not get when you settle down."
- "Social life."

- “There is room for mistakes.”

2) ***"For you, what are the worst things about being a teenager?"***

The majority of teenagers felt that the worst things about being a teenager were “school” and “schoolwork”, including GCSEs and A levels. Others replied:

- “Answering questions about my future.”
- “Being treated as a kid.”
- “Being treated as an adult.”
- “Doing loads of school work but not being paid yet.”
- “Everyone is looking at me when out with friends.”
- “Fast spreading, malicious rumours.”
- “Not a lot of money/cannot earn a lot.”
- “Parental expectations.”
- “Wanting to impress parents.”
- “Wanting more freedom.”

3) *"What are you most looking forward to when you are an adult?"*

The majority responded with the answers "freedom" and "owning my own house." Others replied:

- "A car."
- "Being independent."
- "Building a career."
- "Having children."
- "Doing stuff on my own terms."
- "Getting an actual job, not like McDonald's."
- "Having money."
- "Not being 'on the tracks' of the stages of school."
- "Travelling".
- "Working for myself and making an income".

4) *"What should your parents do to improve their communication with you?"*

The majority responded with the answer 'don't shout'. Others replied:

- "Understand me better."

WISE WORDS FROM OUR PANEL OF EXPERT TEENAGERS

- "Don't immediately start shouting when you don't get your way. Instead, work out the issue and resolve it like civilised humans."
- "Don't assume things but talk to me instead."
- "Listen to what I have to say."
- "Don't talk via my other parent, but directly to me."
- "Wait until you've heard the full story."
- "Don't butt in with pre-formed opinions or ideas."
- "Don't just stick to your own opinion if you lose an argument or if you've been proven wrong just because you don't want to back down."
- "Don't say the same things over and over again otherwise it turns into a heated debate."
- "Be less emotional and more logical. More 'cause and effect' as opposed to 'this is how that makes me feel."
- "Don't shout at me, it makes me angry."
- "Create a safe environment so I can say anything."
- "Treat me as an adult."
- "Have 1 on 1 conversations."
- "Talk about their experiences."
- "Don't talk early in the morning."

- "Communicate without bringing strong emotions into it which leads to breakdowns in conversations."
- "Seek clarity over my actions prior to assuming the worst."

5) *"Imagine, several years down the line, that you are a parent. What would you do differently compared to how your parents parented you?"*

The majority responded with the answer "have a less strict bedtime." Others replied:

- "Always talk to my child calmly and not assume malicious intent when they do actions that hurt me."
- "Don't get too mad if they get in trouble."
- "Give them more independence."
- "I would bear in mind that the world would have changed."
- "I would not take my children's apps away."
- "More open conversations."
- "Same rules for all children."
- "Shout less."
- "Spend more time with my children."

- "Wider options, not just academic."
- "Wouldn't spoil my kids like my parents have me."

6) *"Thinking about arguments, how does it make you feel when your parents argue with you?"*

The majority responded with "upset", "angry" or "frustrated". Others replied:

- "Annoyed."
- "Disappointed."
- "Distressed."
- "Fine."
- "Impactful conversations."
- "Not a nice thing."
- "Pissed off."
- "Sad."
- "Unfair."
- "Very one sided."
- "With one parent it's fine, feels more akin to a debate. With the other it feels pointless and simply hurtful as nothing is achieved."

7) *"Thinking generally, can you give examples of things your parents have done well in their parenting that work for you?"*

There was an interesting mix of answers to this question:

- "A lot of freedom."
- "Are happy as long as I try my best."
- "Being chilled."
- "Cared about the right things."
- "Communicating with me."
- "Encourage hard (school) work."
- "Encouraged and pushed me to carry on."
- "Encouraging me to take opportunities when presented (joining sports teams and the like)."
- "Facilitated my social life."
- "Focused on my happiness."
- "Good diet."
- "Given me enough money, within reason, for my discretionary spending."
- "Helped with homework."

- "I don't have to seek permission for certain activities and justify their costs if they fit into what I have saved from my job and monthly allowance."
- "Let me go out."
- "Made a good effort."
- "Not too much pressure."
- "Often put me first."
- "Supported me."
- "Treated me fairly with siblings."
- "Tried very hard to provide and care for me."

8) "*What do you see your parents' role as nowadays, now that you are no longer a young child but instead a teenager?*"

There was an interesting mix of answers to this question:

- "Be there to talk to."
- "Domestic life activities, although I've had to shoulder more (rightfully) as time goes on."
- "Give me a place to sleep safely."
- "Give me more responsibility to work things out myself."

WISE WORDS FROM OUR PANEL OF EXPERT TEENAGERS

- "Guidance when things don't go quite right."
- "Guiding me into adult life."
- "Help me with life skills e.g. applying for jobs, bank accounts, driving licence."
- "I still rely on them."
- "Help me make the right decisions."
- "Help to share their (own) experiences as a teenager."
- "Help when I need it."
- "Making sure I don't die and do good in school."
- "Make things run smoothly."
- "More adult-like conversations."
- "Provide food and a home."
- "Strong encouragement to do activities that are good for me which will help when I no longer have a framework."
- "Talk more on an adult-to-adult basis."
- "Teach me about mortgages and pay slips."
- "The same but giving me more independence."
- "To do things that I can't do e.g. admin."
- "To support and care but not do everything for me."

- "Transitioning me, especially age 10 to 18 years."
- "What to do and what not to do."

9) *"How do you feel when you picture yourself as an adult?"*

The majority of teenagers came back with the responses "excited" and "happy". Others replied:

- "Be sad to leave childhood behind me."
- "Extra independence is nice but a trade-off for extra things to do."
- "Fairly neutral."
- "Good."
- "Having a job that I enjoy."
- "Having freedom."
- "I can't picture myself as too busy focusing on exams at the moment."
- "I feel close to the stage already and it doesn't feel there will be a sudden change due to university making the change more gradual."
- "If I'm feeling down then I get a negative outlook and worry about the pressure of work and bills."

- “Like time is passing too quickly.”
- “Like the idea of having a family.”
- “Like the idea of being a professional.”
- “Lots of good things to come.”
- “Miserable.”
- "Mostly I have a positive outlook."
- “Nervous.”
- “Not too different.”
- “Worried.”

10) *“Thinking generally, what could your parents do to make your life easier?"*

There was an interesting mix of answers to this question:

- “Don't nag me about homework as I never get into trouble and always do it”.
- “Fewer chores.”
- “Give advice.”
- “Have more privacy.”
- “Help with transport to school (but then I'd have less freedom).”

- "I know what I'm doing as my parents have given me the platform."
- "Stop taking my phone, it's how I communicate with friends."
- "The expectation to cook dinner or do family activities creates challenges when I have pressures at school, for example, tests. I wish there was an option to be more flexible."
- "Try and bond and do things with us more."
- "Understand me more."

11) *"Can you think of anything that scares you in life?*

The majority responded with 'not achieving my full potential'. Others replied:

- "A basic 9-5 job that I hate."
- "Adult life is terrifying... it hits you quite fast."
- "Being burgled."
- "Death of a loved one."
- "Exams."
- "My future frightens me."
- "Not achieving what I want."

- "Not becoming successful."
- "Not becoming what I or my parents want me to be."
- "Not knowing what will happen next."
- "The unknown."
- "Not knowing how to prepare for the future."
- "Not having people to talk to."
- "Reflecting back in 25 years to find that it all went wrong."
- "The rise of easy-to-fake media is always in the back of my mind."
- "Worried that a missed grade will mean I'm not able to get into university or do an apprenticeship."

12) *"Lastly, how do you think the general public perceives teenagers?"*

There was an interesting mix of answers to this question:

- "Almost any age group is negatively perceived by other age groups."
- "Annoying, disruptive, loud, etc."
- "Generally positive, with some being initially cautious, particularly of large groups late at night."

WISE WORDS FROM OUR PANEL OF EXPERT TEENAGERS

- "Negative views."
- "Teachers and parents do have sympathy."
- "People get older and forget what it was like to be a teenager."
- "People judge too quickly."
- "People complain about the new generation but they're similar to the previous one(s)."
- "The public think we are all thugs."
- "The world has changed so teenagers have had to change. But underneath we're quite similar to previous generations."
- "Some are dangerous."
- "Spoilt and lazy/not hard working."
- "That they are mischievous, unpredictable people."
- "They think that we have it so easy because it's 'so much easier than the 80's'. But that isn't true."
- "Watch the news and see problems."

A few other comments were noted in the interviews that I thought deserved a mention:

"My parents support me. But they are still the people you most want to impress." Young Person.

WISE WORDS FROM OUR PANEL OF EXPERT TEENAGERS

"It's a balance between being treated as a kid and an adult." Young person.

"There are things that you don't want to tell your parents but it's good to tell them." Young person.

"My most positive and most negative conversations are with my parents. Which can make me feel quite anxious." Young person.

(During arguments) "I've felt the most sad, distressed I've ever felt." Young person.

"It's super beneficial to have people around that have been through the teenage years." Young person.

"Most important time of life, it shapes you." Young person.

CHAPTER 15: DISPENSING WITH COMMON COMPLAINTS

Teenagers can't seem to win, as there are so many discriminatory complaints bantered around against this age group. When they aren't being the butt of a joke, often made by their parents, they are getting bad press from the media.

There is no excuse for anyone to jump on the bandwagon, automatically blaming teens before looking into their actions. Instead, we should be challenging the age-old ethos of 'let's blame it on the terrible teens'.

Below, we will explore some of these common complaints.

(1) *"They really Push my Buttons!"*

Surely, it's up to us how we interpret our teens' reactions and whether we allow them to 'push our buttons'? We are responsible for our own thoughts and actions and can therefore decide if we want to react or respond. We need to keep ourselves in check. Is it our ego reacting here or is it our heart responding? Let's not forget that teens aren't yet capable of seeing things from another person's perspective as their ability to do so is still under construction.

When using a testy voice towards us, we need to remind ourselves of the working of the teen brain. It would hardly be fair to expect them to be able to fully control their emotions when we know that the part of their brain responsible isn't yet fully developed and won't be for several years. If we liken this to toddlers, do we expect them to be able to know their times tables? Of course not, they can just about talk coherently, let alone work out something this complex.

For those that habitually spoil their teens, this behaviour isn't surprising. We can't really blame them for acting up. It's no wonder they expect us to kowtow to them if they aren't given any boundaries.

When your teen speaks loudly, without shouting, he may not even know he's doing so. We know that he can't control his emotions. And when feeling under pressure, this is how he shows that he's stressed. This is a signal for you to provide him with the support needed. Avoid shouting back at him or telling him off. So he can learn from his actions, calmly explain that he's raising his voice and that he needs to lower it.

(2) *"My son only grunts at me."*

When I asked a friend's teenage son why he thinks teens grunt, he replied that it was due to them being too tired to talk and it's easier to grunt than to formulate proper sentences. This is understandable, considering they spend much of their day feeling tired. Often living in their heads, teens have an awful lot to deal with, including mood changes. So, surely it must be easier to give a monosyllabic response? It's also possible that they may not be in the mood to talk. Then there is the theory that young teens may be embarrassed to speak when their voice is breaking as this causes crackling noises. Similarly, they may be in a situation where they are embarrassed and want to shut down the conversation as quickly as possible. We also have to consider that they are at the stage where they want to distance themselves from us, so they won't make an effort to talk, unless it suits them.

(3) "*He never listens to me.*"

He does listen. But with the average person speaking approximately 15,500 words a day, it comes as no surprise that some aren't remembered or even understood.

Have you checked that your teen is in listening mode? Perhaps he's deep in thought or struggling with an emotional issue which is momentarily stopping him from hearing outside noises. Is he glued to an addictive screen? In which case he definitely won't hear coherently. Can he actually hear you as you shout a message up the stairs? Maybe he's further away than you think or behind a closed door.

If you think he doesn't listen, try these simple tests. Suggest an idea to him and listen out for him to mention or dip back into the same conversation a few days or weeks later. Chances are that he will. Or use an expression that he wouldn't normally use which seems slightly out of place for a teenager. Then wait and see if he either uses it at a later date or queries what you mean. If he responds to either of the above suggestions, then you will see that he does listen to you. Along these lines, I'm sure that you can think of a time when you have told your teen off for doing something only to find him telling you off for doing the same thing a few days/weeks later. In which case he must have heard you in the first place.

Make sure that you aren't too busy multitasking and that you are speaking coherently so that he can understand what you are saying. Due to his immature cognitive ability, he will often take things literally. He may think you mean something different than what you're saying. Something spoken in jest or sarcastically can easily be misinterpreted and result in a different outcome than the one that you had expected. For example, you inform your teen that you're thinking of going out, but he thinks that you mean right now, immediately. Ergo, just make sure that you give him clear information so that he understands you.

Caught up in our busy lives, we don't always take the time to fully explain things clearly to our teens. As a result, they go away confused and aren't able to act upon our request.

When giving instructions, it can be useful to ask your teen to repeat back the main points, including anything he's agreed to, as this avoids him later saying he didn't understand you.

To avoid your teen saying he doesn't remember your instructions, keep it simple. Teens can't handle too many instructions at once, so just give one at a time.

If you are talking in a disrespectful manner, being rude, shouting, or frightening your teen, he's likely to switch off. The same applies to topics that are emotionally difficult for him to discuss. Don't be surprised if he can't remember the conversation later as he may have unintentionally blocked it out.

When it comes to listening, be a good role model. From a young age, unless told otherwise, children will naturally mirror their parents' communication skills.

Try different ways to communicate and give him the chance to react and respond. You can leave him a note on the fridge, leave him a voicemail, write him a letter, or send him an email or text.

Lastly, don't overlook the fact that often he may be tired, or like us, have cognitive overload.

(4) *"Does he ever wash? It doesn't smell like it!"*

During puberty, teens sweat more than they did when they were younger, due to their apocrine glands which previously lay inactive. The apocrine glands are stimulated upon hormonal changes in the body. A type of sweat gland, they are found in the scalp, armpits, genital areas, and nipples, and are released as an emotional response, in times of stress or sexual excitement. They secrete an oily fluid, which doesn't smell but when the bacteria found on our skin breaks down the protein in the fluid it causes a rather unpleasant odour. Oddly enough, this odour acts as our sexual scent, aiding sexual attraction and differing for each human being.

Some teens hate to shower, so will avoid them as much as they can. Another explanation is that whilst washing, your teen's mind is elsewhere. Resulting in him not using enough soap or choosing the wrong item whilst in the shower. This is easily rectified with a gentle reminder on personal hygiene, or a reminder of which products should be used.

(5) "*Why is he so selfish?*"

Research carried out at UCL, London, found that it isn't until the latter years of adolescence that our teenagers' brains are able to comprehend the idea of putting themselves in other people's shoes, which may explain why they often appear less selfish as they grow older. This further supports the notion that teens are not yet fully capable of taking charge or being responsible for all aspects of their lives. It also raises the question of whether they can truly cope with the demands of viewing situations from another person's perspective. Thereby, what we perceive as egocentrism is, in fact, a form of psychological protection, shielding them until they are able to function independently.

In situations where parents are separating or divorcing, we have to question whether it is fair to burden a young teen's shoulders with explanations about the reasons behind such decisions, especially when they may not fully understand. Similarly, in cases where a parent has suffered the loss of a loved one or has lost their job, is it right to use their teen as a crutch or counsellor? In these situations, teens can appear selfish as they often don't know how to cope, both because of their cognitive limitations and their own distress from the separation, loss, or financial adjustments, which can make their lives feel unbearable.

Another argument that explains why teens appear selfish is that, in their struggles for independence and their quest to find their own identity, helping others simply falls by the wayside.

Experts suggest that because teenagers are cared for throughout childhood, they may not yet feel the need, or have the capacity, to consistently consider others. As their brains mature, they gradually become more aware of those around them.

As we noted earlier, teens rely heavily on their amygdala until their PFC is fully developed. Since the PFC is responsible for complex functions like considering how actions affect others, it's no wonder teenagers can often appear selfish. This is especially evident during the throes of an argument when their emotions are running high.

Another explanation why a teen appears selfish is that he may have grown up in a household where parents exhibit selfish behaviours or where there is a power struggle between them, so he copies these patterns by default.

Instead of being frustrated or annoyed when your teen behaves selfishly, sit him down and calmly explain how his actions affect others, and why it's important to consider other people's feelings.

I posed the question of 'Why are teens often seen as being self-centred or selfish' to a teenager I know.

His response was that this type of behaviour could be due to the world that teens are brought up in and that they are witnessing this type of behaviour from others.

(6) *"Why doesn't he ever want to talk to me? I keep asking him to."*

There are many reasons why our teens don't want to talk to us. Most have to do with either our timing or the way we speak to them.

At times, our teens may be too scared to talk as they fear our responses and are worried that they may be judged or questioned. They may not be in the right frame of mind to further explain or defend themselves, making them apprehensive in their response. The previous Chapter on Communication covers this topic in detail.

Teens are often overburdened with homework, tutoring, chores, and extracurricular activities, leaving little time for themselves. As their downtime is so precious they want to spend it wisely. Therefore, talking to their friends or getting on with their own personal tasks take priority, leaving little time for their parents.

Something we need to question is whether we use our teens' lack of desire to talk to our advantage. It's easy to put the blame onto them for not wanting to talk as this frees us up to do other things, and effectively, lets us off the hook. The trouble with this approach is that, before we know it, it's bedtime and we haven't given our teens the chance to talk, even if they wanted to.

Teens that are struggling with issues outside their control can become fearful. Making them withdraw from life, leaving them temporarily unable to talk to us.

One of the common comments that I hear parents make about their sons is that they don't talk as much as they'd like them to. If this is the case for you, then try using phrases along the lines of 'I need a little more feedback so I can understand what's going on.' Or, using a gentle, non-demanding voice, 'Please can you fill me in a bit more so I can sort things out for you,' as opposed to 'You never bother to talk to me!'

(7) *"To my friends, I call my son my little Monster!"*

Like their parents, teenagers are human beings and not monsters. So why do people call them so? Perhaps they don't take the time to understand them or perhaps they want to make situations 'all about them' instead of their teen. Maybe they just can't cope with their own teens, so instead make them a laughing stock to avoid placing any blame upon themselves. Sadly, there are many parents who lack compassion, understanding, and empathy.

Adolescence spans approximately 14 yrs, (ages 10 to 24), during which time teens experience a wide range of emotions that they must learn to navigate. If we compared this to living with a partner for 14 yrs, wouldn't they also experience similar emotions, albeit not necessarily all in the same day or week, as is often the case?

(8) "*Why is my son always tired?*"

Reasons for this may be down to health problems or one or more of the following common issues:

Not enough:

- Exercise.
- Food.
- Fluids.
- Exposure to daylight.
- Fresh air.
- Sleep.

Or from suffering from:

- Anxiety. After the hormonal rush you can feel drained.
- Depression.
- Lack of a healthy sleep routine.

The overconsumption of sugar can lead to a drop in blood sugar levels, resulting in faintness, dizziness, sleepiness, anxiety, brain fog, irritability, mood swings, and even symptoms of depression. Action on Sugar, using UK Government data, reported that teenagers are consuming up to three times the recommended daily amount, which could easily explain why so many feel wiped out or emotionally all over the place (Action on Sugar, 2016).

It's a good idea to check how much sleep your teen is getting as they may need more hours than you might think. The same goes for the amount of food they eat. Doctors suggest that teens who exercise regularly need to consume more food than those who are more sedentary. Since they are growing so fast, they generally require more calories than they did before puberty. For example, an active male teenager needs just under 3,000 calories a day, while a less active one needs only a couple of hundred calories less.

(9) "My teen is always moody!"

Our teens are constantly struggling with a tidal wave of emotions. Many of which they can't yet fathom. As their brains start to develop further, they are faced with new adult emotions and challenges, causing additional stress and confusion. To make matters worse, they don't always know why they are feeling the way they feel. One minute they experience anger or disappointment, and the next euphoria. Due to their inability to control their emotions, it's not surprising that teens cope by either lashing out or becoming withdrawn. If they choose to become withdrawn, then we perceive them as being moody. Conflicts with parents, siblings, peers, and teachers will send them on an emotional roller coaster ride. If teens don't regularly communicate to us how they are feeling, then we don't necessarily know the reasons behind their emotions. So, when we see changes in our teen's behaviour, we label them as 'moody'.

When under pressure, be it at home or school, teens can feel overwhelmed as they aren't able to fully articulate their feelings, putting a strain on their moods.

Thanks to their highly emotional brain, teens can interpret neutral situations as negative ones. Their amygdala really doesn't help as it responds when danger is sensed and, to protect them, makes situations appear dangerous or threatening, even when they aren't.

Thrown into adulthood, whilst at the same time mourning the loss of childhood, can't be easy for our teens. Caught in the void between their old world and their new, makes them feel vulnerable, and no doubt will be fraught with moments of both horror and excitement. Coping with all the challenges and responsibilities that come with being a near adult must, at times, be overwhelming.

Then there is the profound sense that they aren't being understood or truly heard by adults and the world around them. Nor, in the majority of cases, being respected. Which would make anyone feel moody.

For some, the teenage years are a time when romantic relationships are being explored, creating an emotional yo-yo effect, making them appear moody.

Skipping meals or experiencing irregular meal times can also lead to erratic moods. Blood sugar levels that rise and fall rapidly will also affect teens' behaviours.

Lastly, we shouldn't overlook the fact that our teens may be suffering in silence with mental health conditions such as depression.

(10) "I can't believe how stupid my son is and how many risks he takes!"

Risk-taking in teens can be explained by the following factors, including:

- Boredom. A lack of stimulation can drive teens to seek excitement through risky behaviour.
- Dopamine and the reward system. Increased dopamine activity during adolescence makes teens more likely to pursue new and pleasurable

experiences. This can lead to a cycle of seeking out risky behaviours to maintain dopamine levels.

- Impulsivity. Higher dopamine levels, combined with immature brain development, can lead to snap decisions without thinking through the consequences.
- Lack of healthy outlets. Without positive outlets to seek excitement, teen's may turn to unhealthy or dangerous ones.
- Lack of experience with consequences. Many teens haven't yet had enough opportunities to learn how actions lead to outcomes, especially negative ones.
- Lack of positive role models. Without healthy behaviour modelled by older peers or adults, teens maybe more prone to copying risky behaviour.
- Teens are more likely to focus on perceived positive rewards rather than the potential risks. For example, they may believe that smoking may help them gain acceptance in their peer group, or that gate crashing a late-night party will lead them to meeting girls and impressing friends.
- A sense of invincibility leads teens to believe that nothing bad will happen to them which lowers perceived risks.
- An underdeveloped PFC leads to reduced cognitive control and a limited ability to think logically or to see the bigger picture.

- Risky behaviour can be a way to test boundaries or push back against societal or parental expectations.
- Rewards outweigh risks. Teens' brains are more focused on short-term rewards than long-term consequences, which can lead to risky decisions.
- Need to be noticed. Some teens take risks to gain attention or feel seen.
- Rebellion. Taking risks can be a way of asserting independence or expressing frustration with parental control.

The majority of research links risky and impulsive behaviour of teenagers, in activities such as sensation-seeking ones, to the underdevelopment of their brain structures. That said, there is also a fair amount of research which claims that the neurohormone dopamine is responsible. Even though there are many theories as to why teenagers take risks, as brain research is still in its infancy, there seems to be no real definite answers.

But risks shouldn't be ignored. As parents, it's our job to teach our teens how to navigate the pitfalls of risky behaviour. To satisfy their need to experience highs from thrill-seeking activities, we can encourage safe, positive ones. This is especially useful during testosterone surges, when they need to expel excess energy and fulfil their quest for self-identity.

When your teen wants to plan an activity, sit him down and talk through the risks. Ask him about his action plan.

Make sure that he's equipped with the information he needs at the start. As he begins to take risks in a planned manner, ask him to report back to you so he can see the bigger picture, and you can see any pitfalls. This way he will feel more confident about taking on risks as he knows that he is supported. Admittedly, there will be times when our teens may take on risky activities without us knowing, especially when their peers are present. We can tackle this by having regular conversations, during which, we can highlight the value of thinking things through and employing a risk-assessment procedure.

And although teens may well weigh up the possible outcomes before taking on any risky activities, the outcomes they seek may not coincide with those that we find acceptable. If they can't or won't plan properly, our explanation of consequences may fall on deaf ears. Sometimes it's better to let them learn from their own mistakes. (Please note that I'm not condoning that your teen deliberately learns from dangerous or major mistakes such as drug or alcohol abuse, crime, inappropriate sex, hazardous driving, violence or suchlike, but am relating to minor risks.)

By setting rules and boundaries, giving reminders, and keeping an open dialogue, we can monitor our teens' actions and step in if necessary.

(11) "My son is so stubborn. He won't take any of my advice!"

Teens often think that they know more than their parents. In some cases, they do, especially as our advice can sometimes be biassed or just erroneous. Just because we think we have a good idea doesn't necessarily make it so. In some scenarios, could it be that we too are being stubborn?

In order to carve out their own identity, away from the family unit, it's necessary for teens to reject the ideas and advice of others. Given that they aren't supposed to be an extension of their parents, if they always heeded the advice of others, wouldn't this contradict their urge to stand on their own two feet and be their own man? Their rejections encourage their innate quest to become independent and self-reliant. We know that in order for them to learn and grow they will have to make mistakes, which means that they will have to ignore advice given. So what we see as stubbornness, is really just growth.

(12) "How can I engage my son more at school?"

When it comes to good role modelling for education, both parents need to be engaged. As boys need male role models, dads need to be engaged in their studies just as much as their mums. Actions that dads can take, such as being seen reading, helps encourage a love of reading and learning. Like their female counterparts, our teens need to receive books and study-related gifts so that they can engage and be encouraged to enjoy their schoolwork. And we need to teach them that doing well at school doesn't mean they are 'nerdy' or 'aren't masculine enough'.

By helping your teen plan a career that appeals to him, he can work out the steps needed, including any necessary qualifications. To aid him, help him break down his achievement goals into tiny steps, rewarding him as he goes. Researching his favourite role models can inspire him to excel at school. To encourage him to act, demonstrate how his effort will be rewarded, such as how his wages will allow him to enjoy favourite pastimes.

For those struggling with school work, we need to make sure that there aren't any barriers that are invisible to us, such as dyslexia.

(13) "Any tips for when things get too much for me?"

When things get tough, I'm a great believer of putting things into perspective. Although the teenage years can be challenging for both teens and parents, if we reflect back in time, about 80 years, we see things in a different light and realise that things really aren't that bad.

Imagine, as some of your relatives did, living through the Second World War. At the start, and throughout the war, children were sent away from towns and cities from all over the UK to live with total strangers. Your teen could well have been one of the 4 million evacuated to the countryside during the Blitz, with the idea that they would be safer away from the main areas that were being bombed, or likely to be. Your teen would be living with temporary parents who were not vetted in any way. And, as you weren't allowed to visit, you would not have known whether he was happy or safe. Nor if he was being used as a workhorse, had enough to eat, had a decent bed to sleep in at night, or if he was being abused in any way. You may have feared him forgetting you or even preferring his 'new parents'. You would also worry about his reactions on his return home on seeing the bombed-out ruins of his old house. And thoughts such as '*Will he even recognise me?*' or '*Will I recognise him?*' will no doubt plague your mind. Imagine how you would feel if you had to make the decision to send your teen away in the first place?

(14) Case Scenario *"My son has become unruly. He's smashed up his brother's iPad and is now refusing to spend time with his grandparents. He's also shouting at me a lot and swearing. He never used to be like this, it's only recently. I'm not allowing him to participate in online gaming anymore. What else can I do? Should I take his phone away?"*

It sounds like your son is in pain and is suffering greatly. He's lashing out as he's angry and is no doubt struggling to control or even understand his feelings. This loss of control is no doubt scary for him.

When he's in a calm mood, I suggest you find a way to connect to him. Keep calm and find a safe space for him to open up and talk. Really listen, using True Focused Listening. After he's spoken, you can tell him that you understand that he's in pain and upset, that you want to help and that you still love him. Consider using the mirroring technique covered earlier in the book. Explain that his swearing and his behaviour in general isn't acceptable and tell him why.

If communication between you both has broken down completely, consider engaging a counsellor, mentor, or therapist, either at school, via his GP, or privately. Alternatively, there are reputable online organisations that he can contact via text or phone for support whilst he's working through his problems.

In the meantime, try to find out from either your son or others in the family, including his grandparents, what has been going on and why he doesn't want to visit them. Has something happened on one of his visits? Perhaps his grandparents have said or done something to upset, hurt, or offend him. Or he's acted similarly to them and feels guilty.

As far as taking away his phone, I suggest not. He needs his support network of friends. Furthermore, he can use it to access online help such as counselling. Teens are ostracised if they aren't able to keep up with friends on group chats etc. which is another reason why I don't believe in taking away phones. Moreover, he may not be in a hurry to come to you for help in the future if you do so. And, by allowing him to keep his phone, you are able to contact him. There are other ways to tackle this such as restricting his usage and restricting the number and type of apps or websites he visits, setting consequences if he violates the rules.

When it comes to forbidding his online gaming, you may see this as a way to punish him, however before you decide, consider the following facts:

In Hertfordshire's County Council's 2023 Young People's Health and Wellbeing Survey, when asked what their coping strategies were when it came to stress, the top answer for boys was playing computer games. (Followed by listening to music, exercising, talking to family, and talking to a friend.) So, we can clearly see that it's common for males to use computer games as a way to relax and escape from everyday life.

As far as the iPad goes, I suggest that he pays for it to be replaced. If he doesn't have any money saved up, then perhaps he can get a part-time job or earn money by doing jobs around the house, for your friends, or for neighbours. Having him take responsibility for replacing the iPad is a positive step to empowerment.

Moving forward, make sure that you have established boundaries and rules and that your teen understands them. Reserve judgement and avoid dishing out consequences until you have found out why he's acting this way. Chances are, there are things that are going on, or have been, without your knowledge.

As harsh as this sounds, we chose to have children. To give them life. So, we need to take full responsibility for them.

And instead of moaning about our teens, let's respect them and be grateful that we are experiencing minute parts of their metamorphosis from child to adult. If we take a moment to consider all the people around the world who cannot have children or have lost them, our complaints become less significant.

LESSONS IN CARTOONS

The following five cartoons help illustrate the challenges faced by our teens and acts as a reminder of the importance of engaging our brain before we speak.

1. It's biology not laziness. Their hormones are at work.

2. Clothes help teens be who they want to be.

3. Teens push back to explore their own thoughts.

4. It's not defiance, just a shifted sleep clock.

5. Emotional control is still a work in progress.

CHAPTER 16: PARENTAL NEEDS — IF WE LOOK AFTER THEM, WHO LOOKS AFTER US?

"*It's no wonder that people joke about parenting being the hardest job in the world, it's the most important role in life and we don't want to mess it up. We care so deeply about our children that we want to get it right. Preferably, first time around!*"

ACCEPT THINGS WHEN YOU'VE DONE YOUR BEST

Parenting and worrying seem to go hand in hand. Whether its worrying about a decision made or wondering if we've done enough for them. If we've made decisions with love in our hearts, not anger or bitterness, given it our best, then we need to sit back and accept that we've done our best and should not persist in condemning ourselves. Getting things right doesn't happen overnight. It takes years of hard work. But in order to be better parents tomorrow, we need to be open to learning.

Previously, I mentioned the pitfalls of comparing our teens to others. Now we need to touch on comparing ourselves to other parents, especially our friends. When we see our friends acting in ways that differ from our own it can make us second guess ourselves. Giving way to feelings of insecurity and even stupidity. Just because they are more assertive or command more respect, doesn't mean that we should suddenly change how we think or act. We can see how their ways sit with us, but more often than not, it will not sit right and will be out of character for us. If areas of your parenting are working fine, then don't start second guessing yourself. Don't look for inadequacies that aren't there or allow fear to creep in and unsettle you. Take heed of the saying, 'If it ain't broke, don't fix it'.

Ride Out the Storm

We have to be realistic. Our teens won't always, or even often, think that we are wonderful parents, however hard we try. In fact, there will be times when no matter how hard you try, your teen will think that not only are you out to make his life a misery, but are, in his eyes, the devil incarnate. You may even get to the point when you think that you both speak a different language. However, please be mindful that you aren't alone. Take a deep breath and think of all the other parents that are struggling too. No doubt, the storm will soon pass, and the seas will once more be calm. Have faith, for tomorrow is another day and an exciting opportunity for a fresh start. And, although your teen will not usually admit it, and you may not always feel it, you do play a *crucial* role in his life.

When things get tough, it's good to remember that there is a fountain of overflowing love that comes with the gift of your child which you can tap into whenever you need to.

YOUR FEELINGS

When your teen says something that hurts your feelings, take a deep breath. Let the episode pass, wait a few minutes, then revisit it. It will be very difficult to respond sensibly if you don't take a few moments out for yourself. In a kind and caring voice, explain that he's hurt your feelings and then listen to what he has to say. It's important that you are able to express how you feel but not if it steamrollers your teen's thoughts along the way. If in doubt how to respond, always come from a place of love and with an open heart and you will find the correct way.

There will be times when you are excited about something, and your teen will be nearby. However, you may find that he isn't at all interested in what you have to say. This may not be a reflection on you personally, just that he's deep in thought and his mind is elsewhere. Alternatively, he may not fully understand the situation or why you feel this way. If he doesn't engage in your excitement, just remember that he isn't responsible for your happiness. No one is, except you. Then, phone a friend or just enjoy the moments of your elation.

People's moods can have a subconscious effect on those around them. As discussed previously, teens, through no fault of their own, are often in a low mood, which, in turn, can dampen your mood too, often without you even realising it. Don't place blame upon your teen but merely be aware and find ways to uplift the both of you.

MISTAKES

When it comes to small mistakes, let's face it, who hasn't made some stupid ones. Either due to tiredness or not thinking things through, there is no shame in that. Life is about making mistakes and learning from them. You may be surprised to find that your teen appreciates that you too make mistakes and are open and honest about them. Rather than chastising ourselves, which is something best avoided in front of our teens as we don't want them copying, we can use our mistakes to teach about life's pitfalls by explaining how we dealt with certain situations.

UN-TASKING

"Just because we are called the Human Race doesn't mean our whole life needs to be one."

Un-tasking is the act of unravelling the daily habit of multi-tasking. (It may not be a word in the dictionary but it's one I've made up to suit the purpose.) A couple of years ago, I was watching a Korean T.V. series, and as I can't speak any Korean I had to use subtitles. Concentrating on reading every word, I noticed how thoroughly engrossed I became. Being hooked on the beautiful story, I became totally and utterly absorbed. I stopped looking at my phone, stopped thinking about the washing up piled in the sink, and peacefully blocked out my to-do list. In the past, I would have been severely tempted to put the T.V. on pause to stop and carry out one of these tasks and then return back to the T.V. several minutes later, if at all. After watching each episode, I felt like I had given my brain a mini holiday. I really could see the benefits. Most importantly, it reminded me of the importance of single tasking, decluttering our brain, and focusing on the task at hand.

BURNOUT

"Don't glamourise busyness!"

We are so busy running up the down escalator of life that we've turned ourselves into machines, making ourselves unhappy in the process. It seems that the busier we are, the more important we feel. Which, when we think about it, is rather ridiculous. We need to take stock and focus on the important things in life. For the majority, this is health, both mental and physical, family, and friends. But when it comes to mothers, we woefully have a bad habit of putting ourselves, and therefore our health, last, often failing to address this essential area of our lives.

When Googling the definition of the word 'Burnout', I landed on Psychology Today's website and was rather impressed. Most websites, and most people in general, define burnout to be a work-related problem. However, Psychology Today website explained the word as:

Burnout is described as a state of emotional, mental, and often physical exhaustion brought on by ongoing or repeated stress. While it more often stems from work-related challenges, it can also affect other areas of life, from parenting or caring for others to maintaining close relationships (Psychology Today, 2022).

Note the word *parenting*. It's great to see in black and white that it's acceptable for people to admit that they are struggling with parenting. No shame attached and preferably no blame either.

To evade burnout, we need to take positive steps to avoid getting too far down the path of self-destruction. So how do we accomplish this? In simple terms we make sure that we look after ourselves. This isn't an act of selfishness, unless taken to the extreme, but an act of survival. As a parent, we need to take care of others, and in order to do so we must firstly take care of ourselves. If we don't receive enough love and support, then we will be pouring from an empty cup. For many, this isn't easy, and a practice that needs constant attention. Yet, if our physical and mental needs aren't met, our teens won't be either. To think clearly, give our full attention, and be able to keep calm, even on the receiving end of vented anger, we need to be in a good place. Furthermore, by demonstrating the importance of self-care, we become good role models.

PARENTAL NEEDS – IF WE LOOK AFTER THEM, WHO LOOKS AFTER US?

If you find yourself struggling, then please do look at getting some help and support. A GP is a good first point of call as they can refer you on to organisations or signpost you in the right direction. Alternatively, a counsellor or therapist. You don't have to go it alone. There is no stigma attached to asking for help, but sadly there may be a few heads nodding if your teen is struggling due to your own suffering.

Read on and you will see tips on self-care covering several areas of your life.

SLEEP

I'm sure you have noticed that when you are in a really good mood, feel relaxed, or have had a really good night's sleep, preferably all of the above, that your cheery disposition not only lifts your mood but also the mood of others around you. Meaning, if you are kinder to yourself, you become kinder to others. Which is why, one of the most important things you can do for yourself, and your family, is to get enough sleep. Sleep should be made a priority as you can't function properly without it, no matter how much you fool yourself. Professionals now realise that sleep isn't so much a luxury as a *necessity*. So, you should never feel guilty about fitting in a much-needed extra hour whenever you feel the need.

PARENTAL NEEDS – IF WE LOOK AFTER THEM, WHO LOOKS AFTER US?

RELAXATION

"Give yourself permission to be kinder to yourself."

One vital aspect of parenting, especially for single parents juggling so much, is the ability to regularly relax and wind down. It's important to take time out *every day*, even if it's just for a few moments. Relaxing in the spa on a daily basis sounds wonderful, but unfortunately, it's totally unrealistic for most of us. Yet a longer shower, a few stolen moments in the car, or a 10-minute read before starting supper is doable. It's important to set realistic goals, otherwise, we become discouraged and end up abandoning the whole idea, losing out on well-deserved me time. We shouldn't *deny ourselves*, and therefore our family, the opportunity to be a more relaxed and more present parent.

Our minds and bodies need time to unwind, relax, and recharge. Time set aside to process thoughts calms our mind and helps diminish our worries. So, set aside some time either first thing in the morning, at lunchtime, or during the evening.

Recently, I attended an online meeting. At the halfway mark, the speaker told us to take a short break, in fact, she said, 'I give you my permission to take a break, get a breath of fresh air or just have a cup of tea.' It was amazing the effect these words had on not just myself but others. When the meeting resumed, we discussed the fact that we were 'allowed' a mini break without having to fill the gap with tasks such as the washing up. It was as though we needed permission to look after ourselves.

When parents are stressed, it's easy to forget it this can negatively affect their parenting abilities. Happy and chilled parents are more likely to be less judgemental, more insightful, more flexible, and project a sunnier outlook in all situations. Contrarily, stressed out parents are more likely to snap at others, enforce control, install self-doubt, stifle creativity, and on the whole bring a negative attitude to the table.

I'm not going to address our physical well-being as I want to concentrate on our mental well-being. To achieve a good state of mental health we need to be grounded, have a strong supportive network, and be open to being honest with ourselves. Alongside this, we need to know who we are as individuals. As a starting point, we need to know our strengths and weaknesses. When contemplating our attributes, we should do so with compassion and honesty and avoid becoming so focused on our weaknesses that we lose sight of our strengths. Like Jacob Marley, we all wear a chain made up of fears and limitations: some links passed down from previous generations, others forged during our lifetime. This chain prevents us from being who we truly are. Take time to discover yourself. Break the chain so you can focus on your well-being and parent the best way you can.

When it comes to parents, especially mothers, we rarely consider our own feelings. Yet, it's imperative that we do so for our own sanity. It's essential to 'check in' with ourselves on a regular basis, taking time out to go within as this prevents us from inadvertently expressing feelings of resentment, jealousy, or anger, towards others, including our teens. We can ask ourselves questions like, 'How do I feel?', 'How has this affected me?', 'What do I really want to do?', 'What's really bothering me?' instead of waiting until something major happens. Connecting with ourselves on a regular basis makes us happier, which in turn helps us become better parents, and demonstrates skills that are important to pass onto our teens.

We are so busy in our daily lives and so caught up with thoughts of *what's next on the agenda* that we forget to stop and take stock. If we allow our needs to go unmet then issues, such as anger, frustration, low mood, irritability, and anxiety can start to set in.

TOUGH ON YOU, TOUGH ON THEM

"Even without trying, parents teach by example. Like a mirror, our behaviour is reflected back to us through our teens."

Being too hard on yourself

People that are naturally hard on themselves struggle to easily forgive themselves. They pile on the pressure until near breaking point. Inadvertently, they can pass these traits down the line to their teens. If this behaviour resonates with you then take a step back and reflect. Don't chastise yourself further; instead, take time out to see if you want to tackle changing your habits.

However well we mask our feelings, our teens, who are naturally more intuitive than us, can easily pick up on them. For this reason, if you are a very anxious person then your teen may feel unsettled and worry that something isn't right or is unsafe as he will accept this as the norm. The same goes for being too self-critical. He may think it's readily acceptable in society and behave similarly.

Below are some of the tell-tale signs of being very self-critical. Note there is a crossover between these signs and the signs of being a perfectionist:

- A regular habit of putting yourself down.
- Bad decisions regarding choice of friends and partners.
- Beating yourself up over small mistakes that have hardly any consequences.
- Being too hard on others.
- Continuous self-berating over your mistakes, even if you have ratified them.
- Depression.

- Disappointment in yourself.
- Inability to forgive yourself and others easily.
- Inability to relax and rest.
- Lack of acceptance of yourself.
- Lack of self-control.
- Lack of self-esteem.
- Low self-confidence.
- Non-existent self-care.
- OCD.
- Over stretching yourself for others.
- Procrastination.
- Self-doubt.
- Taking yourself and life too seriously.
- Unable to be truly happy.

Being a Perfectionist

Although some consider being a perfectionist to be beneficial, this trait brings various negative repercussions. By practising perfectionism, paradoxically, we can end up putting unnecessary pressure on our teens. When we strive to be perfect, we unintentionally set high expectations for ourselves, often unrealistic ones, and unwittingly we set them high for others too. And when others don't live up to our expectations, we become disillusioned as we consider anything less than perfect to be failure. Even when others try their best it's never good enough. In the case of our teens, they are left struggling as they don't know how to please us as they feel that we are never satisfied. As a result, they have to choose whether to keep trying, knowing that they can never please us, or decide to stop trying altogether. Either way, they miss out on the praise and validation that they crave and deserve. Although this type of behaviour isn't to be condemned, it needs to be noted as it can influence offspring to follow suit, making them perfectionists too.

While perfectionists are busy trying to make sure everything is perfect, they can, unwittingly, end up controlling others, and life in general. In their strive for the world to fit into their mindset, they create stress for both themselves and those around them. Perfectionists come from a judgemental standpoint, pointing out the smallest of mistakes in others, which, although not intentional, comes across as criticism. Another trait of the perfectionist is their tendency to procrastinate for fear of failure.

If you are the type of person who sets the bar very high for yourself and is never satisfied with your own achievements, then maybe it's time to go easy on yourself. Chances are, you are doing the best job you can with the knowledge you have of yourself, the task at hand, and the tools available to you. One suggestion is to see each accomplishment as a brave step in the right direction, instead of just a piece of the puzzle that is yet to be completed, as it may never be completed to your satisfaction. Rather than being results-driven, go for progress by taking small steps, as little changes are often enough. Celebrate each milestone along the way, no matter how small. And remember, it's important to give yourself a pat on the back on a regular basis.

STRENGTHS AND WEAKNESSES WORKOUT

A strengths and weaknesses list can be a valuable tool in our journey of self-discovery, aiding us in becoming better parents. I suggest that you create a list for yourself to celebrate your strengths and be accepting of your shortcomings as this allows you to put some of your gremlins to bed.

To explore both lists, it's best to write them down so you can see them in black and white. Using a large sheet of paper, A4 is ideal, split the page into two separate columns. Title one column 'Weaknesses' and the other 'Strengths'. Firstly, tackle the weakness list, making sure that you are looking at it in a fun and positive light. List anything that comes to mind. You can return to the list later, adding or removing items as you wish. Don't use the exercise as an excuse to disparage yourself. Next, complete the strengths list, making sure you realise how wonderful you really are! It's always better to end on a high when carrying out these exercises, which is why it's best completed in this order. You can ask friends or family members to add ideas to your strengths list as I'm sure they will mention ones that you had never thought of or didn't realise you even possessed. Over time, return to the list and take pride as you either move items from the weaknesses to the strengths side or add to the strengths list. Some items may stay on the weaknesses list but that is okay, we are all human and can't, however much we try, be perfect.

SELF-CARE CHECKLIST

"When it comes to looking after ourselves, it's not a case of we can't find the time, but a case of we can't afford ***not*** *to find the time."*

The following list is a self-care checklist containing ideas to work on in your own time. They will enhance your life and help reduce your stress levels. The items aren't in any particular order so use them as you wish. Read through the list daily, choosing the ones that jump out at you.

- Ask for help when you need it.
- Connect with your inner child and have fun.
- Cut down on the phrase 'I *should....*'.
- Decide what's important in your life and don't stress over the little things that aren't important.

PARENTAL NEEDS – IF WE LOOK AFTER THEM, WHO LOOKS AFTER US?

- Don't take on more than you are able to do at any given moment.
- Embrace some form of relaxation for your mind. Whether it's meditation, mindfulness, yoga, sketching, painting, or other activities.
- Exercise in a way that works for you. Just keep moving as it boosts endorphin levels and offers numerous health benefits, including clarity of thought.
- Follow a healthy/sensible diet (but don't go on a diet as dieting isn't necessarily beneficial for everyone). Don't get paranoid or beat yourself up when it comes to food.
- Fill your life with positive people and limit the amount of contact you have with the negative ones.
- Connect with your inner child and have fun.
- Get enough Sleep for *your* needs.
- Get in touch with your creative side.
- Give yourself permission to relax.
- Help someone less fortunate than you. For example, consider volunteering as it helps raise self-esteem and self-confidence. Boosting your C.V. at the same time.
- Laugh every day.
- Listen to music or a relaxing podcast.

PARENTAL NEEDS — IF WE LOOK AFTER THEM, WHO LOOKS AFTER US?

- Keep tabs on your mental health.
- Look for fulfilment. Be it a paid or unpaid job or a major hobby.
- Never be hard on yourself. Your parenting journey includes making mistakes, and like our teens, we have to make them in order to learn and grow as individuals. Our strength lies in learning from them.
- Practise gratitude. Gratitude calms us, provides a shortcut to acceptance, slows down our thoughts, and helps us to focus on the important things in life.
- Practice self-love.
- Relax and unwind. Find some me time every day. No excuses.
- Spend time in nature to keep you grounded. Try walking, running, yoga in the garden, golf, gardening, photographing nature, or other outdoor activities that you enjoy.
- Surround yourself with a support network - partner, friends, family, neighbours, work colleagues, or online or off-line groups.
- Switch your mobile phone off or have zones in the house where mobiles aren't allowed.
- Regularly take time out and go within, asking for help and guidance when you need it.

PARENTAL NEEDS – IF WE LOOK AFTER THEM, WHO LOOKS AFTER US?

- Treat yourself on a regular basis. Be it the item of clothing you've been eyeing up or the massage your body craves.
- Write a journal of your thoughts and feelings.
- Set yourself clear boundaries and say no to family and friends unless it's an emergency.
- Set yourself boundaries within the workplace.
- Use a friendly listening ear, be it a partner, friend or counsellor/therapist, whenever you need to.

A common issue for parents is our desperate need to relax once our teens are in bed. But the older they get, the later the bedtime, alluding to us often going to bed before them. We can resolve this by tweaking our timetable to ensure we take time out during the day, or early evening. Perhaps a restful lunch break at work, a soothing podcast whilst washing up, a relaxing commute home, a cheerful catch-up with a friend, a bath full of bath bombs, a blasting of your favourite songs, or a feel-good film. Be creative in finding ways that work for you as you deserve it.

WHEN THERE IS NO SUPPORT BETWEEN PARENTS

In households where one parent doesn't support the other parent, life can be difficult for any teen. Naturally, children will follow the lead of their parents, copying bad habits as well as good. If they witness their mother or father being put down or being disrespected by the other parent this will give out negative messages such as, 'Hey son, I don't respect your mum/dad so why should you.' Or 'It's O.K. son to shout at your mum/dad'. Alternatively, the teen, or rather piggy in the middle, may feel torn and want to defend one of his parents, causing countless issues, including guilt and fear.

Teens witnessing arguments between parents that either live together or apart, can suffer long-term. They can internalise their worries and become withdrawn or end up struggling with depression or anxiety. If they externalise their worries, they can portray antisocial behaviours such as hostility, delinquency, or aggression. These behavioural outcomes can carry on, even if the parents end up parting, and a new respectful partner comes on the scene, as, unfortunately, a new partner doesn't always cancel out any unhealthy patterns learnt, no matter how loving they may be. In the scenario of a new partner, parents will need to be patient, allowing their teen time to adjust in order to accept them.

SINGLE PARENTING

Whilst I appreciate that there are differences between single and solo parents, for ease, when I refer to single parents in this section of the book, I mean both single and solo parents.

PARENTAL NEEDS — IF WE LOOK AFTER THEM, WHO LOOKS AFTER US?

According to ONS, in 2022, there were 19.4 million families in the UK, of which lone-parent families accounted for 15%, equating to 2.9m families. Of these, 84% were headed up by a lone mother (approximately 2.5m families), whilst 16% were headed by a lone father (around 457,000) (ONS, 2022).

In 2021 there were 111,934 opposite-sex divorces and 1,571 same-sex divorces (ONS, 2021). With the average duration of an opposite-sex marriage being just over 12 years, and same-sex marriages being just under 6 years, there will most likely be children involved. Although for the majority, divorce or separation is the main reason why parents become single parents, others sadly lose their partners along the way. Then there are those that choose to go it alone, deciding to have children without a partner, a brave decision.

So, what's it like being a single parent? We know that parenting isn't always easy and for single parents the job is even harder, and sadly, even in the 21st century, there is still an unvirtuous stigma attached. Without a committed partner at home to support them, single parents tend to experience a higher degree of loneliness, exhaustion, and poverty. Unfairly, when it comes to their finances, single parent families are nearly twice as likely to end up in poverty compared to coupled ones.

The absence of a permanent partner can at times create an imbalance in the home, as parenting alone can be emotionally intense. Not having a partner to bounce ideas off, lighten the load, both mentally and physically, help with childcare, and set rules and boundaries, can make parenting even more demanding. With no partner to act as a buffer, should situations get hot under the collar, or be an advisor or sounding board, then life can test the strengths of the single parent. Which is why, if you fit into this category, it's even more important to look after yourself.

Time, financial constraints, and lack of childcare can greatly impact much-needed time out. This lays a heavy burden on the shoulders of single parents, often leaving them both mentally and physically exhausted. Not to say that there aren't some amazing single parents out there who are doing a fantastic job balancing work and home life and finding time for themselves, but realistically, this isn't the majority.

When it comes to being present for their children, it would be unfair to say that single parents are less likely to be available, as this isn't true. In fact, I have met many single parents who are far more present for their children than ones with partners.

Without a partner at home, it's easier for single parents to unintentionally lean on their teens, making them their emotional crutch. Although this happens in two-parent families, it's more likely to happen when there isn't a second adult around. We don't want our teens to become our sounding board, accountant, nor counsellor. Hence, we need to avoid off-loading our worries onto their young shoulders as inadvertently, this off-loading can send subliminal messages which our teens read as blame, making them feel responsible for their parents' problems. In addition, they can easily worry that their own actions have caused the problems in the first place as they aren't capable of fully understanding situations. This is a notion that is often depicted on T.V., where children ask if they've done something wrong when they see their parents argue or decide to part ways.

Equally, we should avoid putting the other parent down in front of our teens. It isn't appropriate now and may not be even when they become adults. Our relationship with other people, including ex-partners and family members, is separate from our child's relationship with them so our experiences and emotions will be very different. So, let's leave our teens out of our dramas and our gossip as much as we can and avoid oversharing our life with them, and instead, have a heart to heart with a friend, family member, or counsellor/therapist. For the short duration, we should let them be a teen and not a small adult.

Whether through separation, divorce, or bereavement, when it comes to adapting to a one parent family, teens will no doubt be traumatised. Sadly, due to loss or being in an unhealthy, unhappy, or toxic environment, or to avoid physical or mental harm, parents may not have had a choice about whether to bring up their children on their own. If the latter reason was your choice, you may feel, when you see how your teen reacts, that your decision has backfired. This doesn't mean that you have made a wrong decision, it just means you can't always avoid the rocky road. Keep communicating with your teen, and if he needs professional help, then seek it. If he refuses help, consider going yourself. Either to an adult counsellor, or one that specialises in teens as they can offer insights into what your teen is experiencing.

The Millennium Cohort Study, conducted by The Institute for Public Policy Research, informs us that in all family structures, providing affection and security in a nurturing environment helps our teens thrive. IPPR's key finding is that "children growing up in non-traditional family forms can succeed if warmth, stability and consistent parenting are present" (Dixon et al., 2006).

Co-Parenting

Co-parenting brings its own set of rules and challenges. Yet, the need to put our children first can sometimes be challenging as sadly too many parents struggle to maintain good relationships after they separate. This isn't surprising as they've made the decision to separate because they can't live together any more.

Whilst it's usually best to maintain a good relationship with an ex-partner, realistically it doesn't often happen. But, if possible, for our teens' sake, we should try to keep on good terms with our ex-partner to keep the lines of communication open, meeting up as and when needed, and , if necessary, on neutral territory as this will make our teens happier and their lives easier. In the case of irreconcilable relationships, help, in the form of mediation or counselling, can be enlisted.

When it comes to a dangerous or abusive ex-partner, it may not be healthy to maintain contact. In which case, you may need to limit interactions or sever all ties.

Being a co-parent can be both challenging and mentally draining at times, especially if your ex-partner doesn't pull their weight, undermines your decisions or generally has a totally different approach to parenting that doesn't sit well with you. If you fit into this category, then don't waste your time or energy telling your ex how to parent if you think they will ignore you. Instead, just be the best parent and role model you can, knowing that, as your teen grows, he will see the wood from the trees. Shortfalls and disappointments will eventually become clear, and your style of parenting will win out in the end.

Many single parents feel that they are the ones that shoulder most of the burden as they do the lion's share of the work. There is however a silver lining here. If you are in this situation, then you will be the one that experiences the golden moments, including ones where your hard work has paid off, and you will be the one that your teen can rely on and turn to if needed. And when this happens, make sure that *you* take all the credit.

CHAPTER 17: PET HATES AND REFLECTIONS

PET HATES

Parents can't always remember everything. It's hard enough remembering the dentist appointment, what to add to the shopping list, who to pay, and who to phone. Which is why I have designed a quick and easy chart to remind you of your teen's pet hates. Let's face it, we all have them, and our teens are no different. But if we had a gentle reminder, it would help us avoid unnecessary conflict. After all, there's no point pushing someone's buttons if we don't need to.

You can copy the chart below into your notebook and jot down anything that comes to mind. For example, some teens hate their parents asking their friends certain questions, eating particular foods, or visiting certain places. You can either complete it with your teen, on your own, or ask your teen to fill it in. You may only have a couple of ideas to start with, that's fine. You can add more at a later date and cross off ones that no longer apply. Pet hates can change, so it's worth revisiting every few months.

Because the list is personal and unique to your teen, I recommend keeping it confidential, only sharing with others if your teen is happy to do so.

'PET HATES' CHART

NAME	**LIST OF PET HATES**
Joseph	*Being called 'darling'*

REFLECTIONS

Although similar to the Pet Hates chart above, this is a private one, just for parents. It's a reminder of all the things we love about having a teenager. As with the Pet Hates Chart, copy it into your notebook, then feel free to choose from the suggestions below or create your own ones. Perhaps start by being grateful for your teen, as the practice of gratitude on a regular basis benefits us in many ways. It helps us to become more content with our lives and thus calmer individuals, improving both our mental and physical health.

- When he opens up to me, I gain a deeper insight into his world.

- I appreciate the many lessons he's taught me.
- He challenges me to think outside the box.
- I enjoy adult-like conversations with him.
- I can relate to him as a near-adult.
- I feel proud of how I raised him.
- I'm proud of who he's become.
- I'm proud of his achievements.
- I now have more time for myself now that he's getting older.
- He's helped me gain a deeper understanding of adolescents.
- I admire his compassion, honesty, and strong sense of morals.
- I love how he helps and supports his friends.
- He makes my heart flutter.
- He lights the candle in my heart.
- He's shown me the true meaning of love.
- His bigger picture sometimes exceeds mine.
- His life gave purpose to mine.
- The sound of his voice is still my favourite sound.
- I love seeing this wonderful young man emerge.

'REFLECTIONS' CHART

NAME	REFLECTIONS
Oliver	*He makes me laugh*

CHAPTER 18: 'ON CHILDREN' – POEM BY KAHLIL GIBRAN

Below is my favourite parenting poem. By Kahlil Gibran, also known as Gibran Khalil Gibran, it beautifully depicts how best to parent our children, highlighting that even though they need our love and support, they are separate, unique individuals and not mere reflections of us. It also reminds us of the need to be flexible and adaptable in order to support them as they grow and prepare to take flight.

On Children By Kahlil Gibran (1883-1931). From The Prophet (Knopf, 1923).

And a woman who held a babe against her bosom said,
Speak to us of Children.
And he said:
Your children are not your children.
They are the sons and daughters of Life's longing for itself.
They come through you but not from you,
And though they are with you yet they belong not to you.

You may give them your love but not your thoughts,
For they have their own thoughts.
You may house their bodies but not their souls,
For their souls dwell in the house of tomorrow, which you cannot visit, not even in your dreams.

You may strive to be like them, but seek not to make them like you.

For life goes not backward nor tarries with yesterday.
You are the bows from which your children as living arrows are sent forth.
The archer sees the mark upon the path of the infinite, and He bends you with His might that His arrows may go swift and far.
Let your bending in the archer's hand be for gladness;
For even as He loves the arrow that flies, so He loves also the bow that is stable.

CHAPTER 19: CHILDREN'S RIGHTS: A FOUNDATION FOR RESPECT

Childhood is often considered the happiest time of our lives. But surely this depends on the individual, their circumstances, life experiences, and the people who dominate in their lives, such as parents, friends, family, and teachers? Although we can't control how others treat our teens, we can control how *we* act. Therefore, if we want this statement to hold true, it's up to us to put the wheels in motion to make it happen.

The Universal Declaration of Human Rights contains 30 articles outlining people's most fundamental rights and freedoms. Written for people of all nations and proclaimed in 1948, it is a milestone document in the history of human rights. Below, I have noted a few excerpts as a reminder of how we, amongst others, should be treating our teens. It also serves as a reminder of how adults should be treated too:

Article 1: We are all born free. We all have our own thoughts and ideas and we should all be treated the same way (Amnesty International, n.d.).

Article 5: No one has the right to inflict torture, or to subject anyone else to cruel or inhuman treatment (Amnesty International, n.d.).

Article 11: Everyone accused of a crime has the right to be considered innocent until they have fairly been proven to be guilty (Amnesty International, n.d.).

Article 18: Everyone has the freedom to think or believe what they want, including the right to religious belief (excerpt) (Amnesty International, n.d.).

Article 19: Everyone has the right to their own opinions, and to be able to express them freely. We should have the right to share our ideas with who we want, and in whichever way we choose (Amnesty International, n.d.).

(Note: this is Amnesty International UK's version, which may differ slightly in wording from the original United Nations version.)

CHAPTER 20: SUPPORT RESOURCES

Below is a list of websites offering further information and support for you and your teen. Please note some organisations may be regional. (I'm not affiliated with any of them and take no responsibility for the content on their websites nor actions of their staff or volunteers.)

MENTAL HEALTH:

Anxiety UK (www.anxietyuk.org.uk)
Offers support and resources for those affected by anxiety disorders.

Barnardo's (www.barnardos.org.uk)
A children's charity providing practical support, protection, and advice, for young people and families.

Childline (www.childline.org.uk)
A free, confidential helpline and online service for children and young people needing someone to talk to about any issue.

Give Us a Shout (www.giveusashout.org)
A free, 24/7 text messaging support service for anyone of any age struggling to cope.

Mind (www.mind.org.uk)
Provides advice and support for anyone experiencing mental health problems.

No Panic (www.nopanic.org.uk)
Offers help and support for those living with anxiety disorders, panic attacks, and phobias.

NSPCC (www.nspcc.org.uk)
The UK's leading child protection charity, working to prevent abuse and help children in danger.

Papyrus UK (www.papyrus-uk.org)
A UK charity focused on preventing young suicide. Provides confidential support through HOPELINEUK for those under 35 struggling with suicidal thoughts. Available 9 am to midnight via phone or text. They also help family members, friends, healthcare and education professionals, and emergency workers.

Samaritans (www.samaritans.org)
Provides confidential support 24/7 by phone, email, or letter for anyone in distress or struggling to cope.

SANE (www.sane.org.uk)
Provides emotional support and information to anyone affected by mental illness.

Sleep Foundation (www.sleepfoundation.org)
Provides expert advice and research on sleep health, including tips for improving sleep habits — essential for mental and physical wellbeing.

Teen Talk (www.teentalk.org.uk)
A UK-based service offering confidential emotional support and counselling for young people.

The Calm Zone (www.thecalmzone.net)
Offers information, support, and resources, to prevent suicide. For people of all ages.

The Children's Society (www.childrenssociety.org.uk)
Works to support vulnerable children and young people across the UK.

The Hope Line (www.thehopeline.com)
Provides support and advice for students and young adults struggling with thoughts of suicide, self-harm, or emotional distress.

The Mix (www.themix.org.uk)
Offers free, confidential support for young people under 25, including advice on mental health, money, relationships, and more.

Togetherall (www.togetherall.com)
An anonymous online community where people support each other with mental health issues.

YoungMinds (www.youngminds.org.uk)
UK charity dedicated to improving the mental health of children and young people through information, support, and advocacy.

If you need *urgent help*:
Text Shout for free on 85258 – a 24/7 confidential text support service connecting you with trained volunteers.
Call Samaritans any time (available 24/7) on 116 123 for confidential emotional support.

APPS

BeeZone (www.bee.zone)
A free meditation and relaxation app from the Brahma Kumaris with no adverts.

Calm (www.calm.com)
A relaxation and mental wellness app with tools for meditation, sleep stories, soothing music, and breathing techniques. Designed to help users manage anxiety, stress, and improve emotional wellbeing.

Happify (www.happify.com)
Happify offers science-based activities and games designed to reduce stress and build resilience, aiming to improve overall mental well-being through engaging, evidence-based exercises.

Headspace (www.headspace.com)
A popular mindfulness and meditation app that offers guided meditations, breathing exercises, and sleep support. Useful for teens and adults looking to reduce stress, improve focus, and sleep better.

Smiling Mind (www.smilingmind.com.au)
Smiling Mind provides mindfulness and meditation programs for all ages, including teens. It helps manage stress, improve focus, and support emotional health.

Please check each app's privacy policy before use to ensure it meets your preferences.

SOCIAL MEDIA AND ONLINE SAFETY:

Internet Matters (www.internetmatters.org)
A UK charity offering free resources to help parents keep children safe online, with advice, and interactive lessons.

Netflix Film: *The Social Dilemma*
A documentary revealing how social media platforms manipulate users, impact mental health, and spread misinformation, highlighting the real-world consequences of these effects.

NEWS STORIES:

Ed Farmer

Ed Farmer tragically died after a university initiation ceremony involving excessive alcohol. His death raised serious concerns about student safety and initiation practices. (www.bbc.co.uk/news/uk-england-tyne-45979243)

Felix Alexander

Felix Alexander tragically took his own life after enduring bullying. His death raised awareness about the serious impact bullying can have on young people. (www.theguardian.com/society/2016/oct/05/felix-alexander-mother-lucy-open-letter-worcester)

Molly Russell

Molly Russell tragically died by self-harm while suffering from depression influenced by harmful social media content. An inquest confirmed these factors contributed significantly to her death. (www.bbc.co.uk/news/uk-england-london-63073489)

Disclaimer:
The cases mentioned here are based on publicly available news reports and are included to raise awareness about issues affecting young people. I recognize that many others have faced similar situations but may not have been in the public eye. I include these stories with sensitivity and respect, mindful of the individuals and families involved, and with compassion for all affected.

AUTISM:

ADDitude Magazine (www.additudemag.com)
A trusted source offering articles, expert advice, and practical tips for living with ADHD and related conditions.

ADD-vance (www.add-vance.org)
A UK charity offering support and training for adults and families affected by ADHD.

National Autistic Society (www.autism.org.uk)
The UK's leading charity for autistic people and their families, providing support, information, and guidance.

NHS (www.nhs.uk)
Official health information and advice on autism, ADHD, and ADD diagnosis and management.

DOMESTIC ABUSE:

National Centre for Domestic Violence (NCDV) (www.ncdv.org.uk) Offers free legal support to survivors of domestic abuse to help them quickly obtain protection orders.

National Domestic Abuse Helpline (www.nationaldahelpline.org.uk)
Free, confidential, 24-hour helpline offering support and guidance for women experiencing domestic abuse.

NHS (www.nhs.uk)
Provides medical advice and guidance on recognising and responding to domestic abuse.

Refuge (www.refuge.org.uk)
Provides specialist services to women and children experiencing domestic violence, including emergency accommodation and advocacy.

Victim Support (www.victimsupport.org.uk)
Offers emotional and practical help to anyone affected by crime, including domestic abuse.

Women's Aid (www.womensaid.org.uk)
A national charity working to end domestic abuse against women and children, offering advice, refuges, and a live chat service.

SINGLE PARENTS' SUPPORT:

Gingerbread (www.gingerbread.org.uk)
A UK charity supporting single parents , providing expert advice, expert-advised practical help and campaigning for the rights of single parent families. Their website offers guidance on everything from benefits and child maintenance to work and wellbeing.

TED TALKS:

Dr Jean Twenge – *iGen: The Smartphone Generation* (Jan 2018, ~13 min) (https://www.ted.com/talks/jean_twenge_igen_the_smartphone_generation_jan_2018)

Dr Twenge outlines how growing up with smartphones shapes teens' behaviour, including effects on social interaction, mental health, and generational trends.

Dr Thomas Curran – *Our dangerous obsession with perfectionism is getting worse* (Jan 2018, ~15 min)

(https://www.ted.com/talks/thomas_curran_our_dangerous_obsession_with_perfectionism_is_getting_worse)

A timely talk exploring how rising perfectionism, driven by social media, school, and culture, is harming young people's mental health, and how to tackle the issue.

REFERENCING

Action on Sugar. (2016). Latest NDNS data shows children, teenagers and adults consume two-to-three times more sugar than is recommended. [online] Available at: https://www.actiononsugar.org/news-centre/sugar-in-the-news/2016/items/latest-ndns-data-shows-children-teenagers-and-adults-consume-two-to-three-times-more-sugar-than-is-recommended.html [Accessed: 18 June 2025].

Amnesty International UK. (n.d.) *Universal Declaration of Human Rights (UDHR)*. Available at: https://www.amnesty.org.uk/universal-declaration-human-rights-UDHR [Accessed: 28 June 2025].

Arain, M., Haque, M., Johal, L., Mathur, P., Nel, W., Rais, A., Sandhu, R., & Sharma, S. (2013). Maturation of the adolescent brain. *Neuropsychiatric Disease and Treatment*, 9. 449–461. https://doi.org/10.2147/NDT.S39776 [Accessed: 30 October 2022].

BBC Bitesize. (n.d.) *The teenage brain: How can neuroscience help us understand teenagers?* Available at: https://www.bbc.co.uk/bitesize/articles/z6vkrj6 [Accessed: 19 October 2024].

Casey, B.J., Jones, R.M. and Hare, T.A. (2008). The adolescent brain. *Annals of the New York Academy of Sciences*, 1124, pp.111-126. doi: 10.1196/annals.1440.010 [Accessed: 29 March 2023].

The Children's Society. (2022). "Positive family relationships are key to children's subjective well-being. A greater focus is needed on family well-being as a whole."
The Good Childhood Report Summary 2022.

https://www.childrenssociety.org.uk/sites/default/files/2022-09/GCR-2022-Summary Report.pdf. [Accessed: 01 May 2023].

The Children's Society. (2022). *The Good Childhood Report 2022.* In 2022, more children were unhappy with school than any other aspect of life. [Accessed: 01 November 2023].

The Children's Society. (2022). *School is also the place where most children spend most of their time, and, as such, has the greatest capacity to identify the issues children are facing and be part of the solution.* The Good Childhood Report 2022. [Accessed: 01 November 2023].

The Children's Society. (2022). *Official Website.* [online] Available at: https://www.childrenssociety.org.uk [Accessed: 01 June 2023].

The Children's Society. (2022). *Understanding self-harm.* [online] Available at: https://www.childrenssociety.org.uk/what-we-do/blogs/understanding-self-harm [Accessed: 05 November 2022].

The Children's Society. (2023). *In 2023, more children completing our annual survey were unhappy with school than any other aspect of their lives they were asked about, but there is huge potential for schools to support and protect children's wellbeing.* The Good Childhood Report 2023. [Accessed: 01 October 2024].

The Children's Society. (2023). *The Good Childhood Report 2023.* Available at: https://www.childrenssociety.org.uk/good-childhood [Accessed: 24 May 2025].

The Children's Society. (2023). *Understanding self-harm and how to help*. Available at:

https://www.childrenssociety.org.uk/what-we-do/blogs/understanding-self-harm [Accessed: 19 May 2025].

The Children's Society. (2024). *Children and young people who are currently growing up in the UK are doing so in challenging times. The Good childhood Report* 2024. [Accessed: 01 April 2025].

The Children's Society. (2024). The *Good Childhood Report.* (pdf) Available at: https://www.childrenssociety.org.uk [Accessed: 12/03/2025].

Curran, T. and Hill, A.P. (2022). Young people's perceptions of their parents' expectations and criticism are increasing over time: Implications for perfectionism. *Psychological Bulletin*, 148(1-2), pp. 107–128. https://doi.org/10.1037/bul0000347. [Accessed: 07 May 2024].

Dixon, M., Reed, H., Margo, J., and Pearce, N. (2006). *Freedom's orphans: Raising youth in a changing world.* Institute for Public Policy Research. Available at: https://www.ippr.org/articles/freedoms-orphans-raising-youth-in-a-changing-world [Accessed: 28 February 2024].

The Duke of Edinburgh's Award. (2021). *Annual statistics: April* 2020 – *March* 2021. [online] Available at: https://www.dofe.org/about/research/ [Accessed: 08 June 2024].

The Duke of Edinburgh's Award. (2023). *Annual statistics: Year ending March* 2023. [online] Available at: https://www.dofe.org/about/research/ [Accessed: 8 June 2024].

The Guardian. (2018). *Children's lack of sleep is hidden health crisis, experts say*. Available at: https://www.theguardian.com/lifeandstyle/2018/sep/30/childrens-lack-of-sleep-is-hidden-health-crisis-experts-say [Accessed: 20 October 2022].

The Guardian. (2020). *UK has experienced 'explosion' in anxiety since 2008, study finds*. [online] 14 September. Available at: https://www.theguardian.com/society/2020/sep/14/uk-has-experienced-explosion-in-anxiety-since-2008-study-finds [Accessed: 15 March 2024].

Harvard Health Publishing. (2024). The adolescent brain: Beyond raging hormones. *Harvard Health Blog*. Available at: https://www.health.harvard.edu/mind-and-mood/the-adolescent-brain-beyond-raging-hormones [Accessed: 21 February 2024].

Hertfordshire County Council. (2023). *Young People's Health and Wellbeing Survey*. (online - URL no longer active). [Accessed: 10 June 2024].

Hopkins Medicine. (n.d.). Anatomy of the brain. [online] Available at: https://www.hopkinsmedicine.org/health/conditions-and-diseases/anatomy-of-the-brain [Accessed: 05 February 2023].

Ingalhalikar, M., Smith, A., Parker, D., Satterthwaite, T. D., Elliott, M. A., Ruparel, K., Hakonarson, H., Gur, R. E., Gur, R. C., & Verma, R. (2014). Sex differences in the structural connectome of the human brain. *Proceedings of the National Academy of Sciences*, 111(2), pp. 823–828. https://doi.org/10.1073/pnas.1316909110 [Accessed: 17 May 2023].

Kaczkurkin, A.N., Raznahan, A. and Satterthwaite, T.D. (2018). Sex differences in the developing brain: insights from multimodal neuroimaging. *Neuropsychopharmacology*, 44(1), pp.71-85. https://doi.org/10.1038/npp.2018.229 [Accessed: 15 May 2025].

Lanjekar, P. D., Joshi, S. H., Lanjekar, P. D., & Wagh, V. (2022). 'The Effect of Parenting and the Parent-Child Relationship on a Child's Cognitive Development: A Literature Review', *Cureus*, 14(10), e30574. doi: 10.7759/cureus.30574. Available at: https://www.ncbi.nlm.nih.gov/pmc/articles/PMC9678477/ [Accessed: 17 October 2024].

LeDoux, J. (2015) 'The amygdala is not the brain's fear center', *Psychology Today*, 28 August. Available at: https://www.psychologytoday.com/us/blog/i-got-mind-tell-you/201508/the-amygdala-is-not-the-brains-fear-center [Accessed: 12 February 2023].

Lowry, C., Leonard-Kane, R., Gibbs, B., Muller, L.-M., Peacock, A., & Jani, A. (2022). 'Teachers: the forgotten health workforce', *Journal of the Royal Society of Medicine*, 115(6), pp. 216–219. doi: 10.1177/01410768221085692. Available at: https://journals.sagepub.com/doi/full/10.1177/01410768221085692 [Accessed: 13 March 2023].

Merriam-Webster. (n.d.). *Communicate*. Merriam-Webster.com Dictionary. Available at: https://www.merriam-webster.com/dictionary/communicate [Accessed: 13 October 2022].

MQ Mental Health. (2021). *75% of mental illnesses start before the age of 18, and 50% of adult mental health problems begin before 15*. Available at: https://www.mqmentalhealth.org [Accessed: 13 May 2025].

Neuroscience News. (2025) 'Study Confirms Early Brain Differences Between Sexes', *Neuroscience News*, 7 January. Available at: https://neurosciencenews.com/neurodevelopment-sex-differences-28318/ [Accessed: 17 May 2025].

Newlove-Delgado, T., Marcheselli, F., Williams, T., Mandalia, D., Davis, J., McManus, S., Savic, M., Treloar, W., & Ford, T. (2021). *Mental Health of Children and Young People in England 2021 – wave 2 follow-up to the 2017 survey*. NHS Digital. Available at: https://digital.nhs.uk/data-and-information/publications/statistical/mental-health-of-children-and-young-people-in-england/2021-follow-up-to-the-2017-survey [Accessed: 14 December 2021].

NHS Digital. (2018). *Mental health of children and young people in England*, 2017. [online] NHS Digital. Available at: https://digital.nhs.uk/news/2018/one-in-eight-of-five-to-19-year-olds-had-a-mental-disorder-in-2017-major-new-survey-finds [Accessed: 31 October 2022].

NHS Digital. (2022). *Mental Health of Children and Young People in England 2022: Wave 3 follow-up to the 2017 survey*. [online] 29 November. Available at: https://digital.nhs.uk/data-and-information/publications/statistical/mental-health-of-children-and-young-people-in-england/2022-follow-up-to-the-2017-survey [Accessed: 14 January 2025].

Nook, E.C., Zaki, J., and Somerville, L.H. (2021). '*Negative emotions are murkier, less distinct in adolescence*', *Association for Psychological Science*. Available at:

https://www.psychologicalscience.org/news/releases/negative-emotions-are-murkier-less-distinct-in-adolescence.html [Accessed: 07 July 2021].

Nook, E. C., Sasse, S. F., Lambert, H. K., McLaughlin, K. A., & Somerville, L. H. (2018). *The Nonlinear Development of Emotion Differentiation: Granular Emotional Experience Is Low in Adolescence*. Available at: https://journals.sagepub.com/doi/10.1177/0956797618773357 [Accessed: 26 March 2024].

The Holy Bible, King James Version. (n.d.). Proverbs 18:13. Available at: https://www.kingjamesbibleonline.org/Proverbs-18-13/ [Accessed: 17 October 2022].

NSPCC. (2022). *Domestic abuse and children*. NSPCC. Available at: https://www.nspcc.org.uk/what-is-child-abuse/types-of-abuse/domestic-abuse/ [Accessed: 31 May 2025].

Office for National Statistics (ONS). (2021). *Divorce statistics: 2021*. https://www.ons.gov.uk/peoplepopulationandcommunity/birthsdeathsandmarriages/divorce/bulletins/divorcestatistics/2021 [Accessed: 20 January 2024].

Office for National Statistics (ONS). (2022). *Families and households in the UK: 2022*. https://www.ons.gov.uk/peoplepopulationandcommunity/birthsdeathsandmarriages/families/bulletins/familiesandhouseholds/2022 [Accessed: 20 January 2024].

Office for National Statistics (ONS). (2022). *Domestic abuse in England and Wales overview: November 2022*. Office for

National Statistics. Available at: https://www.ons.gov.uk/peoplepopulationandcommunity/crimeandjustice/bulletins/domesticabuseinenglandandwalesoverview/november2022 [Accessed: 31 May 2025].

Office for National Statistics (ONS). (2024). *Crime in England and Wales: year ending December 2024*. Office for National Statistics. Available at: https://www.ons.gov.uk/peoplepopulationandcommunity/crimeandjustice/bulletins/crimeinenglandandwales/yearendingdecember2024#main-points [Accessed: 31 May 2025].

Psychology Today. (2025). *Burnout definition.* [online] Available at: https://www.psychologytoday.com/us/basics/burnout [Accessed: 17 July 2022].

Roaten, G.K. and Roaten, D.J. (2012) 'Adolescent Brain Development: Current Research and the Impact on Secondary School Counseling Programs', *Journal of School Counseling*, 10(18). Available at: https://files.eric.ed.gov/fulltext/EJ981198.pdf [Accessed: 18 March 2023].

Royal College of Psychiatrists. (2021). *Record number of children and young people referred to mental health services as pandemic takes its toll.* [online] 23 September. Available at: https://www.rcpsych.ac.uk/news-and-features/latest-news/detail/2021/09/23/record-number-of-children-and-young-people-referred-to-mental-health-services-as-pandemic-takes-its-toll [Accessed: 14 November 2021].

Russell, M. (2022). *The biggest gift a child can have*. [YouTube video]. The Children's Society. [Accessed: 15 January 2023].

Samaritans. (2022). *Personal communication via email*, November 2022.

Samaritans. (n.d.). TV *advertisement*: "*Every* 90 *minutes*" [television advert].

Samaritans. (2023). *Young people and suicide*. Available at: https://www.samaritans.org/about-samaritans/research-policy/young-people-suicide/ [Accessed: 19 May 2025].

Scientific American (2016) *Brain Differences in Boys and Girls: How Much Is Inborn*? Available at: https://www.scientificamerican.com/article/brain-differences-in-boys-and-girls-how-much-is-inborn/ [Accessed: 17/05/2025].

Shan, Y., Abel, J. H., Li, Y., Izumo, M., Cox, K. H., Jeong, B., Yoo, S.-H., Olson, D. P., Doyle, F. J., & Takahashi, J. S. (2020).*Dual-color single-cell imaging of the suprachiasmatic nucleus reveals a circadian role in network synchrony*. Neuron, 108(1), pp.164–179.e7. https://doi.org/10.1016/j.neuron.2020.07.012 [Accessed: 3 May 2021].

Sky News. (2024). "UK *Teenagers Are Facing a Happiness Recession," and*

"UK *Teenagers Rank Last for Life Satisfaction in Europe*." Quoted by Mark Russell, The Children's Society, August 2024.

Sleep Action. (2022). *Why teach about sleep*? Available at: https://sleepaction.org/training/education/why-teach-about-sleep/ [Accessed: 20 October 2022].

Tarokh, L., Short, M., Crowley, S. J., Fontanellaz-Castiglione, C. E. G., & Carskadon, M. A. (2019).*Sleep and Circadian Rhythms in Adolescence. Current Sleep Medicine Reports*, 5(4), pp. 181–192. Springer. https://doi.org/10.1007/s40675-019-00155-w. [Accessed: 20 October 2022].

Uhls, Y.T., Ellison, N.B. and Subrahmanyam, K. (2017). *Benefits and costs of social media in adolescence. Pediatrics*, 140(Suppl 2), S67-S70. https://doi.org/10.1542/peds.2016-1758E. [Accessed: 28 January 2023].

UNICEF. (n.d.). Adolescents. UNICEF DATA. Available at: https://data.unicef.org/topic/adolescents/overview. [Accessed: 01 May 2025].

University of Pennsylvania School of Medicine. (2017). Gray matter density increases during adolescence, study finds: Study reveals new methods of characterizing differences between youth and adult, male and female brains. *ScienceDaily*. Available at: www.sciencedaily.com/releases/2017/05/170526084524.htm [Accessed: 02 April 2023].

Way, N. (2024). *Rebels with a cause: Reimagining boys, ourselves, and our culture*. New Haven: Yale University Press [Accessed: 9 June 2025].

Way, N. (2011). *Deep secrets: Boys' friendships and the crisis of connection*. Cambridge, MA: Harvard University Press [Accessed: 9 June 2025].

Way, N. (2024). 'Why boys need close friendships and emotional connection', *Harvard EdCast*, 9 May. Available at: https://www.gse.harvard.edu/news/edcast/2024/05/why-boys-need-close-friendships-and-emotional-connection [Accessed: 9 June 2025].

Wilson, T.D. (2002). *Strangers to ourselves: Discovering the adaptive unconscious*. Cambridge, MA: Harvard University Press.

World Health Organization (WHO). (2021). *Adolescent mental health*. [online] Available at: https://www.who.int/news-room/fact-sheets/detail/adolescent-mental-health [Accessed: 02 January 2025].

YoungMinds. (2019). *Lack of early support for young people's mental health puts pressure on GPs*. Available at: https://www.youngminds.org.uk/about-us/media-centre/press-releases/lack-of-early-support-for-young-people-s-mental-health-puts-pressure-on-gps/ [Accessed: 31 October 2022].

Note 1: *Every effort has been made to ensure that all references and citations are accurate and properly credited. If you notice an error or omission, please contact the publisher at connect@alexpezaro.com and we will review and correct it in future editions where appropriate.*

Note 2: *Several citations from The Children's Society's Good Childhood Report across multiple years have been consolidated or generalised to avoid repetition and improve clarity.*

INDEX

INDEX

Thank you for reading. I hope you found this book both insightful and empowering. Together, we can change the world – one teen at a time!

If you'd like to say connected, you can find me on **Instagram: @pg_author (Penny Goodwin)**

For feedback, publishing enquiries, bulk orders, or stocking requests, please visit: www.alexpezaro.com

Printed in Dunstable, United Kingdom

72594795R00262